DATE DUE			
MY 15 '75			
JA 15 '79			
MY pd '80			
JUL 6 1981			
OCT 6 1981			
MAY 16 1986			
NOV 5 - 1992			
DEC 3 1993			
4 1998			

DEMCO 38-297

WALT WHITMAN
THE MAN AND HIS WORK

WALT WHITMAN
THE MAN AND HIS WORK

BY
LÉON BAZALGETTE

*Translated from the French
by Ellen FitzGerald*
Department of English, Chicago
Normal College

Cooper Square Publishers, Inc.
NEW YORK
1970

Originally Published 1920
Published by Cooper Square Publishers, Inc.
59 Fourth Avenue, New York, N. Y. 10003
Standard Book No. 8154-0352-6
Library of Congress Catalog Card No. 72-128770

Printed in the United States of America

TO THE MEMORY OF
MY FATHER
BEST TYPE OF THE COMMON AVERAGE FOR
WHOSE STORIES OF THE WAR AND OF
LINCOLN I DEDICATE THIS TRIBUTE TO
THE POET OF THE WAR AND OF LINCOLN

PREFACE

M. BAZALGETTE's introduction, so expressive of the deep feeling which inspired him to build a French dwelling for Whitman, explains why this elaborate structure should become our own. To advance a taste of a personality is the main purpose of M. Bazalgette's biography and he surely succeeds. This enthusiastic rendering of Whitman's life into a complete dramatic unit, its lights and shades fully balanced, suggests that Whitman, in our neglect of him as a poet, may have been lucky after all; for here he transcends the mere bounds of a literary figure, and becomes a complete national asset, the man in whom was incarnated the whole life of America. So thoroughly does M. Bazalgette create a superman for us that Whitman becomes as impressive as Milton to Blake and the reader is tempted to paraphrase Blake's beautiful exclamation:

<blockquote>And did this man really dwell among us?</blockquote>

Whitman has never lacked devoted biographers in his own country, and by this free ample use of their work M. Bazalgette may raise the question of his sharp emphasis on American neglect of him. Admitting that Whitman is a negligible force with the American masses, as compared with Longfellow and Whittier, whose saintlike faces bless every American child at his school tasks, whose verse is as familiar as the portraits, Whitman himself is responsible, much more than the American people.

There is a profound paradox in this whole issue between

PREFACE

Whitman and the people he exalted. They could but interpret him according to their light. They had been used to literary expression from men of simple lives and Whitman inaugurated very unprofessional literature in a very professional way.

A poet who announces himself as:

> Turbulent, fleshy, sensual eating, drinking and breeding,

is only one with Hamlet and several other characters in Shakespeare who were really trying to make their world better. Trained readers know how to value such confessions but the average man takes these literary conventions seriously, and hence misses the really great message of the poet. For this reason I have felt justified in abridging M. Bazalgette's treatment of the New Orleans episode, not that it may not be true but that it is a mystery which neither H. B. Binns nor he can clear by elaborate guess work; I have also as much as is consistent with the unity of the book lightened his emphasis on the *Leaves of Grass* conflict. Again the people were led by their normal light. They had always known that Democracy was good and America great. What they were unprepared for was that a subject profoundly moral like sex should be made merely objective and scientific. Again only the trained in art know that the nude is beautiful.

But M. Bazalgette's biography may do much toward a right reading of Whitman, for the whole of his work is part by part built into this firm structure and needs to be read and reread now if ever. That much neglected piece *Primer for Americans*[1] has its real place. It might well have been the foundation of Mr. Mencken's *The American Language*. *Specimen Days* and *Drum Taps* and the whole of Whitman's relation to the war and his interpretation of all war may force upon the American people the thought that if Whitman cannot be with Longfellow and Whittier, he

[1] It appeared for the first time in the Atlantic Monthly, 1904.

PREFACE

can be with Grant and Lincoln, as forces in our history.

Had M. Bazalgette written his biography in 1919, or had someone else felt that a new interpretation of Whitman is needed, not because it is his centenary year but because the world is little better than chaos for the want of his great philosophy, I feel sure that the interpretation of Whitman would be first political, and that all that he wrote is subordinate to this. History has proved Whitman true. His centripetal personality, his poetical conception of science, his experiments in verse are each and all less than that in war or peace, or, at the council table his mystical conception of man and institutions is the only politics to live by. Whitman is the greatest romantic because he wrote a new *Contrat Social:* America as he conceived it is the great romance. Whether or not he was aware of it, the long foreground Emerson spoke of included the best French philosophy from Rosseau, and Blake's glorious idea of America as another portion of the infinite. These have been the two motives in offering this biography as a centenary tribute. Not the least of M. Bazalgette's praise of Whitman is Whitman's power to recreate the soul. Surely it came from his prophet power to dream of things to come. Now more than ever this soiled world needs his faith; now more than ever America must make his faith her own:

And thou America,
For the scheme's culmination, its thought and its reality,
For these (not for thyself) thou hast arrived.

Thou too surroundest all,
Embracing carrying welcoming all, thou too by pathways broad and new,
To the ideal tendest. . . .

Is it a dream?
Nay but the lack of it the dream,
And failing it life's lore and wealth a dream,
And all the world a dream.

E. F.

TABLE OF CONTENTS

PREFACE vii
AUTHOR'S INTRODUCTION xv

PART ONE

ORIGIN AND YOUTH

LONG ISLAND (1819–1841)

CHAPTER		PAGE
I.	BIRTHPLACE AND ANCESTORS	3
II.	WEST HILLS FARM	19
III.	YEARS OF YOUTH AND APPRENTICESHIP . .	29

PART TWO

THE MULTITUDINARY LIFE

NEW YORK (1841–1855)

IV.	LITERARY BEGINNINGS	45
V.	THE MAN OF CROWDS	54
VI.	TO THE SOUTH AND TO THE LOVE OF WOMAN	72
VII.	"WALT WHITMAN, A COSMOS" . . .	91

PART THREE

"LEAVES OF GRASS"

BROOKLYN (1855–1862)

CHAPTER		PAGE
VIII.	THE GREAT DESIGN	115
IX.	THE FIRST SONG	131
X.	WALT INSULTED	141
XI.	EMERSON AND WHITMAN	152

PART FOUR

THE WOUND DRESSER

WASHINGTON (1862–1865)

XII.	AT THE BEDSIDE OF THE DYING	171
XIII.	THE WOUND	179
XIV.	THE COMRADE HEART	186
XV.	HYMNS OF THE WAR AND OF LINCOLN	193
XVI.	O'CONNOR'S LASH	202

PART FIVE

THE GOOD GRAY POET

WASHINGTON (1865–1873)

XVII.	THE GREAT COMPANIONS; PETER DOYLE, THE CONDUCTOR	209
XVIII.	FIRST VICTORY OF "LEAVES OF GRASS"	222
XIX.	THE STRICKEN OAK	234

PART SIX

THE INVALID

CAMDEN (1873–1884)

CHAPTER		PAGE
XX.	THROUGH ABANDONMENT AND SORROW	247
XXI.	THE NATURE BATH	260
XXII.	ACROSS THE CONTINENT	265
XXIII.	ANOTHER PERSECUTION	271
XXIV.	DAWN OF GLORY	279

PART SEVEN

THE SAGE OF CAMDEN

CAMDEN (1884–1888)

XXV.	THE INVALID AT HOME	289
XXVI.	THE SOUL OF WALT	294
XXVII.	DAYS IN THE COTTAGE	304

PART EIGHT

THE SETTING SUN

CAMDEN (1888–1892)

XXVIII.	A NEW ASSAULT FOILED	313
XXIX.	MEDITATION AT TWILIGHT	325
XXX.	HOUR OF APOTHEOSIS	334
XXXI.	THE DELIVERANCE	344
XXXII.	A PAGAN FUNERAL	349

AUTHOR'S INTRODUCTION

> . . . . . But I do not undertake to define you,
>   hardly to understand you,
> I do at this moment but name you,
>   prophecy you,
> I do only proclaim you!

THE America which dreams and sings, back of the one which works and invents, has given the world four universal geniuses: Poe, Emerson, Thoreau, and Whitman. However great her other poets and thinkers may be, they have, after all, but a national significance and do not so deeply touch the heart of humanity. And among these four figures, one of them more and more dominates the group: it is Walt Whitman.

Poet, seer, one hesitates to define him. He is both and much more besides. Through him a whole continent is suddenly an exultant voice. In listening to him, one seems to hear some huge rough rhapsodist from the antique world who had passed over America to confess the desires, the marvels, and the faith of the Modern Man,—the Vedic hymns of our age, fresh, rich, multiple. They thrill with the birth of an era.

So ample are his proportions that America, aside from a handful of followers, has never known his supreme significance. She ignores him. Little it matters perhaps! She has plenty of time to know him, when, at the seventh day, she rests from her labours. And he has plenty of time to wait. Has he not said somewhere, thinking of his own case: "The proof of the merit of a poet may be strictly deferred to the day when his country shall have absorbed him as lovingly as he absorbed his country."

In awaiting that time the world is about to offer to Walt Whitman another testimony. The conviction of some fine minds, expressed in many languages, is that he should be considered indisputably not only as the first of American poets, but as the most powerful poet and the most modern of the whole nineteenth century. A conviction at which one may smile "*a priori*"; it grows nevertheless from day to day.

Many, who do not share this, may avow that there is no one in modern times so wonderfully vast. His verse has to an astonishing degree the quality which only a dozen sovereign geniuses before him possessed: that of speaking to the whole world. They answer, stronger than any other voice the aspiration, the needs, the fervour, everything belonging to a young humanity, everything directed to the future. His work is big with revelation as decisive for Europeans as for Americans. These may try in vain to appropriate Walt Whitman; he escapes them; passes all frontiers, and speaks to all the people of earth.

It is not the purpose here to present an "exotic," but to remove the barrier which denies us a living source of beauty and of love at which generations may be refreshed. In a way, Walt Whitman is much closer to us than if he were of our blood. He does not emerge from the shades of time or the fogs of space, like some imposing figure, all solitary and afar. He is a big elder Brother who clears our way after having breathed our atmosphere, travelled our roads, experienced our appetites, ruminated our thoughts. We would wrong him less in ignoring him than in transforming him into a poetical curiosity. The reader may easily see that this work has not been for me a mere literary enterprise: something very different indeed. It is the fruit of a communion with his work, his character, so close and fervent that I seem to have lived for years near him. One must not be surprised then to meet here traces of my personal feeling toward both. If I have succeeded in understanding, and making understood (of that I am not very sure), this individuality of a new type it is only by having loved him so much. Whatever emotion of beauty or humanity the future may hold for me, I feel indeed that this prolonged contact with such a revealer will remain the great impression of my life.

In France, Walt Whitman for twenty-five years has roused, among those able to read him in the original, a small number of vivid admirers. Though it is not rare to-day to see his name cited, he still remains unknown to the public. Since this ignorance is bound to disappear some day, is it not better to introduce him whole in his work and his life than by fragments and sketches? At least this method has seemed to me surer and more in keeping with his importance. Hence this volume, dedicated to the man, and conceived as a kind of introduction to the reading of *Leaves of Grass*. It goes without saying that these pages have no interest, if they have any, except in relation to that great Book: it is that especially which has to be explored to understand him who built it.

I am not unmindful of any in this country who have honoured Walt Whitman and I honour them in turn, at the beginning of this work. To the name of Gabriel Sarrazin shall always be linked the honour of having first saluted Whitman amply and magnificently and of having sounded his depths. Precious to me is the encouragement which I have received since the idea possessed me of building, to the measure of my strength, a French dwelling for the American bard. What I owe to my predecessors, to the biographers of Walt Whitman, to his friends who published their memoirs, and especially to those who edited the *Camden Edition* and to my friend, Horace Traubel, is sufficiently evident in the following pages dotted with references. It was never my intention to put out a work of erudition, but to print a full-length portrait, as real and living as possible, of a man about whom one may cram volumes without defining completely. The matter is inexhaustible. I would at least try to present an advance taste of his personality.[1]

This work, such as it is, slowly and tenderly pursued, I offer to-day with the hope of conveying to other minds the marvellous revelation contained in the personality of Walt Whitman. How many times I stopped in writing these pages, disconcerted by the grandeur and wonder of the figure that I feel so near, persuaded that I was not permeated enough by his especial atmosphere and his intimate significance. What does the sailor who courses the sea all his life know of it?—I say to myself. The surface. He has been able to take some soundings; but what is that to the leaping abyss? In reality the ocean remains to him unknown; and I well understand the unwonted scruple of an Addington Symonds who was unable till the last moment to complete the work which he had long prepared on the man more revered than all, to whose mastery he yielded and whose book he absorbed verse by verse. I have nevertheless persevered, ruled by an instinct stronger than all scruples. O may I not have failed! Above all, may I not have weakened the character of the great Liver, the character whose reality seems to baffle the effort of painters!

October, 1907.   L. B.

[1] The author notes specially these biographers: H. B. Binns, Bliss Perry, Horace Traubel.

PART ONE
ORIGIN AND YOUTH
LONG ISLAND (1819–1841)

I
BIRTHPLACE AND ANCESTORS

AT THE close of the last century, an American artisan-poet summed up in one page his many-sided life. For long years he had been an invalid and he knew his end was near; he faced it in perfect peace and he was happy in casting a last backward glance on himself and the incidents of the journey whose last stage he was completing. He died the following year.

This summary, laid down by an old man, is enough to show us that like many of his countrymen, he pursued a wide range of occupations: he was a printer, country school teacher, carpenter, volunteer nurse, and besides he made poems. But who would suspect all the depth and immensity which these simple and almost commonplace lines concealed, where might be recognized the description of an individual who, whatever he was, at least was akin to hundreds of others? How perceive that from this page emerges a monument of solitary proportions, a life of the simplest bigness, the amplest, fullest, most extraordinary which has perhaps been lived on earth? A life open, joyous, expansive, multitudinary, enjoying deep draughts yet imperturbed and natural, a life which has passed outright into a strange, phenomenal book, without parallel in its origin, character, significance. A life which makes the great adventurers or busiest captains of modern industry appear indeed poor, the more one has penetrated its depth and seized its ensemble. A life which seems to break the word to live in order to recreate it with new meaning.

To describe this life, it will suffice to follow this table of contents penned by Walt Whitman when close to death.

But at the very opening of the first chapter a strange uneasiness overcomes you: the difficulty of including the thousand aspects of a life at once so individual and so universal appears well nigh insurmountable. The fear of marring, distorting, or clouding this great figure makes you falter in the attempt. A momentary awe is felt before this mystery which is alike vast and very simple.

To conquer this disquietude we shall cling narrowly to the truth which, in his life is so beautiful that to respect it scrupulously is the surest means of exalting the man. The truer one remains, the vaster is his measure. And in carefully maintaining exactitude, we shall try above all to keep that central interior truth, which shall be unaffected by the omission of a date or an incident. Never the practice of subordinating detail to mass is more essential than for a fulllength portrait of a Walt Whitman.

To depict such a man living, it is necessary to show him in the concrete reality of his daily life. It is to preserve the colour, the atmosphere of the life lived and its natural savour, that I efface myself as much as possible, in the humility of a compiler, behind those who were in personal contact with him and caught him on the spot. The subject is too big for a biographer to seek pretext for making an effect.

There is one chief fact, of which we are never to lose sight in these pages: the identity of the man and his book. Identity realized to a degree heretofore undreamed of and so perfect that all effort to sever them would be vain. "Reading him in his printed pages, seeing him near the fireside, are all one,"[1] says one of his friends. The second of his biographers likewise noted: "His body, his outward life, his inward spiritual existence and poetry, were all one; in every respect each tallied with the other, and any one of them could always be inferred from the other."[2] A similar appreciation is from one of the great companions of his life who declares

[1] Bucke, Traubel, and Harned: *In Re Walt Whitman*, p. 117.
[2] Bucke: *Walt Whitman*, p. 51.

BIRTHPLACE AND ANCESTORS 5

that Walt Whitman every day is the "living commentary" of his book.[1] So we shall unceasingly evoke the work to explain the man, and reciprocally, when we try to define the poet-prophet. If this point of view is misconceived, both will be for us an enigma.

It is but artificially and for a moment that we can separate the book from him who thus conceived it, without doubt in order to give himself more fully still than in life. This one—the poem-individual—is essentially indissoluble; the individual appears in reality great as a poem, the poem offers itself to us as an individual. Let us recognize here that the novelty of the subject excludes the precise methods of biographers, and that a more scientific rigour is not to be expected in the recital of the life of Walt Whitman than he himself put into the living of it.

Whatever may be the value of the book left by the American bard—and in truth it is incalculable—it is no exaggeration to affirm that the man seems still more extraordinary. "Walt Whitman in his person is greater than his book or what his book imports," says one of the intimate friends of his old age. "He is made of that heroic stuff which creates such books."[2] In reality, they are both but the visible and invisible aspect of the same Personality. No detail shall be idle which compels us to penetrate further into the comprehension of the living himself. The chapters of his life are the natural steps which lead us to the threshold of his poem, that we may enter in the right mood. Without this, we should undoubtedly stray long about the house before finding the door.

The essential is that the man become familiar to us and reveal himself to us as he appeared to all who saw him pass along the pavements of New York, Washington, Philadelphia. We can in full measure understand the great Elizabethan dramas, the Odyssey, the Song of Songs, or the

---

[1] John Burroughs: *Birds and Poets, The Flight of the Eagle*, p. 213. See also *Notes* of the same, p. 13.
[2] *Camden's Compliment to Walt Whitman*, p. 23.

Rig Veda with knowing scarcely anything of their authors. I do not believe that we could fully appreciate *Leaves of Grass*, ignorant of him who projected his all-powerful personality in this ode-epic of the modern Me.

The Atlantic! From it he came, the old Northman; the far distant murmur of the ocean responded to his first cries; the tumult of its leaping waves formed the accompaniment of his first meditations; the rhythm of its tides, the undulation of its shores dictated to him the law of his poems; its breezes toughened his skin; its salt penetrated his flesh. He exhales an odour of the sea god; he expresses the ample roughness of one. He, himself, in his old age loved to be compared to some sea captain retired to his cabin, and dreaming of the voyages of the olden time. Walt Whitman might have been a sailor like the Williamses and the Kossabones of his maternal line had he not preferred the more audacious venture, the sea of humanity. . . .

Long Island stretches opposite the North American continent, like a fish with its head about to strike into the midst of it, as if snapping Manhattan Island where rises New York. From Brooklyn to the promontory of Montauk, which marks one of the two extremities of its tail, this gigantic cetacian measures nearly one hundred and twenty-five miles by an average breadth of twelve to thirteen miles. A chain of irregular hills which runs the entire length of the island and separates it into two ridges outlines its dorsal fin.[1] The Indians called it Paumanok and Walt Whitman adored the rude sonority of this name.

Large, uncultivated stretches—forests of spruce, waste land, sand, salt marshes—communicate to this territory a wild, rough aspect. The south coast is bounded by flats, with immense lagoons, and in front of these straits and long bars of sand, natural dikes sustain the assaults of the Atlantic. Innumerable cone-shaped little islands

---
[1] I. Hull Platt: *Walt Whitman*, p. 1.

sprinkle the large south bay. To the east, on the stretches of the promontory which push into the open sea, are lighthouses. During storms, these bars have often seen shipwrecks, and these redoubtable, whitish looking shores keep the secret of many a tragedy of the sea. Region of winds and waves, region rude and little attractive, impress of a splendid desolation; immensity confronts one on every side, and an incessant subdued or furious clamour of the waves seems like an echo of it. The odour of marsh grass fills the bays. Not long ago all kinds of water game and fish abundantly stocked these shores, inhabited by a race of men fierce and hard like the Vikings, long since extinct.

In violent contrast with this arid and solitary coast, the region of hills and the northern slope which they shelter, especially toward the centre, are smiling and cultivated. It is a country of hills and vales, pastures and woods—where abound the oak, fir, walnut, chestnut, acacia. Numerous fruit trees, springs, little streams of pure and shining water, and villages of low-built houses with their impressive little cemeteries remind one of Normandy, or of the English Suffolk, "the Constable country." The environment here is essentially peasant and patriarchal; and at the commencement of the nineteenth century this fertile middle part of Long Island richly nourished its farmers.[1] Little country roads wound between hedges, binding the pastures and farms whose door yards were gay with lilacs. The numerous windings of the land formed infinitely varied perspectives. Beyond the waters of the strait, the coast of Connecticut is faintly outlined. The north coast, picturesque and indented, is a safe shelter of coves and inlets.

Such is the double character, savage and soft, maritime and pastoral, of this island-whale, which an immense bridge now binds to New York. Time has much modified without destroying the charms of its undulating fields and the fierce splendour of its coasts.

---
[1] J. Hull Platt: *Walt Whitman*, p. 2.

At the humble beginnings of the great migration which brought Northern Europeans to the settlement of a new continent, two currents of different origin were diffused in Long Island. From New Amsterdam (the future New York) the Dutch advanced toward the centre of the island, occupying all the western part, and notably Queens County. A little later, toward 1650, some English colonists, quitting the settlements of Massachusetts and Connecticut, crossed the sound to settle in Suffolk County, situated to the east. These two contingents, very distinct in origin, to which were added some Indians who were found toward the promontory of Montauk, and a small number of blacks, constituted the "Paumanackers" or Long Islanders. Thus the basis of the population of the island was allied directly to two great stocks which formed the foundation of the American nationality and whose fusion has determined the predominant character of the people. Whatever has been the importance of the other initial contingents, like the Scotch-Irish, the Swedes, or the Huguenots, and some modifications which the after currents have carried to that secret chemistry in which a new people is elaborated, the contributions of the Netherlands and of Great Britain remain the essential ones. And kept apart by its insularity from the great floods of immigration, and of the vast enterprises which transformed the continent, Long Island was able for a long time to conserve these two elements of its population in an almost pure state, and to remain like a fragment of Primitive America, the base and security of future America. The people of the villages applied themselves to agriculture, stock raising, fishing, ship building. They were renowned as excellent farmers and hardy sailors. Toward 1820, the entire island did not possess sixty thousand inhabitants[1]: to-day Brooklyn alone counts nearly a million and a half.

In the middle part of the island, about three miles from the village of Huntington, and slightly to the east of the

[1] H. B. Binns: *Life of Walt Whitman*, p. 3.

limit of Queens and Suffolk counties, which marked also the beginning of the line of cleavage of the two nationalities, is situated the village of West Hills, to which belonged the patrimonial farm of the "Whitman homestead" where the great-grandfather, the grandfather, and the father of the poet had lived, cultivating their estate.

The origin of the American Whitmans goes back to the time of Elizabeth. The acknowledged ancestor was a certain Abijah Whitman of whom old England saw the birth about the year 1560, and whose three sons crossed the Atlantic. The first, Zechariah, who was born in 1595 and became a clergyman, sailed in 1635 in the *True Love*, and settled in Milford, Connecticut. Five years later, the second son, John, who was born in 1602, embarked in the same vessel, and steered toward Weymouth, Massachusetts. He died in 1692, having had five daughters and five sons, all living in 1685; one of the latter, Samuel, lived to be a centenarian[1] and another, Reverend Zechariah Whitman, of Hull, Massachusetts (nephew of the other Zechariah) was a graduate of Harvard (1668), whom the annals of Dorchester describe as a *Vir pius, humilis, orthodoxus, utilissimus*.[2] It was, one believes, the posterity of John which spread across New England and the whole of America the name of Whitman, borne by thousands of individuals, living proof of the vigour and fecundity of the original stock. The third son of Abijah, Robert, born in 1615, came to America in the *Abigail* in 1635, married in 1648, and lived till 1679.

It is the first of the three brothers who interests us here for to him is attached the geneology of the poet. A son of the Reverend Zechariah of Milford, named Joseph,[3] crossed Long Island Sound sometime before 1660, and settled in

---

[1] Bucke: *Walt Whitman*, p. 14.

[2] O. L. Triggs: *Selection from Walt Whitman*, Introduction, p. xvi.

[3] It appears that this Joseph Whitman was not the son of the Reverend Zechariah Whitman of Milford, who died without children. He may have come from Stratford, Conn., and should have seen the light of day in England (Bliss Perry: *Walt Whitman*, pp. 2-3). It is a geneological point which no doubt future biographers will clear up.

the village of Huntington, which was founded in 1653 by the colonists of Massachusetts upon land bought from the Indians.[1] It is only known that he won a fair subsistence, that he lived some thirty years and was named by his fellow townsmen for different public employments.[2] It was he, or perhaps one of his sons, whose name remains unknown,[3] who bought the farm of West Hills. This unknown son himself had a son named Nehemiah, born about 1705, who married Sarah White, who lived from 1713 to 1803[4]. The oldest of their four sons, Jesse, was born in 1749 and died in 1803. He married, in 1775, Hannah Brush, daughter of Tredwell Brush, and had by her three sons, one of whom, Walter, was born July 14, 1789, the very day of the taking of the Bastille, and who was the father of the poet.

An exceptional vigour appears to have been the chief characteristic of the family. The Whitmans were in general tall and solidly built. One pictures them as tranquil and rather grave, very firm of character and chary of speech, exclusively occupied with their land and their cattle: rude men whom no power on earth could move and who seemed to partake of the tranquil force of the elements. They were remarkable for their longevity and their fecundity: from the ancestor who came from England to the family line of Walt, large families were an uninterrupted tradition. There are accorded to his great-grandfather, Nehemiah Whitman, twenty-two grandsons and granddaughters, and beyond these others of whom trace has been lost.[5]

It was a race of ample and rich virility, built for enduring work, and without the least trace of feebleness or degeneracy. It contributed fundamental and massive qualities, which make builders of cities. Although among the Whitmans of

---

[1]Bliss Perry: *Walt Whitman*, p. 2.
[2]*Id.:* p. 3.
[3]Bliss Perry (*Walt Whitman*, p. 3.) cites a John Whitman, Sr., who filled some municipal functions between 1718 and 1730, and who might be, according to him, the father of Nehemiah.
[4]*Camden Edition, Introduction*, pp. xii–xiv.
[5]*Id.*, p. xii.

New England a number were ministers, professors, and graduates of Harvard or of Yale,[1] those of Long Island always remained outside the liberal professions. Good farmers, excellent citizens, some among them artisans, not one among the descendants of Zechariah has left traces of mental distinction. All were and remained of the people, manual workers, farmers "with little or no formal culture and with no marked artistic tastes in any direction."[2] Their posterity form "an uninterrupted succession of simple workingmen, the best although the most obscure foundation of democracies."[3] They enjoyed, however, a certain ease and belonged to "that class which worked with their own hands and marked by neither riches nor real poverty." From father to son for nearly a century and a half their farm of West Hills gave them a living. They were hospitable, solicitous of ease and of the education of their children, and their reputation in the county was excellent.[4] From the beginning the property which they possessed must have been considerable, and Nehemiah knew how to augment it. But because of a succession of adverse circumstances it came much diminished into the hands of Walter, the father of the poet.

Some individuals of the family are distinguished by a few unlooked for characteristics. For example, Sarah White, the great-grandmother of Walt, seems to have realized the ideal of a virago. Of dark complexion, chewing tobacco like an old man, brusque and erect, she showed to strangers a repellent countenance, and was tender only to the little Negroes always hanging at her skirts. A consummate horsewoman, she was seen, after she became a widow, riding out every day to visit her land and to direct her slaves, swearing like a pagan when she found them at fault. She died at the age of ninety.[5] Hannah Brush, grandmother of the poet,

[1] O. L. Triggs: *Selections, Introduction*, p. xvi.
[2] *Camden Edition, Introduction*, p. xvii.
[3] *Id.*: p. xviii.
[4] John Burroughs: *Notes*, p. 120.
[5] *Camden Edition, Introduction*, p. xx.

was an orphan, reared by her Aunt, Vashti Platt, proprietor of an important farm and of numerous slaves, in the eastern part of the island. She was a school-teacher for a time and besides an excellent seamstress, a woman of the old school, fair and robust, of natural distinction, fine, intelligent, and gay.[1] As she had lived through the Revolutionary period down to 1834, her grandson, who knew her till he was fifteen, heard her recount her memories and knew from her the fiery spirit which animated his ancestors of that great epoch.[2] During the war of Independence, the Whitmans were notably among the most enthusiastic "rebels" of the island. Many among them had served under Washington, some as officers, such as the son of Nehemiah who was killed as lieutenant at the Battle of Brooklyn: an event the poet was to interpret in one of his poems, *History of a Centenary*.[3] Major Brush, uncle of Hannah Brush, expiated in an English prison the ardour of his patriotism.

If the Whitmans belonged to the most vigorous British element in one section, their neighbours, his mother's family, the Van Velsors, who lived nearly three miles from West Hills, on the boundary of Queens County, could equally pass for typical representatives of the old Americanized Dutch. The Van Velsors, like the Whitmans, lived for many generations upon the same farm, situated in a picturesque corner at the border of the solitary road which rises from Cold Spring Harbour, a small port opening upon the sound.

The date of their arrival in the county is uncertain; but the first of the name had certainly come with the Dutch colonists of New Amsterdam, who were dispersed in the west of Long Island. The ancestor, the farthest removed whom one can name, is the legendary "Kossabone, Old Sea Wolf," who died at the age of ninety. Walt, in one of his poems,

---

[1] *Camden Edition, Introduction:* p. xx.
[2] Triggs: *Selections, Introduction,* p. xvi.
[3] *Camden Edition, Introduction,* p. xix.

BIRTHPLACE AND ANCESTORS 13

evoked, from family traditions, his impressive death in his great arm chair, facing the sea and the vessels, his dying eye following their evolutions.[1] It is conjectured that Mary or Jenny Kossabone, who married the great-grandfather of the poet, Garrett Van Velsor, a cloth weaver, deceased in 1812, was his granddaughter. The second of the six issues of this marriage was "Major" Cornelius, who united with Naomi (shortened to Amy) Williams, one of the six children of "Captain" John Williams and Mary Woolley. Naomi Van Velsor died in 1826 and the Major in 1837. The poet knew them in his infancy: and it was of them that Whitman's mother, Louisa Van Velsor, was born.

Despite their proximity and their life so closely alike, and the identity of their aspirations, the Van Velsors and the Whitmans differed remarkably one from the other. Among the Whitmans, the British stock, the chief trait was firmness of character, verging almost upon hardness; the maternal ancestors were indebted to their Low Country origin for their abundant vitality and joviality. Among the farmers of Cold Spring a good humour dominated, a bonhomie, a warm, communicative cordiality, natural to a people in possession of the art of living: they had something more flush, more plastic, more varied, and more open, than their neighbours. There must be added to these characteristics an indomitable spirit of hardness, and of liberty which had so magnificently proved the race in the mother country and which persisted in the new world. The Van Velsors were farmers, stock raisers, artisans, sailors. Cornelius, the one who stands out as the most picturesque of the group, offers the perfect type of the Americanized Hollander. His grandson describes him for us as stout, red, jovial, frank, with a sonorous voice and a characteristic physiognomy,[2] "the best of men," affirms someone in the neighbourhood who knew him well.[3] The

---
[1] *Leaves of Grass*, p. 395.
[2] *Complete Prose*, p. 5.
[3] Bucke: *Walt Whitman*, p. 15.

Van Velsors were noted for their blood horses, which they reared and cared for themselves.[1] The Major always owned beautiful horses and his sons followed his example.[2] His wife, Naomi Williams, belonged to a family which from father to son were sailors. Her father, John Williams, a kind and charitable man fond of good cheer, was Captain and joint owner of a schooner plying between New York and Florida, and his brother was likewise a sailor. Both perished at sea.[3] Naomi is pictured as truly adorable with a presence of sweetness and intimate charm. Generous, hospitable, knowing how to care for her children, of elevated soul, deep, intuitive, she showed herself in every way the worthy spouse of the excellent "Major." Her grandson kept a particularly touching memory of her, which one day inspired this strophe:

Behold a woman!
She looks out from her quaker cap, her face is clearer and more beautiful than the sky.

She sits in an armchair under the shaded porch of the farm house,
The sun just shines on her old white head.

Her ample gown is of cream-hued linen,
Her grandsons raised the flax, and her grand-daughters spun it with the distaff and the wheel.[4]

The Williamses were probably of Welsh stock. The poet, however, made little of this origin: and whatever may be the likelihood of it, one must acknowledge that nothing particularly celtic appeared in the forming of Walt Whitman.

An influence on the contrary, of which he acknowledges indubitable traces in him, was that of the Van Velsors, the good people of Holland. It is but right that he felicitates himself in yielding to it. No European race has carried across the world a blood more precious, a more energetic principle of

---

[1] *Complete Prose*, p. 5.
[2] John Burroughs: *Notes*, p. 78.
[3] *Complete Prose*, p. 5.
[4] *Leaves of Grass*, p. 355.

vitality and fecundity, than that of the Netherlands, which notably constitute, chronologically and characteristically, the founding of the state of New York. "Not the Scotch-Irish stock itself, or the Jewish, is more dourly and stubbornly prepotent in human society than is this Dutch strain in America. . . . These original stocks tinge and saturate humanity through generations. . . . Few realize how the Dutch element has percolated through our population in New York and Pennsylvania. As late as 1750 more than one-half of New York State were Dutch. The rural Dutch to-day almost always have large families of children, and form in every respect the most solid element in their community. In New York City and in Brooklyn and Albany it is superfluous to say that to belong to a Dutch family is to belong to blue blood, the aristocracy. . . ."[1] In the United States the Hollander has carried his realist instinct, positive and earthy, his solid intelligence, his methodical spirit, his passion for independence, and above all his magnificent physical qualities of health and of poise. Destined to assist in building the foundation of the American edifice, he was the guarantee of its aplomb, and its solidity, as his brothers of the Southern hemisphere assure the future of the South African Federation. Without the British element, it is probable that the United States would not exist to-day: but without the Dutch element it is certain it would not have attained its present grandeur. Bucke is thus right in affirming that New Yorkers should be as proud of the ship *Goot Vrow* and the debarking of the first Dutch, as the inhabitants of New England are of the *Mayflower* and of Plymouth Rock.[2] The race of Netherlands is above all a mother-race. Its presence upon a new soil was a blessing to the nation which one day should develop there.

Other influences marked the spot where the poet was to be born, and affected particularly his parents. The sect of

[1] Bucke: *In Re Walt Whitman*, p. 197. W. S. Kennedy: *Reminiscences of Walt Whitman*, p. 89.
[2] Bucke: *Walt Whitman*, p. 17 (Note).

Quakers or Friends was strongly implanted in Long Island, which was to become one of their centres. The shoemaker, George Fox, its founder, when on his pilgrimage in America met attentive auditors among the Paumanackers and his word had awakened echoes in the soul of this rude and independent population when he came in 1672, to preach to the people in the open air, as in the time as the Apostles.[1] Many recollections of that time still live in the memory of the Islanders when Walt was a child. One of the great Quaker figures, the preacher, Elias Hicks, was born on Long Island and had evangelized it. He was a radical spirit who, finding the doctrine of the society too formalistic, had fomented a dissent. Hicks despised creeds, churches, and every organization of the religious life. Religion for him consisted in spiritual emotion, in a "secret, ecstatic silence," which in obedience to a Divine Law speaks in the depth of the individual conscience. All exterior manifestations were in his eyes but lies. "Seek the truth only within yourself": such was one of his essential precepts. "He is the most democratic of the religionists—the prophets,"[2] wrote Walt Whitman in a brief tract which he tardily consecrated to Elias Hicks, to carry out an idea of his youth in rendering homage to one who had expressed the religious aspirations of his ancestors. Thus the Hicksites were affirmed as the left of quakerism, which was itself the extreme left of the rich variety of sects issuing from the Reformation.

It is important to know the expressly original and heterodox character of this society of Friends, which represents sentiment extremely adverse to dogma. They have neither ministers nor sacraments. The divinity of Christ and the authority of the Scriptures mean much less to them than the "interior light" which illumines the conscience of every man upon earth, and which they made the rock of their doctrine.

The Quakers were people of ultra simple manners, in-

---

[1] *Complete Prose*, p. 477.
[2] *Id.*, p. 457.

BIRTHPLACE AND ANCESTORS 17

flexible and opinionated, headstrong, narrow, fundamentally pacifist, abhorring oppression under all forms, political as well as spiritual: all in all, religious individualists. Their exclusive obedience to the appeal from within, which they judged a divine order manifested to man, gave to their character a special stamp, a rigidity which manifested itself in their habits and their social conduct. They were looked upon with suspicion by the other sects, who disapproved of their excessive independence—and found themselves, notably in colonial times, in radical opposition to the Puritans. Opposed to these, who leaned toward intolerance and theocracy, quakerism represented the origin of the most modern principles, such as the separation of church and state, equality of all religious denominations, free trade, justice to the aborigines. The Friends were discontented with England, and reached America to find themselves cruelly persecuted by the Puritans of New England.[1] By the strength of their obstinacy, they succeeded in doing away with the proscription of heretics in Massachusetts. The prosperous Quaker colony of Pennsylvania became the hive from which swarmed through the West the bearers of the libertarian spirit, the pioneers.[2] Such is the spirit, synonym of the fierce and irreconcilable independence, of the old Quakers who, under a rude surface, bore the vital element of democracy and of the modern world. These men queer, but simple and great, despite their absurd narrowness, who refused to uncover before any one, were he the president of the United States, who thee'd and thou'd everybody, and forbade any inscription upon their graves, were the stoics of our age and the ancestors of the more recent free, religious thinkers. The country might esteem itself happy which in its beginnings had them, for from them came men like Thomas Paine and Lincoln.

With the Whitmans as with the Van Velsors, the sect

---
[1] *Complete Prose*, p. 477.
[2] John Fiske: *The Dutch and Quaker Colonies in America.*

numbered adherents or met sympathy. The grandfather Whitman, Jesse—who likewise knew Thomas Paine[1]—had been in his youth the intimate companion of Elias Hicks, to become later his admirer. The father of the poet followed his sermons assiduously: and Walt himself remembers to have been present, as a small child, at one of his last preachings.[2] The whole family was more or less tinged with quakerism. On his mother's side traces of it manifest themselves: Amy Williams, if she was not perhaps a true Quakeress, as her grandson has told us, inclined strongly toward the sect.[3] This particularly sane and strengthening atmosphere of the society of Friends the poet could absorb by all his pores from his family and in his travels about the island. We see how this spirit of independence and heterodoxy would reappear in him, enlarged, transmuted, and what invisible and strong bonds, beyond the most patent divergencies, attached to the old Quakers the most modern and most enfranchised of men. In his pages on Elias Hicks one sees these secret affinities very closely, so that one can there recover the advances of religious individualism in its march beyond Christianity.

---

[1] H. B. Binns: *Life of Walt Whitman*, p. xxv.
[2] *Complete Prose*, p. 465.
[3] H. B. Binns: *Life of Walt Whitman*, Appendix A, pp. 347-348.

II

THE WEST HILLS FARM

On June 8, 1816, Walter Whitman married Louisa Van Velsor, a daughter of one of the farmers of Cold Spring.

Like his fathers, Walter Whitman cultivated the farm of West Hills. But the support it yielded the family in his boyhood was meagre, and at fifteen he left the farm for New York to apprentice himself to carpentry. When he returned to the country he undertook the business of general building and carried his tools to the different parts of the island where his work called him. He was considered a first-rate craftsman, doing conscientious, durable work. "Not a few of his barn and house frames"—wrote Bucke in 1883—"with their seasoned timbers and careful braces are still standing in Suffolk and Queens Counties and in Brooklyn, strong and plumb as ever."[1]

He was a kind of giant, measuring more than six feet, said a man of the neighbourhood, of physique as solid and massive as his buildings, with countenance serious and rather taciturn. Morally he was fundamentally honest, calm, and rigid, a man of great firmness. His features bespoke strength and sincerity, that kind of serene and austere primitive energy so often seen in portraits of men of "the antique time," so strikingly unlike the restless mobility and fatigue of contemporary faces. There is, moreover, lurking about the mouth and eye, a certain hardness. Walt confesses that, in his youth, he often had tempestuous discussions with his father, roused by his parental authoritativeness: little storms which the excellent mother, natural peace maker,

[1] Bucke: *Walt Whitman*, p. 15.

always dispelled.[1] In a poem wholly penetrated with impressions of his childhood, a certain little interior picture evokes a scene of this kind which might well have been inspired by a memory of the paternal home.[2] Like his kindred Walter Whitman was rather slow and placid, but once without command of himself he was violent as a cyclone. His son, nevertheless, kept affectionately close to him till his death, and could write truthfully of his father and mother: "As for loving and disinterested parents, no child or man has ever had more reasons to bless and to thank them than I." He was a fine, a true Whitman, this husband of Louisa. However, his strong qualities do not seem to have favoured him in his struggle for existence. Unlucky or too honest, perhaps without a sense of business, the good workman knew constant care and, in dying, left nothing to his family for patrimony except regret.

His wife, Louisa Van Velsor, was, if we are to believe her son, a wife and mother of exceptional character; when we look at her portrait, we must credit his enthusiastic testimony, who declared he saw in her "the most suave woman whom he had ever seen or known or expected to know."[3] It is one of those faces from which sovereignly radiates beauty and an infinite benevolence. Something unspeakably amiable and powerful, at the same time tender and strong, looks out from this good old face, still agreeable and smiling at sixty. It is easy to believe one's self looking at the magnificent and fecund image of earth or of the mother of men, equal to any task, like that of bringing forth a new race. How eloquent this face, rich and racy of the peasant, which reflects a light of interior contentment and eternal youth. She had nine children and lived poor. She was an "ample woman" according to Whitman's expression, who glorified in her person the virtues of the women of the Dutch race, serene, maternal, and fruitful.

---

[1] *Camden Edition, Introduction*, p. xvi.
[2] *Leaves of Grass*, p. 283.
[3] See the daguerreotype reproduced: *The Wound Dresser*, p. 47.

THE WEST HILLS FARM

She was, to be sure, a simple, illiterate woman, whose world was her household. But like her mother, she possessed intuitive qualities very intimate and almost divine, which belong to superior women. In her letters to her family, which she could write only with difficulty, she reveals incomparable spiritual gifts.[1] She irregularly followed religious exercises, a little indifferent to the denomination of the church which she frequented: she pretended to be a Baptist, but, in reality, her preferences drew her rather toward the Quakers. Like her husband, she did not practice and was content to affirm her sympathy for the same sect, in going to hear Elias Hicks. Religious observance of any kind in the home there was none.[2] To those who saw her only in her old age, she appeared elderly, grave, "imposing and contained," full of "simple, organic energy."[3] She was in truth a typical example of those "powerful, uneducated persons" whom her son was to exalt.[4] She was far superior to her husband[5] and Walt Whitman confessed himself indebted to this admirable woman for his more intimate qualities; his genius did not prevent his acknowledging himself the spiritual son of this humble housewife. And it was the clear perception of this debt, proudly confessed, which strengthened the bond which united them. An exceptional tenderness, beyond a filial attachment, always existed between Walt and his mother. "He never speaks of her," says his friend John Burroughs, "without love and passion flooding his face."[6] His correspondence, his conversation, his works in prose and in verse are sprinkled with allusions to his "dear mother," all proving a passionate affection and a respect almost religious. When he writes to her, he seems to become a little child telling her his love and his daily

---
[1] Bucke: *Walt Whitman, Man and Poet*, Cosmopolis, June, 1898, p: 687:
[2] Bucke: *In Re Walt Whitman*, p. 38:
[3] *Camden Edition, Introduction*, p. xxii:
[4] Bucke: *In Re Walt Whitman*, p. 353:
[5] *Camden Edition, Introduction*, p. xxii.
[6] John Burroughs: *Notes*, p. 121.

thoughts. And after her death, he characterized her from the depths of his sorrow, "the most perfect and most magnetic character, the most rare combination of the practical, moral and spiritual, the least selfish of all whom he had ever known. . . ."[1] He has otherwise immortalized her in the monument which he has dedicated to her among his *Songs of Parting* in a strophe the sorrow of which is so poignant.[2]

In these two beings so representative of their origin, two complementary races united. We shall see later what this fusion signifies, when it comes to be realized in the life of their offspring, with the addition of genius and even of something more than genius. The maternal contribution tempered with its experienced optimism and benevolence and generous affectionateness, whatever he may have had of severity and of tension, of the rigid and narrow in the character of the Whitmans; and in one point at least, the inclinations of the two families combined and drew them toward spiritual independence.

The union of these two races was therefore the extraordinary promise of a completer human type, one profiting by all the power of a new soil. It is not an artifice of the panegyrist to see the exceptional natural advantage which attended the coming of this truly predestined man. Abysmal mystery of hereditary transmissions, successive minglings, as in a series of crucibles, the slow and sure human preparation! These words of Doctor Bucke, the biographer of the poet, are here invested with particular authority: "No conclusion of modern science is surer than this: that there is no great man without great ancestors, that to produce a supreme personality it is first necessary that exceptional stock be prepared. Then indeed many shall be called for the one who is chosen."[3]

It may be asserted that this exceptional stock was veri-

---
[1] *Complete Prose*, p. 274 (Note).
[2] *Leaves of Grass*, p. 376.
[3] Bucke: *Walt Whitman, Man and Poet*, Cosmopolis, June, 1889, p. 687.

tably "prepared" when Walt was born, May 31, 1819, at the West Hills farm, second son of Walter Whitman, the carpenter, and of Louisa Van Velsor. He found in his cradle the enormous strength and health accumulated by his family, nowise diminished like the family fortune, but increased each generation. He was the issue of a race of manual labourers, peasants, artisans, sailors, of individuals skilled in various kinds of business, but equally mingling with the earth and sea, with the air, with elemental things. He belonged to the chosen race of the common people, sprang from a soil admirably virgin, to be converted into intellectuality and art. Not one of his family had been affected by culture, falsified by an excessive development of sensibility, vitiated by the miseries of urban life. Nothing but a natural soil about this young branch. He was an off-shoot, sprouting from the most authentic American trunk, from the very heart of the race. And to be indeed of pure race, signified for an American, to be the issue of a mixed blood; likewise, in a democracy real and not fictitious, to be of high birth, one must come from average people, the sanest portion of the mass, and not from titled and privileged men. In this respect the infant of West Hills was of high birth. His forebears, women as well as men, represented the nucleus of individuals superior in energy and vitality, by which the United States was truly to be built. They were great personages of the people. Walt much later had the right to be proud of them, and in truth he was. He could well, in his candid, limitless pride say

> Well begotten, and raised by a perfect mother . . .

and reflecting on all his ancestors, dedicated from century to century to great primordial labours, could proclaim:

> I come from people in their proper spirit.

The location of West Hills is particularly pleasant. It is a retired spot among hills where vegetation is luxuriant. In the midst of orchards are farms, prairies, old roads bordered with dense tufted hedges, and shaded here and there with great trees. Insects, birds, springs, game, and flowers abound; here unfolds the very heart of the farm region of Long Island.

As for the estate of the Whitmans—"it was," according to their descendant, "a fine domain, five hundred acres, all good soil, gently sloping east and south, about one-tenth woods, plenty of grand old trees." There were, he further tells us, "broad and beautiful farm lands of my grandfather (1780) and of my father. There was the new house (1810), the big oak a hundred and fifty or two hundred years old; there the wells, the sloping kitchen-garden, and a little way off even the remain sof the dwelling of my great-grandfather (1750–'60) still standing, with its mighty timbers and low ceilings. Near by, a stately grove of tall, vigorous black walnuts, beautiful, Apollo-like, the sons or grandsons, no doubt, of black walnuts during or before 1776. On the other side of the road spread the famous apple orchard over twenty acres, the trees planted by hands long mouldering in the grave (my uncle Jesse's), but quite many of them evidently capable of throwing out their annual blossoms and fruit yet."[1]

The primitive ancestral home still remains and is to-day used as a wagon shed. The newer one where the poet was born is now occupied by a farmer and life has not left it. It is a small two-story house, a little stoop in front. Its sloping walls, its grassy court before the entrance, the lilac bush decorating its front, the barrier of wood and the well curbs near by, give it a stamp savouring of the rustic and the antique. The habitation is humble in appearance but comfortable.[2] Aside from a wing built on the right, it is still as it was built nearly a century ago. And in a region which the proximity of the enormous metropolitan city transforms

---
[1]*Complete Prose*, p. 4.
[2]H. B. Binns: *Life of Walt Whitman*, p. 8.

little by little into a suburb, the place still retains the charm of solitude and of nature.

West Hills is near enough to the sea for its confused noises to be heard; especially on peaceful nights, after a storm, the muffled and distant rumbling of the waves produce a marvellous effect. Walt always kept the echo of the "mystic surf-beat of the sea." Very near the farm is the elevation, Jaynes Hill, the culminating point of the island. From this height, which is perhaps but a hundred yards, a marvellous panorama of fields, wood, hills, bounded by the waters of the sound on one side, by the ocean on the other, surrounds and subdues you. More than once in his youth the poet made its ascent to impregnate himself with space and wind, to embrace the immense horizon of land and sea. The whole region abounds in striking and varied perspectives.

As for the life which the family of the old farm lived at the beginning of the last century, it is described in these lines, by John Burroughs, the earliest of the Whitman biographers, and who had in the writing of his books advice and suggestions from Whitman himself:

> The Whitmans lived in a long story-and-a-half farm-house, hugely timber'd, which is still standing. A great smoke-canopied kitchen with vast hearth and chimney, form'd one end of the house. The existence of slavery in New York at that time, and the possession by the family of some twelve or fifteen slaves, house and field servants, gave things quite a patriarchal look. The very young darkies could be seen, a swarm of them, toward sundown, in this kitchen, squatted in a circle on the floor, eating their supper of Indian pudding and milk. In the house, and in food and furniture, all was rude, but substantial. No carpets or stoves were known, and no coffee, and tea or sugar only for the women. Rousing wood fires gave both warmth and light on winter nights. Pork, poultry, beef, and all the ordinary vegetables and grains were plentiful. Cider was the men's common drink, and used at meals. The clothes were mainly homespun. Journeys were made by both men and women on horse-back. Both sexes labor'd with their own hands—the men on the farm—the women in the house and around it. Books were scarce. The annual copy of the almanac was a treat, and was pored over through the long winter evenings. I must not forget to mention that both these families were near enough

to the sea to behold it from the high places, and to hear in the still hours the roar of the surf; the latter, after a storm, giving a peculiar sound at night. Then all hands, male and female, went down frequently on beach and bathing parties, and the men on practical expeditions for cutting salt hay, and for clamming and fishing.[1]

The Van Velsors lived a similar kind of life. From among his memories, the poet evokes "their vast kitchen and ample fireplace, and sitting room adjoining, the plain furniture, the meals, the house full of merry people, my grandmother Amy's sweet old face in its quaker cap, my grandfather, the 'Major' "—[2] all the dear farm decorations which were so familiar to him in his childhood. Less lucky than that of the Whitmans, the "long irregular house a sombre gray brown, with walls covered in shingles, with the outhouses, the stable, and the vast barn," of the Van Velsors has long since disappeared and "the plow has passed over its foundations."

These last lines date from a journey which the poet made to West Hills when he was sixty-three years old. After having lived and worked, he was seized with a desire to see his native home.

All the religious sentiment which attaches one to a line of ancestors and to a corner of the soil is revealed in the touching page where the old man gives an account of his visit to the little cemeteries, lonely and wild, nature in full swing, conquered by vegetable life, where his relatives were resting:

July 29, 1881.—After more than forty years' absence (except a brief visit, to take my father there once more, two years before he died), went down Long Island on a week's jaunt to the place where I was born, thirty miles from New York City. Rode around the old familiar spots, viewing and pondering and dwelling long upon them, everything coming back to me.—I now write these lines seated on an old grave (doubtless of a century since at least) on the burial hill of the Whitmans of many generations. Fifty and more graves are quite plainly traceable, and as many more decay'd out of all form—depress'd mounds, crumbled and broken stones, cover'd with moss—the gray and sterile hill, the clumps of chestnuts out-

---

[1] John Burroughs: *Notes*, pp. 78–79.
[2] *Complete Prose*, p. 5.

side, the silence, just varied by the soughing wind. There is always the deepest eloquence of sermon or poem in any of these ancient graveyards of which Long Island has so many; so what must this one have been to me? My whole family history, with its succession of links, from the first settlement down to date, told here—three centuries concentrate on this sterile acre.

The next day, July 30, I devoted to the maternal locality, and if possible was still more penetrated and impress'd. I write this paragraph on the burial hill of the Van Velsors, near Cold Spring, the most significant depository of the dead that could be imagin'd, without the slightest help from art, but far ahead of it, soil sterile, a mostly bare plateau—flat of half an acre, the top of a hill, brush and well grown trees and dense woods bordering all around, very primitive, secluded, no visitors, no road (you can not drive here, you have to bring the dead on foot, and follow on foot). Two or three score graves quite plain, as many more almost ribb'd out. My grandfather Cornelius and my grandmother Amy (Naomi) and numerous relatives nearer or remoter, on my mother's side, lie buried here The scene as I stood or sat, the delicate and wild odor of the woods, a slightly drizzling rain, the emotional atmosphere of the place, and the inferr'd reminiscences, were fitting accompaniments.[1]

This same emotion we feel in our turn before the two sketches illustrating Bucke's book, where the etcher Pennell knew how to translate with such intensity and mute and poignant eloquence the anonymous graves where sleep the ancestors who prepared the coming of the poet.

We find ourselves in the presence of origins. And we should interrogate them without haste before following the man in his moving and diverse career; they forever fashioned him and his work; they furnished him a base so solid and so vast in life and in art that each of his steps is firmer, each of his songs freer, by the effort of the generations which preceded him. We encounter them everywhere in the course of his life, blended with his acts and his verse. He owes them his amplitude, his health, and his strength. Walt Whitman is not a magnificent flower blooming suddenly and artificially. He is a product of nature, amplified by the august individuality which was granted him by superaddi-

---
[1] *Complete Prose*, p. 4.

tion. Whence the particular interest which adheres in discovering his roots and the soil into which they penetrate.

This prelude, which holds in germ the motif of the drama, this momentary pause upon the threshold before entering, to give us time to examine the surroundings, the situation, the aspect of the extraordinary dwelling where we are guests, is not meant to please a vain ambition of a biographer. The poet himself commands us not to neglect any of the elements which concurred in his genesis. They contribute truly to one essential part, to an explanation of the wonderful riddle which he is. It is only after having studied all the depth of the influences from soil, from race, from ancestors, from environmment, that we can seize the real meaning of these verses:

My tongue, every atom of my blood, form'd from this soil, this air,
Born here of parents born here from parents the same, and their parents
    the same, [1]. . . .

---
[1] *Leaves of Grass*, p. 29.

III

YEARS OF YOUTH AND APPRENTICESHIP

THE child received the Christian name of Walter, but the family dropped the last syllable, no doubt to distinguish him from the father.[1] This familiar name of Walt was retained and definitely adopted by the poet after the first edition of his book, as truer and more intimate. He wished to be for all but Walt Whitman, as he was for his family, and posterity will not know any other name. And already one writes simply Walt, as one says Jean Jacques.

Walt was four years old when his parents quitted the farm among the hills to live in the big town which was developing at the western extremity of Long Island. It was no longer a time when one was born and died in the same spot, near the bones of one's ancestors, and the mobility of the period encroached even upon them. Circumstances had changed since the close of the Revolution, an epoch of prosperity for the family, and the father came to try his luck in Brooklyn where at that time there was much building. The Whitmans remained in town for twelve years, during which the carpenter followed his trade with varying fortune, without ever becoming rich, to the time when a grave illness of the mother recalled them to the country.

The household of three children—Walt was the second and a fourth was soon to be born—settled in Front Street at the water's edge, not far from "New Ferry" which plied between Brooklyn and New York. It was probable that Walter Whitman speculated in his work, by mortgaging or reselling the little houses which he built: the frequent re-

---
[1] Bucke: *In Re Walt Whitman*, p. 35.

movals of his family seemed to indicate this.[1] After a stay in Cranberry Street they removed to "a pretty house" says the poet—which the father had built in Johnston Street. Then it was to Tillary Street that they migrated. About 1830 we find them at last in Henry Street.[2] It was thus a somewhat nomadic life which the child lived during his first years, though these successive habitations followed close upon one another.

Brooklyn at that time, the humble kernel of the enormous agglomeration now absorbed by greater New York, was still a quiet little village very rural in character.[3] It was there that Walt, to use his own words, quitted his frocks and became a boy bold enough to begin exploring the surrounding world, and to adventure alone into the streets, as far even as the store of the corner grocer, who later became mayor. He seems to have manifested very early independent and vagabond instincts. He was often seen on the neighbouring ferry whose employees took a fancy to the little fellow who went aboard and made a tour with them. The child already yielded to the attraction of moving ships which after were to inspire him with a veritable passion. He watched with astonished eyes the horses which so drolly stepped round and round in the centre of the boat to produce the motive force. It was at the turning of an epoch, and the first steamboat had yet to be used in the service.

Thus from the age that he could take to his little legs he lived the carefree, independent, dawdling life, life in the open with all its risks, a child of the people who blossoms on the streets, drawn to places by his awakening intelligence, the same obscure instinct of migration, of curiosity and adventure which animates primitive humanity in its flight across the world; however futile may seem the remark, in reality it is not, for it matters in the future development of the individual that the first memories of his childhood are not

---

[1] H. B. Binns: *Life of Walt Whitman*, pp. 13-14.
[2] *Complete Prose*, p. 9. Bucke: *Walt Whitman*, p. 8.
[3] *Complete Prose*, pp. 10-11.

YEARS OF YOUTH AND APPRENTICESHIP 31

linked with ideas of confinement, and of subordination to a narrow surveillance. Sixty years later Walt still kept vivid these impressions of his life as a boy, scarcely out of his mother's arms.

This is the place for an incident of his fifth year, a type of anecdote often found in the youth of men of genius, as if to mark them with the sign of their predestination. John Burroughs has told it for us:

> On the visit of General Lafayette to this country, in 1824, he came over to Brooklyn in state and rode through the city. The children of the schools turn'd out to join in the welcome. An edifice for a free public library for youths was just then commencing and Lafayette consented to stop on his way and lay the corner-stone. Numerous children arriving on the ground, where a huge irregular excavation for the building was already dug, surrounded the heaps of rough stone, several gentlemen assisted in lifting the children to safe or convenient spots to see the ceremony. Among the rest, Lafayette, also helping the children, took up the five-year-old Walt Whitman, and pressing the child a moment to his breast, and giving him a kiss, handed him down to a safe spot into the excavation.[1]

The poet in his old age still recalled among the memories of that distant epoch[2] the arrival of Lafayette in Brooklyn. His parents then lived in Tillary Street. The hero with a manly figure and a fine face had come by the Old Ferry and was received with great pomp at the foot of Fulton Street.[3]

Walt at that time went to school, that is to say to the public school. He made but a short stay—about six years—allowed to the children of the common people, forced early into practical life. He also frequented a Sunday school at St. Ann's. And this primary teaching remained the only foundation of methodic and formal instruction of his whole life,[4] to which later he added the treasure of his reading and

---

[1] John Burroughs: *Notes*, p. 80.
[2] *Diary in Canada*, pp. 5–7.
[3] *Complete Prose*, p. 9.
[4] No other instruction was his till his ultimate passing as student to the Jamaica Academy (Long Island) indicated by Bucke, *Walt Whitman*, p. 22, and which in any case must have been very short and almost insignificant. As he taught later at this place, Binns' *Life of Walt Whitman* p. 33, there is perhaps confusion.

his studies. The son of the carpenter was not a privileged one.

In 1831 he was employed as a boy in the office of a lawyer in Fulton Street, where he was given a fine desk and a window nook to himself. His "boss" was very kind and helped him with his writing. He moreover gave his little clerk a ticket to a big circulating library,—which Walt later called the most signal event of his boy life. Then he plunged with delight into every kind of romance: the entire series of *Thousand and One Nights* he went through; then the novels and poems of Walter Scott, without counting other marvels.[1] It was a veritable feast. Next he was placed with a doctor, likewise as errand boy. At fourteen it was time to decide upon a business and he entered as apprentice the composing room of a weekly paper, the Long Island Patriot, to learn the printer's trade. At last he hit upon his work, for through all the ups and downs of his many-sided life it was in printing offices that he long found his principal occupation.

The proprietor of the Patriot, S. E. Clements, paid attention to his apprentices and sometimes took Walt out walking: on Sunday he conducted them to a church which resembled a fortress. In the office Walt had for colleague and friend an old revolutionary character who had seen Washington and who recounted for him many stories of heroic times. After that, he worked on the Long Island Star, the journal of Alden Spooner,[2] who later recollected his apprentice as a notably idle boy:[3] epithet which Walt was to encounter the whole of his life, very unjustly, however.

From these years the poet remembered vividly an impression made upon the mind of the boy observer. One day in January, when walking on Broadway, he saw "a bent, feeble but stout-built very old man, bearded, swathed in rich furs, with a great ermine cap on his head, led and as-

---

[1] *Complete Prose*, p. 9.
[2] *Complete Prose*, p. 10.
[3] H. B. Binns: *Life of Walt Whitman*, p. 20.

sisted, almost carried, down the steps of his high front stoop (a dozen friends and servants, emulous, carefully holding, guiding him) and then lifted and tuck'd in a gorgeous sleigh, envelop'd in other furs, for a ride. Well, I, a boy of perhaps thirteen or fourteen, stopp'd and gazed long at the spectacle of that furswathed old man, surrounded by friends and servants, and the careful seating of him in the sleigh. I remember the spirited, champing horses, the driver and his whip, and a fellow-driver by his side, for extra prudence. The old man, the subject of so much attention, I can almost see him now. It was John Jacob Astor."[1] The son of Long Island farmers in passing the New York millionaire was petrified before the revelation of the enormous display of wealth.

Though living in Brooklyn, during the school and apprenticeship years, Walt did not say good-by to the farm at West Hills nor at Cold Spring. Every summer he returned to pass his vacations with his grandparents to make prolonged stays with them. It was thus that he came to know his gentle grandmother, Naomi, with her quakeress cap, his jovial grandfather, Cornelius, and Hannah Whitman, his other grandmother. A good part of his childhood and adolescence was thus passed exploring in every sense the country and the borders of the island to the point of feeling them as near as if he had not been from them for four years. It is he himself we must question in order to know the impressions which these magnificent months of nature and of liberty left upon him:

Inside the outer bars or beach this south bay is everywhere comparatively shallow; of cold winters all thick ice on the surface. As a boy I often went forth with a chum or two, on those frozen fields, with hand-sled, axe and eel-spear, after messes of eels. We would cut holes in the ice, sometimes striking quite an eel-bonanza, and filling our baskets with great, fat, sweet, whitemeated fellows. The scenes, the ice, drawing the hand-sled, cutting holes, spearing the eels, etc., were of course just such fun as is dearest to boyhood. The shores of this bay, winter and summer, and my doings there in early life, are woven all through L. of G. One sport I was very

[1] *Complete Prose*, p. 12.

fond of was to go on a bay-party in summer to gather sea-gull's eggs. (The gulls lay two or three eggs, more than half the size of hen's eggs, right on the sand, and leave the sun's heat to hatch them.)

The eastern end of Long Island, the Peconic bay region, I knew quite well too—sail'd more than once around Shelter island, and down to Montauk—spent many an hour on Turtle hill by the old light-house, on the extreme point, looking out over the ceaseless roll of the Atlantic. I used to like to go down there and fraternize with the blue-fishers, or the annual squads of sea-bass takers. Sometimes, along Montauk peninsula, (it is some 15 miles long, and good grazing,) met the strange, unkempt, half-barbarous herdsmen, at that time living there entirely aloof from society or civilization, in charge of those rich pasturages, of vast droves of horses, kine or sheep, own'd by farmers of the eastern towns. Sometimes, too, the few remaining Indians, or half-breeds, at that period left on Montauk peninsula, but now I believe altogether extinct.

More in the middle of the island were the spreading Hempstead plains, then (1830–'40) quite prairie-like, open, uninhabited, rather sterile, cover'd with kill-calf and huckleberry bushes, yet plenty of fair pasture for the cattle, mostly milch-cows, who fed there by hundreds, even thousands, and at evening, (the plains too were own'd by the towns, and this was the use of them in common,) might be seen taking their way home, branching off regularly in the right places. I have often been out on the edges of these plains toward sundown, and can yet recall in fancy the interminable cow-processions, and hear the music of the tin or copper bells clanking far or near, and breathe the cool of the sweet and slightly aromatic evening air, and note the sunset.

Through the same region of the island, but further east, extended wide central tracts of pine and scrub-oak, (charcoal was largely made here,) monotonous and sterile. But many a good day or half-day did I have, wandering through those solitary cross-roads, inhaling the peculiar and wild aroma. Here, and all along the island and its shores, I spent intervals many years, all seasons, sometimes riding, sometimes boating, but generally afoot, (I was always then a good walker,) absorbing fields, shores, marine incidents, characters, the bay-men, farmers, pilots—always had a plentiful acquaintance with the latter, and with fishermen—went every summer on sailing trips—always liked the bare sea-beach, south side, and have some of my happiest hours on it to this day.

As I write, the whole experience comes back to me after the lapse of forty and more years—the soothing rustle of the waves, and the saline smell—boyhood's times, the clam-digging, barefoot, and with trowsers roll'd up—hauling down the creek—the perfume of the sedge-meadows—the hay-boat, and the chowder and fishing excursions. . . .[1]

---
[1] *Complete Prose*, p. 7.

The memory of this happy period remained dear as ever to the poet, past the period of his virility. Describing the southern coast of the isle, fatal to so many ships, he noted that, "As a youngster I was in the atmosphere and tradition of many wrecks—of one or two almost an observer." Off Hempstead beach, for example, was the loss of the ship, "Mexico" in 1840 (alluded to as the "Sleepers" in *Leaves of Grass*.[1] Later still he evoked "old Moses," one of the freed slaves of West Hills, "a great friend of my childhood."[2] The sea especially took possession of him at this time with its odour, movement, its noises, its vastness. Already at this period he was inspired to sing of the sea.[3] The perfumes of seaweed and of sea fish clung to him, and he had, he tells us, the look of a "water dog." As a certain captain said of Walt, "I can smell salt water ten miles away in just seeing him."[4] What animal strength and what largeness these intervals of life, wild, exultant, diffusive of unconscious joy, near the sea and on it, were preparing for the individual! And we think of these verses in which this reflection of his childhood is expressed:

There was a child went forth every day,
And the first object he look'd upon, that object he became,
And that object became part of him for the day or a certain part of the day,
Or for many years or stretching cycles of years.

The early lilacs became part of this child,
And grass and white and red morning-glories, and white and red clover, and the song of the phoebe-bird,
And the Third-month lambs, and the sow's pink-faint litter, the mare's foal and the cow's calf,
And the noisy brood of the barnyard or by the mire of the pond-side,
And the fish suspending themselves so curiously below there, and the beautiful curious liquid,
And the water-plants with their graceful flat heads, all became part of him. . . .[5]

---
[1] *Complete Prose*, p. 7.
[2] *Id.*, p, 4½.
[3] *Id.*, p. 88.
[4] O. L. Triggs: *Selections, Introduction*, p. xxii.
[5] *Leaves of Grass*, pp. 282–283.

Walt at sixteen was one of the employes in a printer's office in New York. However, his work—and it was to be always thus with him—absorbs him but little. A fever to know seizes him. He lives intensely these hours in which every generous adolescent burns to measure himself with the world. Quivering with intellectual ardour, he devours a multitude of novels, and indiscriminately all the books which fall into his hands. He frequents lectures in Brooklyn and his neighbourhood, and takes an active part in debates. He goes ardently to the theatre, as much as his means will permit.[1] It is the period of the awakening of all his curiosities. Not content to read and to speak in public, he writes poems and little novels for reviews and journals.

It is about his seventeenth year that there appeared in his life the first of those brusque interruptions which the American temperament and spirit of initiative foster. He abandons his case and reaches his island, where presently he becomes the improvised master of a village school. Without doubt the desire to be near his parents, who had left the city—other children had come to the carpenter, and the birth of the last boy had cost the mother, however robust, months of illness—was not remote from this resolution. According to the custom of that time he "boarded round" in the families of his pupils, where boys and girls mingled, often the same age as the teacher. The recollection of one of them projects a vivid glimmer upon this period of his youth. I transcribe it in all its savour:

> I went to school to him in the town of Flushing, Long Island. He taught the school at Little Bay Side. We became very much attached to him.
> His ways of teaching were peculiar. He did not confine himself to books, as most of the teachers then did, but taught orally—yes, had some original ideas all his own. I know about that, for I had heard of others who tried

---

[1] *Complete Prose*, p. 13.

YEARS OF YOUTH AND APPRENTICESHIP   37

oral teaching. But the plans he adopted were wholly of his own conception, and most successful.

He was not severe with the boys, but had complete discipline in the school. Before and after school and at recess, he was a boy among boys, always free, always easy, never stiff. He took active part in games of frolic. It seemed his object to teach even when we played. . . .

Whitman was very fond of describing objects and incidents to the school. He would not do this privately, but to all hands. He would give quite a good deal of time to any subject that seemed worth while. He was always interesting, a very good talker, able to command the attention of scholars, of whom, by the way, there were seventy or eighty. Our ages ranged sixteen, seventeen, eighteen years old, yet many, too, were young shavers like myself. . . . .

The girls did not seem to attract him. He did not specially go anywhere with them or show any extra fondness for their society. . . .

Walt was a good story teller. Oh! excellent; was both funny and serious. Did I say he had his own notions how to punish a scholar? If he caught a boy lying, he exposed him before the whole school in a story. But the story was told without the mention of any names. No punishment beyond that. He had such a way of telling his story that the guilty fellow knew who was meant. He would do this in the case of any ordinary offence; but, if the offence was grave enough, the whole school was taken into the secret. . . .

My memory of Walt is acute, unusually acute—probably because his personality had such a peculiar and powerful effect upon me, even as a boy. I had other teachers, but none of them ever left such an impress upon me. And yet I could not mention any particular thing. It was his whole air, his general sympathetic way, his eye, his voice, his entire geniality. I felt something I could not describe. What I say, others will also say. I think he affected all as he did me. They have admitted it, yet, like me, can give no definite reasons. No one could tell why. Their memory of him is exactly like mine. There must be something in it; it is not imagination. . . .

Whitman had dignity, and yet at the same time he could descend to sociability. The very moment he stepped across that school door-sill he was master. He had authority, but was not severe.[1] We obeyed and respected him.

---

[1] In a little novel published by Walt in 1841 in which he presents a scene of a brutal schoolmaster, a characteristic passage is found: "That teacher was one little fitted for his important and responsible office. Hasty to decide, and inflexibly severe, he was the terror of the little world he ruled so despotically, punishment he seemed to delight in. Knowing little of those sweet fountains which in children's breasts ever open quickly at the call of gentleness and kind words, he was feared by all for his sternness, and loved by none. I would that he were an isolated instance in his profession."—*Complete Prose*, p. 338.

One thing is sure. As far as Walt's goodness of character goes, you can report me pretty fully and as strongly as you choose. Even back in the school-days, those of us who knew him, his scholars there on Long Island, felt, somehow, without knowing why, that here was a man out of the average, who strangely attracted our respect and affection.[1]

This testimony, so affirmative and so curious, must be placed near that of another Long Islander who was likewise his pupil. Interrogated by Doctor Johnston, one of the English admirers of the poet, an old farmer, named Sandford Brown, formulated in these terms the opinion which he retained of his old teacher:

Walter Whitman, or "Walt," as we used to call him, was my first teacher. He "kept school" for 'bout a year around here. I was one of his scholars, and I used to think a powerful deal on him. I can't say that he was exactly a failure as a teacher, but he was certainly not a success. He warn't in his element. He was always musin' an' writin,' 'stead of 'tending to his proper dooties; but I guess he was like a good many on us—not very well off, and had to do somethin' for a livin'. But school-teachin' was not his *forte*. His *forte* was poetry. Folks used ter consider him a bit lazy and indolent, because, when he was workin' in the fields, he would sometimes go off for from five minutes to an hour, and lay down on his back on the grass in the sun then get up and do some writin', and the folks used ter say he was idlin'; but I guess he was then workin' with his brain, and thinkin' hard, and then writin' down his thoughts. . . . He kept school for a year and then his sister succeeded him.[2]

Whether he was successful or not in teaching where his ascendant personality and his resources could supplement his meagre education, Walt kept up for at least three years this life of village schoolmaster, interrupted by visits to the farm which his parents had retaken since their return to the country. He taught at Babylon at the edge of the Great South Bay where he used to catch eels and lobsters, at Jamaica, at Woodbury, at Whitestone.[3] It was then that in

---

[1] *Fellowship Papers*, 1894. (I. H. Pratt, *Walt Whitman*, pp 6–10.)
[2] J. Johnston: *A Visit to Walt Whitman*, p. 70.
[3] H. B. Binns: *Life of Walt Whitman*, pp. 28–29.

journeying through the island he took possession of it and knew its population. In the course of this somewhat nomadic life how many firesides, how many divers types—fishers, farmers, grazers—he had occasion to visit and to observe! He himself called these years "one of my deepest lessons of human nature behind the scene and in the masses."[1]

In the interval—he was then nineteen years old—the young Whitman realized another of those experiences, the sum of which later made for him an incomparable knowledge of humanity. He loved to print both literally and figuratively. For the year and a half during which he taught, we find him at the head of a journal, the Long Islander, which he founded at Huntington, the market town near West Hills, and which still stands, after more than sixty years. His brother George, who was then ten years older, was co-proprietor. Walt was manager, editor in chief, compositor, pressman, and apprentice, combining in his own person the elements of one edition. Despite his multiple occupations, the work in the office of the Long Islander did not monopolize all his time; sometimes the manager could be seen in the midst of his friends, with a ring suspended from a ceiling by a thread and forcing it to reach a hook in the wall. When the ring was hooked the player won a piece of pie or a five-cent piece.[2] Or perhaps he played a game of whist. His readers were indulgent and Walt was in no hurry. But there were times when he worked uninterruptedly, and again when he merely played. He had to be allowed his own way. That which undoubtedly satisfied him was that his business as printer and his literary talents found opportunity to fuse.

These months in which he printed, edited, and distributed the little sheet came to be a particularly happy phase of his adolescence, and the following lines express this delight:

---
[1] *Complete Prose*, p. 10.
[2] Bucke: *In Re Walt Whitman*, p. 37.

I was encouraged to start a paper in the region where I was born. I went to New York, bought a press and types, hired some little help, but did most of the work myself, including the press work. Everything seem'd turning out well; and (only my own restlessness prevented me gradually establishing a permanent property there) I bought a good horse, and every week went all round the country serving my papers, devoting one day and night to it. I never had happier jaunts—going over to southside, to Babylon, down the south road across to Smithtown and Comac, and back home. The experiences of those jaunts, the dear old fashion'd farmers and their wives, the stops by the hay-fields, the hospitality, nice dinners, occasional evenings, the girls, the rides through the brush, come up in my memory to this day.

Others besides Walt kept the memory of this time. Two years after the death of the poet, some friends, on a pilgrimage to Long Island, found still some villagers who had known the young director of the Long Islander and did not hesitate to evoke his figure. Two of the forefathers of the hamlet clearly remembered his powerful personality, brimful of life, revelling in strength, careless of time and the world, of money and of toil, a lover of books and of jokes, delighting to gather round him the youth of the village in his printing-room of evenings and tell them stories and read them poetry, his own and others. That of his own he called his yawp, a word which he afterward made famous.[1]

Walt was twenty-two when he left his school and his island to return to New York. Other ambitions were stirring within him which teaching could not by its nature satisfy. Adolescence was at an end and with it years of apprenticeship. A vast field of experience was open to him, where we are presently to see him expand in contact with men and things and reach his plenitude.

The proofs which we possess of the poet's youth, beyond those which he himself tells, and the evidences which we are to cite, are of themselves singularly poor. They suffice to prove for us that he already possessed an emphatic personality: the recollection of the first of his pupils is astonishingly

---

[1] I. Hull Platt: *Walt Whitman*, pp. 11–12.

significant in this respect. He showed in his face and his glances something very powerful and very sweet, that inexpressible quality which emanates from certain individuals like an aroma and irresistibly attracts sympathy. Among the young men of the village he appeared different, not by an essential superiority, but very peculiarly a singular lad who avoided grossness of speech, and whom no one could induce to drink or to be part of low games. Without the shadow of pose, but under the rule of an innate instinct, he had a great self-respect which forbade the familiar diversions of the gay youth of his own age.

But above all he was himself. The love of independence which possessed him as a boy, the tempestuous discussions with his father, little inclined to jest on the subject of authority, was confirmed with years. He early left home, and the experience which he already had of the big city tended to fortify his individualistic tendencies. Walt was not an enemy of work, far from it, but he was an enemy of work prolonged and mechanical, foreseen and measured like the day of a cab horse between the shafts. On this head, he was determined to follow his own will and to obey only his own instinct. When he by chance helped in the field, he passed for a do-nothing, because he was seen, as Sandford Brown says, sometimes to put down the scythe, the fork, or the rake to stretch under a tree solicited by a thought which was worth more than the work of fork or scythe: why resist it since it came to him? His Quaker ancestors, did they resist the inner call? Even to his family, with whom he always retained the most affectionate relations, he remained a puzzle. His sweet and intuitive mother, despite the particular bond of tenderness which held her to her second son, did not always understand him. Something in him escaped her.

Besides, he was never certain what to do with his life: Walt was not one of those adolescents who, their studies and apprenticeship ended, make straight toward a box which they occupy till death. He did not know, he waited, he watched the world about him. In the depth of his heart a sea of confused desires moved him, and he experienced their delight and their torture. Under a happy countenance and a tranquil manner he concealed a very vivid sensibility, and his youth already knew profound emotions.

Walt at twenty years had boundless health and unusual strength. He had grown very fast and reached his development at about sixteen years.[1] Tall and broad shouldered, he was the living proof that the blood of the Whitmans flowed in him pure and plentiful. He already impressed one by his appearance of a young athlete,[2] with gray-blue eyes, which looked directly at one, a face oval and regular, a complexion extraordinarily fair, and hair an intense black.[3]

With something of a magnificent abandon, full of animation and gayety, great lover of games and adventure, he gave himself to them with joyous heart once a pleasure party was planned. There was no one more boisterous and more turbulent than he when leading a band of young boys. Wherever his errant life led him, he was easily the chief. Walt was a youth of genuine pluck. Fishing, boating, long tramps afoot were his favourite recreation: he would have nothing to do with hunting. He was never seen in church. There were certain moments when a particular gravity spread over his face: and his companions asked if it was indeed the same youth who in a moment exulted in the joy of living and abandoned himself totally to the intoxication of youth and strength. Already the duality of the man was apparent and marked him with a special sign.

---

[1] *Complete Prose,* p. 16.
[2] Bucke: *In Re Walt Whitman,* p 35
[3] Bliss Perry: *Walt Whitman,* p. 9

PART TWO

THE MULTITUDINARY LIFE

NEW YORK (1841–1855)

IV
LITERARY BEGINNINGS

However eager we are to see the genesis of such an individual, the period of plenitude which opens at the time of his return to the metropolis more powerfully allures us. The years in New York—whose Indian name Manahatta, which means "place around which there are hurried and joyous waters, continually,"[1] was dear to him—the years in which he became conscious of himself, and whence his work has derived, are the marvellous and unique experience upon which his personality rises. It is then that the magnificent and loose drama of his life knits, and our attention tightens in seeing it live and move.

Twelve to fifteen years—the long period preceding the appearance of his poem—suggest more than can be actually verified, a luxuriant life wholly enveloped in a warm light reflected by some facts which have come to us. For the precise facts of Whitman's life to his thirty-fifth year are perhaps rarer than any of its phases. No analyst lived beside him to preserve the history of a man who had no history, of one who lived lost in the crowd, occupied simply in living and absorbing his time. Walt was not revealed to himself and to the world. Some autobiographic pages, a document here and there, allow us at least to conjecture what he then lived through, in the flowering of his manhood. Ten lines of a contemporary, an impression from life, quickly noted, the description of a gesture or a trait of character, many times tell us more of his personality than a journal rigorously kept.

---
[1] W. S. Kennedy: *Reminiscences of Walt Whitman*, p. 64; *Diary in Canada*, p. 55.

Because the information relative to this period is scant we renounce here, more than elsewhere, a rigorous following of the chronology of events in order to express the general sense and the particular nature of an epoch fecund in diverse, intimate, and multiple experience. And we must confess that what was undoubtedly very great in these magnificent years remains impossible to reproduce and must rest in shadow.

In 1841 Walt finally quitted his school-teaching and returned to New York stirred by a new ambition. He had edited a journal, as a youth, and the great town opened, boundless, before his young desire. A great boy of twenty-two who appeared at least twenty-five, of exceptional vitality, and a singular assurance, was thus about to be lost in the eddies of a crowded and eager city. The city should not, however, devour him: it was he who was to absorb it, its men and things, its aspects and crowds, its sufferings and joys.

Walt, in these New York years, lives a mixed life: half labourer, half journalist, he followed a trade, solely for a living, according to a method (or an absence of method) invariable with him. For five years he worked as compositor in printing offices in New York, without allowing himself to be absorbed by his daily task. In summer this incorrigible idler, this lover of air and of sun, often escaped from the workroom to the woods or the shores of his island. And to be able to prolong his sojourn there he does not disdain now and then to hire himself as a gardener, just as simply as he sets type.

In returning to New York, Walt had a desire, which without mastering him—that would have been contrary to his disposition—preoccupied him seriously during the five or six following years: that of "taking up literature!" For Walt was a writer. He had published little tales and poems in periodicals. This vocation was affirmed since his fourteenth year and he continued in his easy way to follow it till he became a new man, a time when all this literature was dispersed like a soft smoke on the horizon.

One would be led to believe, in a life of which one poem

LITERARY BEGINNINGS 47

is the soul, the key, the final solution, that its literary beginnings should have a particular importance. They are hardly that with a Walt Whitman. It is the life experiences of the period we are now entering which are primary and significant in the formation of his personality. The man would be diminished in nothing, if he had not published in his youth. Nor would he be any greater either. He would remain the same to us. His *juvenilia* are like the sprouts of shrubbery which bear no fruit; they may be pulled up without loss.

Whitman has told us himself how the idea of writing came to him: "On jaunts over Long Island as a boy and young fellow nearly half a century ago, I heard of or came across in my own experience, characters, true occurrences, incidents which I tried my 'prentice hand at recording: I published these pages during my occasional visits to New York City." Elsewhere, he confides to us his first impressions as author: his beginnings were described toward 1832 as "sentimental bits" inserted in the Long Island Patriot where he commenced his apprenticeship as compositor. "Soon after, I had a piece or two published in the Mirror of George P. Morris, then a celebrated and elegant journal of New York. I remember with what half-suppressed excitement I used to walk to the big, fat, red-faced, slow moving very old English carrier who distributed the Mirror in Brooklyn: and when I got one, opening and cutting the leaves with trembling fingers. How it made my heart double-beat to see my piece on the pretty white paper in nice type."[1]

From that time on Walt persevered. Exactly at the time of his arrival in New York a story of his published in the August number of the Democratic Review had a vivid success. *Death in the Schoolroom*—a kind of moral story inspired by his experience as schoolmaster—made a sensation and was widely copied in the press.[2] This flattering recep-

---
[1] *Complete Prose*, p. 187.
[2] John Burroughs: *Notes*, p. 80; and H. B. Binns: *Life of Walt Whitman*, p. 33.

tion fortified the literary ambitions of the young man. It was the commencement of his regular collaboration with this review, then in full fashion and in which a pleiad of future great men published: Poe, Hawthorne, Whittier, Lowell, and Bryant. From 1841 to 1845 the signature W.W., or Walter Whitman, frequently appeared in it and the young printer gave copy elsewhere. The New World, in whose composing room he worked on returning to the city, inserted some of his verse. Some sketches, some stories, appeared in Brother Jonathan,[1] in Columbian Magazine, in the American Review, and in the Broadway Journal, directed by Edgar Allan Poe, whom he went to see one day in his office and found kind and attractive but subdued and a bit jaded.[2] He wrote at the same time for journals like the New York Sun, Aurora Tatler, Statesman, the Democrat, the Tribune.[3] At that time the publicist in him expended itself youthfully.

Later, Walt was the last one to be mistaken as to the value of these "crude and boyish" pieces. He would have wished them in eternal oblivion if he had not feared their surreptitious issue. One day he unwillingly decided to publish some of them as appendix to his *Collect*.[4]

A brief examination of these youthful pages is enough to explain why he was reluctant to reprint them. They authorize no hope and prove only what a detestable writer at that distant period the poet of the *Leaves of Grass* proves himself. Nothing is more conventional and more mediocre than these stories of grandiose idea; their naïve and flat form, and their melodramatic manner, are intolerable. The greater part of them, beneath their pathos and inflation, show an intention plainly moralistic. Their author, then in the full crisis of humanitarianism, sought in literature but a means

---

[1] Bliss Perry: *Walt Whitman*, p. 26.
[2] *Complete Prose*, p. 12.
[3] *Id.*, p. 187.
[4] *Id.*, p. 334.

to vivify instruction. His recent biographer, Mr. H. B. Binns, has very closely characterized this phase of his youth: "The moral consciousness of Whitman was then predominant; he was an advocate of 'causes.' But his moralizing sprang out of a real passion for humanity which took the former sentiment; sentiment which was thoroughly genuine at bottom, but which, in its expression at the time, became false and stilted enough to bear the reproach of sentimentality."[1]

Not but that one may discover, very exceptionally indeed, in the banality of these little stories, some ingenious or poetic motive, however inevitably spoiled by awkward treatment. Thus the idea of the widow scattering flowers indiscriminately upon all the graves in a cemetery because she could not find her husband's. Sometimes a passage, a line, holds attention, because it suggests certain fugitive correspondence between the Whitman of five and twenty and the much later one. Thus one of his stories, *One Wicked Impulse*, closes, after the ordinary gamut of incidents frightfully tragic, upon the curious impression of the guilty one who finds in the bosom of nature absolution of his crime. She receives him, the assassin, as she receives the most innocent of the sons of earth, rejecting no one, admitting the most vile to her communion. It is truly interesting to find this as the first indication of the sentiment, which later is to flower so magnificently in the man and his poems—the ardent sympathy for the fallen and the pariahs, the full and entire acceptance of all outlaws. Phrases like these are like an annunciation: "Ah! that good morning air—how it refreshed him—how he lean'd out, and drank in the fragrance of the blossoms below, and almost for the first time in his life felt how beautiful indeed God had made the earth, and that there was wonderful sweetness in mere existence."[2]

---

[1]H. B. Binns: *Life of Walt Whitman*, pp. 34-35.
[2]*Complete Prose*, p. 344.—see also Bucke: *In Re Walt Whitman*, p. 340 (Note); *Camden Edition*, IX, pp. 130-133, 146-148. Bliss Perry: *Walt Whitman*, p. 24.

But how rare are such gleams! The *juvenilia* deserve en masse charitable and purifying oblivion. It is astonishing, above all, to find no point of contact between the real man—such as he already manifested himself—and his writings: what is certain, I believe, is that the latter were but accessory, despite the undeniable sincerity of his reformatory ardour. In any case, it instructs us but in a mediocre way as to his intimate self.

As for the verse pieces of this period, they are poorer and more colourless if possible than the prose. At most only one of them, *The Blood Price,* inspired by his anti-slavery passion is really moving, stands out from its colourless company. Whitman, after his new birth, inclosed with significant quotation marks the word poesy when he applied it to his distant lucubrations, proving all his disdainful pity for this pseudo-lyricism. A purely conventional notion of the poetic form then possessed him: later he declared how much he struggled to free himself from it.

He went even further. Emboldened by his success as story teller and versifier, he wrote, soon after his return to New York, a novel. Here likewise the quotation marks were imposed, for the term seems a bit pretentious in view of this production. *Franklin Evans, A Tale of the Times,* was offered to the world as a "temperance novel." It was published in a supplement of the New World, the weekly in whose composing room the author worked. The journal approved the affair, and the masterpiece—which had been written on command and was paid for in advance[1]—was announced to the public in a sensational manner, of which this is a sample: "Friends of temperance, ohe! Franklin Evans or the drunkard. *A Tale of the Times,* by a popular American writer. This novel, which is dedicated to the temperance societies and to the friends of temperance in the United States, will make a sensation. . . . It has been written especially for the New World by one of the best

---

[1] H. Traubel: *With Walt Whitman in Camden,* p. 93.

novelists of the country, with the intention of aiding the great work of reform, and of snatching young men from the demon of intemperance," etc., etc. . . .[1] This violent acclamation was not vain, for *Franklin Evans* was a great success and was printed, it was said, to the twentieth thousand.

The title alone explains its literary type. It is the terrible and extraordinary history of a young man whom alcohol leads to vice and to all miseries, and who pledges to practise in future the strictest rules of abstinence. Its style is flamboyant with a redoubtable odour of Puritan sanctity. Even Whitman, this crisis passed, may wish that one would keep silent as to this sin of three and twenty. He never spoke of nor showed pride in it himself, even at the time it was written. When any one alluded in his presence to this "novel" he did not hesitate to laugh at it.[2] A short time before his death his intimate friends searched everywhere for this old "stuff"; the author on learning this told them that he "hoped indeed by the grace of God" this search would be fruitless. "I do not know how I came to write it," he remarked, "all that I know is that I was simply in the raw and the unripe, that is all." And he sarcastically pretended that his famous "temperance novel" was written on the table of a saloon with a reinforcement of spiritous liquors.

That it was nothing but an intellectual caprice, is possible; but it appears doubtful whether Walt was at this time an exemplary "water drinker." He was always too richly alive and too free to subject himself to an absolute rule. But he was passionately interested in the problem of hygiene, temperance, and physical culture. The abundant notes,[3] belonging to the period of *Franklin Evans*, confirm this: page after page, even treatises, on walking, swimming, etc. . . . Lost among this declamatory mass some curious paragraphs establish, in spite of everything, a kind of

[1] *Camden Edition, Introduction*, pp. xxiv-xxv; *Id.*, VIII, p. 262.
[2] Bucke: *In Re Walt Whitman*, p. 39.
[3] *Camden Edition*, VIII, pp. 261-274.

concordance between the literature of five and twenty, so ardent to espouse "causes," and the later man. The juvenile tone of the following lines proves the man of plenitude and of triumphant health, who was in truth the young apostle, temporarily embedded in moralism. "What pity may we feel for the flabby, lymphatic, half-grown puny creatures, called men and women, of whom the earth is full! What wonder that such morbid abortions are tempted to kindle within their sluggish systems some sparkler of genial life by transient exhilaration! . . . God's elixir of life is wondrously compounded of sunlight, and pure air and water; of the perfume of flowers, of music, and the continual change of hours and seasons. We drive each other to quaff the fiery fountain which bubbles up from hell by robbing one another of the exhaustless animal joy which our Creator would pour upon us from all living and moving things. To drink to fulness of the nectar which Nature distils is to be intoxicated with health!"[1]

It is necessary to keep in mind in thinking of the future Walt this pitiless disdain of the strong man face to face with the feeble one, the man of the cabinet, the dreamer forgetful of his body, the neurasthenic, who in the midst of these reproofs he induces to swim, to walk, to exercise with dumbbells, to live in the open air. By this single fragment one sees what passion already pushed the young man to defend causes from which he afterward turned. Even in his lay sermons, Walt by instinct repudiates the prudish and posed accent of literature familiar to the family. He could not escape from his excessive and generous temperament, and in this crisis of moralism he remained fundamentally the being of nature described in these lines. From another point of view the memory of the lance broken in favour of abstinence will appear significant when we reply to the accusations of drunkenness and debauch which were hurled later at the great pagan, by malignantly perverting some of his poetical affirmations.

---

[1] *Camden Edition*, VIII. pp. 263–264.

But of all this preaching literature nothing will last. The man issues from it unharmed. It simply demonstrates that in the time of his youth certain racial tendencies sought expression to later retreat and disappear forever. All the Quakers of his line were behind him when he was profuse and enthusiastic for the abolition of slavery, and of capital punishment, and when he combatted alcohol. "I promptly got away beyond all that," he declared one day to his friends. But it was a sentiment very strong while it lasted.[1] How can we doubt it? He had the idea of accomplishing great things, and the ardours of apostolate consumed him. He recognized quickly that he was deceived as to the way, for the venture of *Franklin Evans* had no successor. Already the crowds with their enormous reality circled about him, through him; and their contact, warm, electric, to which he abandoned himself, prepared the metamorphosis from which he would rise a new man.

---

[1] *Camden Edition, Introduction*, p. xxv.

V

THE MAN OF CROWDS

Let us hasten to see the man live very far from these trifles—the work of his early years. Despite his literary aspirations, Walt is not temperamentally a writer. His real self expanded in the open air and in free companionship, in the track of the immense inquiry which he slowly pursues with the view of fathoming his city, his nation, his time.

Profound is the word by which Bucke denominated these New York years, the time in which the poet received his "education." Never has one dreamed of the like. A man sprung from the people is about to prove democracy for himself by compassing at leisure the entire scale of sensations which a great modern city with its surroundings can offer. Endowed with vast and varied appetites, enjoying faculties receptive and extraordinarily communal, this tranquil and uncommissioned inquirer finds himself in the centre of a moving and swarming collectivity, energetic and feverish. The particular emotional intensity which this contact yields him he will one day report to us.

With real simplicity Walt Whitman lets us see most of the experiences of this boundless time. We shall let him express them here in his own words which have a flavour and an accent of truth which no translation can supply:

> Living in Brooklyn or New York City from this time forward my life then identifies itself curiously with Fulton Ferry, already becoming the greatest of its sort in the world for general importance, volume, variety, rapidity, and picturesqueness. Almost daily later ('60 to '70) I crossed on the boats, often up in the pilot-houses where I could get a full sweep, absorbing shows, accompaniments, surroundings. What oceanic currents, eddies, underneath—the great tides of humanity also, with ever-shifting

movements. Indeed, I have always had a passion for ferries; to me they afford inimitable, streaming, never-failing, living poems of the river and bay scenery, all about New York island, any time of a fine day—the hurrying, splashing sea-tides—the changing panorama of steamers, all sizes, often a string of big ones outward bound to distant ports—the myriads of white-sail'd schooners, sloops, skiffs, and the marvelously beautiful yachts—the majestic sound boats as they rounded the Battery and came along towards 5, afternoon, eastward bound—the prospect off towards Staten Island, or down the Narrows, or the other way up the Hudson—what refreshment of spirit such sights and experiences gave me years ago (and many a time since). My old pilot friends, the Balsirs, Johnny Cole, Ira Smith, William White, and my young ferry friend, Tom Gere—how well I remember them all!

Nothing could be more characteristic than this love for the ferries, moving routes between water, earth, and sky, satisfying the appetite for motion and space which tormented the heart of the young man. Throughout his poems how we see them pass and repass with their crowds, with the odour and perspective of the water. Standing by the side of the pilot, Walt was never weary of the breath and press of the people, above the moving waters, seething and rhythmic; one with the great natural force; he watched the human tide as well as the sea. . . . This endless pageant, combined with the odours of the salt air, the noises and colours of the bay, plunged him into a strange intoxication. He was wont to dilate, and to expand in the presence of the landscape and in the thousands of confronting faces, to dream, to be gorged with visions, his eye taking in the bay, his meditation encircling the globe.[1]

In the heart of the city another spectacle equally thrilled him. It was Broadway, the great central artery of Manhattan, carrying along its pavements the most feverish crowd in the world. In the eddies of this human flood Walt was wont to plunge every day, watching its continuous movement with an unceasing and fascinated eye. The tramping, the cries, the oceanic murmur, the files of vehicles, the mass

---
[1] *Complete Prose*, p. 11.

of faces held for the big curious child, at once both actor and observer, an enormous mystery and a whole world of beauty. The pulsations of humanity afoot accelerated his own life and stimulated him to intoxication. Broadway offered him not only the spectacle of anonymous pedestrians, but that of notables of the day. "Here I saw during those times, Andrew Jackson, Webster, Clay, Seward, Martin Van Buren, filibuster Walker, Kossuth, Fitz Greene Halleck, Bryant, the Prince of Wales, Charles Dickens, the first Japanese ambassadors, and lots of other celebrities of the times. Always something novel or inspiriting; yet mostly to me the hurrying and vast amplitude of those never-ending human currents."[1] When Manhattan celebrated some extraordinary occasion, it was also an event for the lover of "populous pavements." At the sight of and in contact with the vast sea of crowds, everything of the naïve, the infantile, and primitive leaped within him as in the presence of a great planetary phenomenon. And what a crowd! New York on a holiday saluting the arrival of some great celebrity, "Manhattan with millions of feet walking upon the pavements," "with all that indescribable human roar and magnetism, unlike any other sound in the universe—the glad exulting thunder shouts of countless unloos'd throats of men."[2] The immense processions with torches, fire works, noise of wild bands, at the time of presidential elections, the crowds free and abounding. . . .

To observe the crowd, Walt selected a choice place: the seat of a Broadway omnibus, by the side of the driver, from where he took in the crowds of the street, as from the pilot's cabin on the ferries he overlooked the waters of East River. He has told us about those famous omnibus jaunts, the joy of his youth and of his mature age, with a picturesque heartiness from which looks out a youthful, candid soul, marvelling at everything:

---

[1] *Complete Prose*, p. 12.
[2] *Id.*, p. 12.

One phase of those days must by no means go unrecorded—namely, the Broadway omnibuses, with their drivers. The vehicles still (I write this paragraph in 1881) give a portion of the character of Broadway—the Fifth Avenue, Madison Avenue, and Twenty-third Street lines yet running. But the flush days of the old Broadway stages, characteristic and copious, are over. The Yellow-birds, the Red-birds, the original Broadway, the Fourth Avenue, the Knickerbocker, and a dozen others of twenty or thirty years ago, are all gone. And the men specially identified with them, and giving vitality and meaning to them—the drivers—a strange, natural, quick-eyed and wondrous race—(not only Rabelais and Cervantes would have gloated upon them, but Homer and Shakespere would)—how well I remember them, and must here give a word about them. How many hours, forenoons and afternoons—how many exhilarating nighttikes I have had—perhaps June or July in cooler air—riding the whole length of Broadway, listening to some yarn (and the most vivid yarns ever spun, and the rarest mimicry)—or perhaps I declaiming some stormy passage from Julius Cæsar or Richard (you could roar as loudly as you chose in that heavy, dense, uninterrupted street-bass). Yes, I knew all the drivers then, Broadway Jack, Dressmaker, Balky Bill, George Storms, Old Elephant, his brother Young Elephant (who came afterward), Tippy, Pop Rice, Big Frank, Yellow Joe, Pete Callahan, Patsy Day, and dozens more; for there were hundreds. They had immense qualities, largely animal—eating, drinking, women—great personal pride, in their way—perhaps a few slouches here and there, but I should have trusted the general run of them, in their simple good-will and honour, under all circumstances. Not only for comradeship, and sometimes affection—great studies I found them also (I suppose the critics will laugh heartily, but the influence of those Broadway omnibus jaunts and drivers and declamations and escapades undoubtedly enter'd into the gestation of *Leaves of Grass*).[1]

Of a whole world of joys and emotions there still remains one of his favourite pastimes at this period, the frequenting of the theatre. From childhood, the stage exercised a real fascination for him. Later, when writing for newspapers, he was on the free list and profited by the privilege to the full.[2] The impression which he received must have been profound, and after having written many times in these autobiographic pages his memoirs of the theatre, he reviewed them again some months before his death.

---
[1] *Complete Prose*, p. 13.
[2] *Id.*, p. 13.

Walt found before the footlights, as in the promenades along the great highways, the sensation of the crowd. The vibrant atmosphere of the great hall crowded with listening spectators, the electric human thrill which the dramatic phenomenon produced, the emotion which reverberated from the stage to the audience, the strong magnetism which freed this exchange, he felt in every minute cell. One easily imagines that the audience was as absorbing as the piece— perhaps more. The spectacle which thrilled him was divided between the auditorium and the play. One feels, in these lines, powerful and peculiar, that sensation of the crowd under the spell of a theatrical performance and his own wild joy in it:

> The old Park theatre—what names, reminiscences, the words bring back! Placide, Clarke, Mrs. Vernon, Fisher, Clara F., Mrs. Wood, Mrs. Seguin, Ellen Tree, Hackett, the younger Kean, Macready, Mrs. Richardson, Rice—singers, tragedians, comedians. What perfect acting! . . . Fanny Kemble—name to conjure up great mimic scenes withal —perhaps the greatest. I remember well her rendering of Bianca in "Fazio." Nothing finer did ever stage exhibit—the veterans of all nations said so, and my boyish heart and head felt it in every minute cell. . . . . Fanny Kemble play'd to wonderful effect in such pieces as "Fazio, or the Italian Wife." The turning-point was jealousy. It was a rapid-running, yet heavy-timber'd, tremendous wrenching, passionate play. Such old pieces always seem'd to me built like an ancient ship of the line, solid and lock'd from keel up—oak and metal and knots. One of the finest characters was a great court lady, Aldabella, enacted by Mrs. Sharpe. O, how it all entranced us, and knock'd us about, as the scenes swept on like a cyclone.[1]
>
> At the date given, the more stylish and select theatre (price, 50 cents pit, $1.00 boxes) was "The Park". . . . English opera and the old comedies were often presented in capital style; the principal foreign stars appear'd here, with Italian opera at wide intervals. The Park held a large part in my boyhood's and young manhood's life.[2] . . . I saw played marvelously at this time all the plays of Shakespere (I read them care-

---

[1]*Complete Prose*, pp. 13–14.
[2]*Id.*, pp. 426–27.

fully the evening before.)[1] Actually I cannot perceive anything more beautiful than the elder Booth in Richard III or Lear (do not know in which of the two rôles he was the better), or Iago (or Pescara or Sir Giles Overreach, to go outside of Shakspere)—or Tom Hamblin in Macbeth—or old Clarke, either in the ghost in Hamlet or as Prospero in the Tempest, with Mrs. Austin as Ariel and Peter Richings in Caliban. Other dramas, and fine players in them, Forrest as Metamora, Damon or Brutus— John R. Scott as Tom Cringle or Rolla—or Charlotte Cushman as Lady Gay Spanker in London Assurance.[2] . . . (I could write a whole paper on Clarke's peerless rendering of the Ghost in Hamlet at the Park.[3] . . . There were many fine old plays, neither tragedies nor comedies—the names of them quite unknown to to-day's current audiences. "All is not Gold that Glitters," in which Charlotte Cushman had a superbly enacted part, was of that kind. . . . I saw Charles Kean and Mrs. Kean (Ellen Tree)—saw them in the Park in Shakspere's King John. He of course was the chief character. She played Queen Constance. Tom Hamblin as Faulconbridge, and probably the best ever on the stage. It was an immense show-piece. . . . The death scene of the King in the orchard of Swinstead Abby was very effective. Kean rushed in, gray-pale and yellow, and threw himself on a lounge in the open. His pangs were horribly realistic. (He must have taken lessons in some hospital.)[4]

It was to the old popular Bowery Theatre, where Booth and Forrest triumphed before an audience of workingmen, that his most moving memories are attached, and this preference for the big drama furnishes a precious index to his character and tastes at this time. The elegant society of New York and Boston then interdicted these two master actors, "probably because they were too robust."

Recalling from that period the occasion of either Forrest or Booth, any good night at the old Bowery, packed from ceiling to pit with its audience mainly of alert, well dressed, full blooded young and middle-aged men the best average of American born mechanics—the emotional nature of the

---

[1] He wrote elsewhere: "As a young fellow, when possible I always studied a play or libretto quite carefully over, by myself (sometimes twice through) before seeing it on the stage—read it the day or two days before. Tried both ways not reading some beforehand: but I found I gained most by getting that sort of mastery first, if the piece had depth (surface effects and glitter were much less thought of, I am sure those times) . . ." *Complete Prose*, p. 515.

[2] *Prose Works*, p. 22.

[3] *Id.*, p. 423.

[4] *Id.*, pp. 511-512.

whole mass aroused by the power and magnetism of as mighty minds as ever trod the stage—the whole crowded auditorium, and what seethed in it and flushed from its faces and eyes to me as much a part of the show as any—bursting forth in one of those long kept up tempests of hand clapping peculiar to the Bowery—no dainty kid glove business, but electric force and muscle from perhaps 2,000 full sinewed men—(the inimitable and chromatic tempest of one of those ovations to Edmund Forrest, welcoming back after an absence, comes up to me this moment). . . . I can yet remember (for I always can for really it is a play) the faces of the leading authors, poets, editors of this time who occasionally peered from the first tier boxes; and even the great National Eminences, President Adams, Jackson, Van Buren and Tyler who made short visits there on eastern tours. A little while after 1840 the character of the Bowery as hitherto described completely changed. Cheap prices and vulgar programs came in. . . . That does not mean but what there was more or less rankness in the crowd even then. For types of sectional New York those days—types that never found their Dickens or Hogarth or Balzac and have passed away unportraitured—the young ship builders, cart men, butchers, firemen . . . , they too were always to be seen in these audiences racy of the East River and the Dry Dock. Slang, wit, occasional shirt sleeves, and the picturesque freedom of looks and manners, with a rude good nature and a restless movement were generally noticeable. Yet there never were audiences that paid a good actor or an interesting play the compliment of more sustained attention or quicker rapport.[1]

The enthusiastic pages which he has given to Booth denote the ineffaceable impression which Walt received from the actor who thrilled his youth: "Although Booth must be classed in that antique, almost extinct school inflated, stagy, rendering Shakèspeare (perhaps inevitably, appropriately) from the growth of arbitrary and often cockney inventions, his genius was to me one of the grandest revelations of my life, a lesson of artistic expression. The words fire, energy, abandon, found in him unprecedented meanings. . . . And so much for the greatest histrion of modern times, as near as I can deliberately judge . . . grander, I believe, than Kean in the expression of electric passion, the prime eligibility of the tragic artist. . . ."[2]

[1] *Complete Prose*, pp. 429-30.
[2] *Id.*, p. 431.

After the theatre whose memories reach back to his boyhood and youth, music was, later, one of the prime passions of the man. Music in the least complex form, melody, Italian vocalism. "The experts and musicians among my actual friends," he wrote in 1891, "claim that the new Wagner and his pieces belong far more truly to me and I to them. Very likely. But I was fed and bred under Italian dispensation and absorbed it and doubtless show it."[1] For a nature like that of Walt, Italian music stripped of all intellectual element, without program or "intentions" was still the simple, concrete life. He was not seeking art as revelation, but wished merely to be swept away with sounds by some prodigious singing bird. In the pure and full single voice of a virtuoso an unspeakable mystery appeared to him. It was for him the supreme efflorescence of a soul delivering its secret. "Beyond all other power and all beauty," he wrote a little before his death, "there is something in the quality and power of the right voice (timbre the schools call it) which touches the soul, the abysms."[2] The voice was for the sensibility of the young man an incomparable revelation, more eloquent and more moving than the face.

Perhaps my dearest amusement reminiscences are those musical ones. I doubt if ever the senses and emotions of the future will be thrilled as were the auditors of a generation ago by the deep passion of Alboni's contralto— or by the trumpet notes of Badiali's baritone, or Betteni's tensive and incomparable tenor in Fernando in "Favorita" or Marini's bass in "Faliero" among the Havana troupe, Castle Garden.[3] . . . I heard, these years, well rendered, all the Italian and other operas in vogue: "Somnambula," "the Puritans," "Der Freischutz," "Huguenots," "Fille d' Regiment," "Faust," "Etoile du Nord," "Poliuto," and others. Verdi's "Ernani," "Rigoletto," and "Trovatore," with Donnizetti's "Lucia" or "Favorita " or "Lucrezia" and Auber's "Massaniello," or Rossini's "William Tell" and "Gazza Ladra," were among my special enjoyments. . . . I yet recall the splendid season of the Havana musical troupe under Mar-

---
[1]*Complete Prose*, p. 515.
[2]*Id.*. p. 499.
[3]*Id.*, p. 427.

etzek—the fine band, the cool sea-breezes, the unsurpass'd vocalism. . . . (The Battery—its past associations—what tales those old trees and walks and sea-walls could tell!)[1]

Not only the play and the opera but the concert in all its forms, the circus, the exhibitions of the music hall singularly attracted this youngster, curious of shows and crowds. The singing of black minstrels, the characteristic dancing of Negroes, popular farces, romances, everything which had a taste of the picturesque and of the natural stirred him. Nothing affected nor conventional in him bridled his candid enthusiasm. He was open to all the impressions dear to the crowd. He even belonged, for some time, to an amateur theatre and acted parts in which he played many small rôles and found a fund of enjoyment.[2]

If, of all the actors whom he had known, Booth particularly struck him, the famous contralto Alboni exercised on him a deep influence. When she was on tour, he went to hear her every time she appeared in New York and vicinity.[3] This copious matron with a voice of the nightingale was for Walt a supernatural bird whose trilling filled him with ineffable delight. And forty years afterward he wrote "I should like well if Madam Alboni and the old composer Verdi (and Bettini, the tenor, if he is living) could know how much noble pleasure and happiness they gave me, and how deeply I always remember them and thank them to this day."[4] So strong were the emotions which the singing of the diva gave him that he wished to leave the trace of them in his poems, where the image of Marietta Alboni ineffaceably remains. . . .

> Splendid orb, Venus contralto, expansive mother,
> Sister of the sublime gods. . . .

---

[1] *Complete Prose*, p. 14.
[2] *Id.*, p. 518.
[3] *Id.*, p. 14.
[4] *Id.*, p. 515.

And elsewhere it is visibly to her memory that he dedicates these verses addressed *To a Certain Cantatrice:*

Here, take this gift,
I was reserving it for some hero, speaker or general,
One who should serve the good old cause, the great idea, the progress and freedom of the race,
Some brave confronter of despots, some daring rebel;
But I see that what I was reserving belongs to you just as much as to any.[1]

One may already know him. This was not a dreamy youth, solitary, retired within himself, this Walt Whitman. These New York years were a phase of life superabundant, expansive, free, joyous, without method or restraint. Neither doubt, nor timidity, nor melancholy attenuated the enormous faculties of this big boy, full of life, attentive and merry—in his way—exulting in every experimentation which multiplied his contact with things and people, and carefree in his enjoyment, like a superb human animal, wild to prove his magnificent health. He was no more retired in his living than in his thinking. In the open air, among passersby, he came to satisfy his thirst for sensation, of knowledge both direct and unlooked for, seeking only to grow by the absorption of things concrete and experienced. He seemed to take possession of a paradise, to inventory a heritage which fell to him. Greedily he assimilates this nourishment, plunges into materialities, responds with a heart smitten at all the mute allurements of his surroundings. These years appear like a gigantic gulping of impressions and emotions.

What surprises and disconcerts at first glance is the universality of his sympathies. Nothing in the ensemble of human affairs was to him negligible, unworthy of his attention. He appeared to have in his constitution of an athlete an athletic absorption. Not only was no aspect of life foreign to him, but he proclaimed himself closely identified with every thing and everybody. He possessed a catholic

---
[1] *Leaves of Grass*, p. 16.

instinct which made him recognize the true riches of things and of beings immersed in the obscure mass and judged too ordinary by passing humanity. The biography of Bucke contains an admirable passage which marvellously verifies the unique character of these experiences of a man with his ear to all the noises of life. We know, moreover, by the word of the poet, that these lines were written by himself.

In the first place he learned life—men, women, and children, he went on equal terms with every one; he liked them and they him, and he knew them far better than they knew themselves. Then he became thoroughly conversant with the shops, houses, sidewalks, ferries, factories, taverns, gatherings, political meetings, carousings, etc. He was first the absorber of the sunlight, the free air and the open streets, and then of interiors. He knew the hospitals, poorhouses, prisons, and their inmates. He passed freely in and about those parts of the city which are inhabited by the worst characters; he knew all their people, and many of them knew him; he learned to tolerate their squalor, vice, and ignorance; he saw the good (often much more than the self-righteous think) and the bad that was in them, and what there was to excuse and justify their lives. . . .

True, he knew, and intimately knew, the better off and educated people as well as the poorest and most ignorant. Merchants, lawyers, doctors, scholars and writers, were among his friends. But the people he knew best and liked most, and who knew him best and liked him most, were neither the rich and conventional, nor the worst and poorest, but the decent-born middle-life farmers, mechanics, carpenters, pilots, drivers, masons, printers, deckhands, teamsters, drovers, and the like. . . .

He made himself familiar with all kinds of employments, not by reading trade reports and statistics, but by watching and stopping hours with the workmen (often his intimate friends) at their work. He visited the foundries, shops, rolling mills, slaughter-houses, woollen and cotton factories, shipyards, wharves, and the big carriage and cabinet shops—went to clambakes, races, auctions, weddings, sailing and bathing parties, christenings, and all kinds of merrymakings (In their amplitude, richness, unflagging movement and gay colour, *Leaves of Grass*, it may be said, are but the putting in poetic statements of the Manhattan Island and Brooklyn of those years, and of to-day). . . . . Walt Whitman expressed the happiness of his life thus:[1]

Wandering, amazed at my own lightness and glee.

---
[1] Bucke: *Walt Whitman*, pp. 19-22.

THE MAN OF CROWDS

In the vast, limitless field of such an education the suggestions of life and of instinct remain the sovereign guide. Walt flowered according to his own inner law, far from methods and admitted conceptions. His culture above all was of humanity and grew in direct contact with concrete things. What others felt or thought before him, always interested this self-educated man least; and he confides to us "that he could himself draw better pictures or descriptions than those that others made;"[1] he asked of his reading only a completory education. However, after all, supreme works of art are also realities, and the all-devouring curiosity of the man could not leave them outside his inquiry. Had he neglected them, his culture such as he conceived it would have been limited, incomplete. Moreover, he absorbed some books, like all else, by direct contact, forgetting, or rather not wishing to learn, the judgment of critics.

Walt read in his own way. He had for a study two places which he preferred to all others: the top of the Broadway omnibus with the tumult of the street serving him as a set-off, or some nook of the seaside far from any human presence. The crowd and the ocean seemed to him better companions for the reading of the great masters rather than the closed and dull solitude of a room. He called his method: proving genius in the open air. "It is," he tells us, "in the presence of outdoor influences that I went over thoroughly the Old and New Testament, and absorbed (probably to better advantage for me than in any library or indoor room)—it makes such difference *where* you read—Shakespeare, Ossian, the best translated versions of Homer, Eschylus, Sophocles, the old German Nibelungen, the ancient Hindoo poems, and one or two other masterpieces, Danté's among them. As it happened, I read the latter mostly in an old wood. The *Iliad* (Buckley's prose version) I read first thoroughly on the peninsula of Orient, northeast end of Long Island, in a

---

[1] Bucke: *Walt Whitman*, p. 21.

sheltered hollow of rocks and sand, with the sea on each side."[1]

Despite this preference for reading in the open air, he passed hours and hours of the winter in the libraries of New York. Walt was not rich and could not always procure the work which he wished to absorb, but his lungs, accustomed to breathe freely, were rebels against the morose and asphyxiating atmosphere of reading rooms. Without the appearance of, and living a life apparently free from every abstract occupation, he read intensely and with all his senses. His chief care was to keep himself in touch with the thought of his time: thus he followed attentively the journals and reviews which all his life he preferred to books—except a dozen of the eternal and culminant ones which he had meditated upon and ended in knowing almost by heart. The enormous mass of magazine articles pencil marked and marginally annotated, found in his room after his death,[2] proclaims the omnivorous reader that he was, just as curious to learn the life of his great confrères of the past, for instance, as to assimilate the geography, the scientific ideas or facts of daily life. There was nothing *a priori* in his tastes as reader: he proposes to be universal student. He copies, extracts, edits, analyzes, notes, comments. And all this desultory knowledge filtered into him like the air, the pageants from without, the people passing by; he did not "furnish" his mind according to the old term; he was assimilated and transmuted. Walt had no desire to be "instructed," to enclose ideas in the lobes of his brain, he made only his inquiry into life; in this inquiry, books and print enter simply as a part, and not the most vital. They were but the accessory, the confirmation. When he conversed with any one—artisan, sailor, etc.,—possessing certain and positive knowledge in the domain of personal experience, he noted with care what he was listening to. Everything to him was good, everything

---
[1]*Leaves of Grass*, A Backward Glance, pp. 432-433.
[2]*Camden Edition*, X, pp. 63-97.

authentic and real. At the theatre, in the street, on boats, in the woods, his constant habit was to record his impressions. Notions, apparently the most insignificant, such as the mention and description of a cartman whom he had met and with whom he was amicably entertained, he registers with as much care as he would have given an historical document. The method which he practised with the view of gathering and condensing this scattered information was as original as his manner of self-instruction; it is thus that he put together the débris of geography by annexing maps, newspaper articles, leaves of white paper, upon which he recorded the ideas received from the mouths of travellers and navigators—the whole bound in a thick solid volume, a veritable magazine of documents, methodically classified, of all the countries of the world.[1]

However absorbed he was by the study of his time and his nation, Whitman did not ignore the traces of the past. He liked to question former civilizations, the better to understand what differentiated them from his own. There was exhibited at this time in Broadway a collection of Egyptian antiquities gathered together by an English physician. Walt surrendered himself to a profound study of this collection by the aid of a "formidable catalogue" and entered into it along with the doctor; more than that, he absorbed books on ancient civilization on the border of the Nile, "its antiquities, its history, how things and scenes really looked and how we judge of them now." In this domain, as when he had studied from concrete life, his method was to go to the heart of things, to squeeze the subject till he was himself saturated. He frequented also the "Phrenological Cabinet" of Fowler and Wells, where were gathered "all the busts, specimens, curiosities, and books possible in this study"[2] and where someone made his phrenological examination one day.

---
[1] *Camden Edition*, IX, pp. xvii–xviii.
[2] *Complete Prose*, p. 517.

He was a frequenter of meetings and never failed to hear the lecturers of the day—men like Bryant and Emerson. He confesses to us that at these mixed meetings, "windy and cyclonic," of reform societies before the war, he "learned much."[1] For not only was he there as auditor but he often spoke. At this epoch Walt, seduced by the multiform activities of his age, pretended to play his part in politics. At the time he published his little stories and verse, that is, between his twentieth and twenty-sixth year, his appearances on the platform were numerous. He threw himself with zest into the conflict of parties as he did into the literary and journalistic world, not as a dilettant, but as an apprentice of life, eager to plunge into all its currents and to learn by stirring them. He proved apt in filling all these human rôles, yet the voice of his destiny was not ready to be heard just then. When he was schoolmaster in Long Island, he was in the campaign in the ranks of the Democratic party, which helped the election of Van Buren to the presidency, and his success as an orator at Jamaica was, they say, vivid.[2] Back in New York, he used to frequent Tammany Hall, the celebrated general Democratic quarters where he knew the political notabilities of the party. In the electoral contest of 1844 which carried Polk to the presidency he was very active. But Walt was not of the stuff of the partisan. He was too calm and too human to be mixed in the raging and vociferous chase of politicians. And this crisis passed just as his literary fever passed. Never could he mix again in politics; he was content to follow attentively its phases, and to keep a live interest in what concerned national affairs. He had seen the "machine" function near enough to know the "springs of action." And he always voted at congressional presidential elections. A little later his sympathies carried him into the Republican party, to be changed again, at the close of his life, to the

---
[1] *Complete Prose*, p. 517.
[2] Bucke: *Walt Whitman*, p. 22.

Democratic. But these fluctuations signify little; they singularly prove that he remained always outside of parties.

One of his joys, perhaps the most natural, the most elementary of all, was to converse, no matter with whom, in the street, on a boat, on the doorstep of a store, no matter where. It was an irresistible need with him to communicate with passersby, to search new faces, to learn what the average humanity thought, to capture it alive, to fraternize. He had to convey a more fervent sense to the word sociability to render it adequate to this propensity. A passerby, a type of man, an individuality! That for him was the marvel of marvels, which he could not but allow himself to contemplate, to study in all its manifestations, to breathe in joyously. A note of the period of his youth—"A new soul which opens to us is better than a novel," is characteristic of his insatiable eagerness which incited him to open the book of environing lives. In that immense library which was New York, one power above all attracted him, that of common lives. In them he found his element; though to intellectuals, bourgeois, parlourmen, he was little drawn. He thirsted for the real man, and for a thinker, or reader: moreover, his taste carried him especially, according to the word of one of his intimates, "toward beings who have the qualities of things of the open air,—the power of rocks, of trees, of hills."[1]

He preferred the conversation of his comrades, the coachmen, to that of the most learned, because they were rude, primitive natures, who brought him news direct from life. "They were," he explained one day to his friend Donaldson, "as a rule, strong men mentally as well as physically. Some were educated, some not; but those who were competent to drive a stage for a length of time on such a street as Broadway, New York, for instance, were men of character and individuality.[2] Any portion of his papers, the bulk of which

---
[1]John Burroughs, *Walt Whitman*, p. 64.
[2]Donaldson: *Walt Whitman the Man*, p. 203.

was inventoried after his death and some published, revealed paragraphs where he comments on the vivid impression which his good friends made upon him. This silhouette, for instance: "Peter X . . ., young boy, tall, strongly built, coachman. Weight 180 pounds. Natural and sincere before me the first time that he saw me. Man of strong will, powerful in gross sensations and appetite . . . I love his refreshing naughtiness, as the orthodox say . . . I never met a man of whom I could judge in forty minutes, more open, ruder, more stubborn, more solid, and freer of the mischievous desire to go into society."[1]

In the course of this multiple existence, the sum of people with whom he mingled is unimaginable. From the bricklayer encumbered at the corner of a road, or the tramp on the streets, to the president or the great poet, William Cullen Bryant,[2] with whom he took long walks and kept most cordial relations—hundreds of thousands of interlocutors, who crossed his path, are lost in the anonymous crowd, titular mistress of this great Lover. And to figure to himself the immensity of his inquiry, it is necessary to evoke the hundreds of thousands whom he intensely observed with the eye of an artist, or a physician, without speaking to them a word, and without their apprehending him. Indeed, no one perhaps had a more extended knowledge of the masses; and we should recognize among his attributes a special sense, truly superhuman, of observation, introspection, whose power was "limited only by the things to be observed."

Such was in its general character and seen only under a limited number of its aspects the enormous education of this uneducated man. Walt had not been able to finish the elementary school; he became, none the less, one of the most endowed men who have trod the earth; made so by the living knowledge and perception of humanity, acquired by personal contact. "Lost in the cosmopolitan flood" of the swarming

---

[1] *Camden Edition*, IX, p. 134.
[2] O. L. Triggs: *Selections, Introduction*, p. xxv.

city to which this countryman, with a complete faith, vowed an enthusiastic devotion, he prepared without knowing it that limitlessness of himself which he was immortally to define and exalt.

Like the giant tramps and idlers of literature, the Hamsuns, the Gorkis, and the Londons, but with a much richer instinct, and in proportions incomparably ampler, he knew all life; he lived it boldly before he expressed it. He was one of the active units of the great whole which he later will sing. The democracy of the New World with its rudeness, its diversity, its tendencies, clear or shadowy, its furious enthusiasm, was ready to be realized in one individual sprung from it, worthy to create its type and its representative.

And what marks above all these crowded, tumultuous, unbridled years is that they flowed in an atmosphere of joy, of fecund mirth. They were "good times," full of "amusement in the mass" according to his own terms. The instinct of his Dutch lineage spoke in him. Walt was a happy man. With the sensuality of a man strong and healthy, every act of his life thrilled him through and through, causing him an emotion of pleasure. But the supreme feast was to find things so beautiful, so rich, so varied, to sport in the marvels, hidden for nearly all, in the heart of the commonplace and the every day. . . .

VI

TO THE SOUTH AND TO THE LOVE OF WOMAN

IT SEEMS rather strange that a man of such queer habits could fill at different intervals the post of editor of a newspaper. At first view, Walt appeared a man the least congenial to such a task. But the very special conditions of American life must be kept in mind and the vast difference between the little sheets of that period and the great dailies of the present time. An editorial chair of the kind Walt occupied at Brooklyn would be thought somewhat similar to the work in France of a sub-prefect.

The truth is that the man proved astonishingly facile in adapting himself, at least temporarily, to all his needs. He appeared almost indifferent to the kind of work which life demanded of him, provided the work respected him. That was the essential point. Aside from that, whatever came his way, he was prepared to take it for a living so long as it left him free for the dearest of his occupations: leisure to observe people and things.

It was at the beginning of 1846[1] that the destiny of the Brooklyn Eagle was confided to Whitman. He stayed with it two years. "I had there," he tells us, "one of the pleasantest sits of my life—a good owner, good pay, easy work, and convenient hours."[2] The Eagle was a modest daily of four small pages; its appearance alone conveys the impression that its editor must have passed undisturbed days. It was a Democratic organ; but this great party, in whose wrangling ranks Walt had combatted up to this time, was about to split. The editor had irreducible principles, and ranged

---

[1]H. B. Binns: *Life of Walt Whitman*, p. 42.
[2]*Complete Prose*, p. 188.

himself on the side of the Radicals, notably on the question of Anti-Slavery, which he took greatly to heart. Hence came quarrels with the orthodox of his party and his chief. There was nothing to do but to leave, and that he did. Walt wished again to gain his living by writing leading articles, but however good the place, the instant that there was a question of sacrificing one of his firm, definite convictions to the demands of the "machine" he took his hat and looked elsewhere. There was no upsetting a man of his character. In the newspaper offices of New York there were always cases for him. And like his forefathers in religious questions, Walt in politics instinctively took the side of the heterodox. Eventually there were other journals. After a stay with the Crescent of New Orleans, where we shall find him presently, he founded at Brooklyn the Freeman, first a weekly, then a daily. And about 1856, after a period of manual labour, he was for a time editor of the Brooklyn Times.

This was, after all, but a livelihood. It goes without saying that Walt did not have the temperament of a journalist. Slowly, creditably, just as he manipulated type, he discharged the duties assigned to him. But the special demands of the work were too contrary to his habitual serenity for him to shine in it. "He had in him too much repose. His employers called it idleness."[1] He was truly a singular editor. "His home (a modest house in Myrtle Avenue, where Walt lived with his parents, then returned to town), we are told, was half a league from the office of the Eagle near Fulton Ferry, and it may be supposed that he preferred to live at this distance that he might enjoy the things to be contemplated and observed, which lay in the course of his daily walk between these two points. Not only he loafed from his house to his office and back again, but even for whole days he forsook his desk, went to bathe and to recreate, leaving the people to settle their affairs as they could,

[1] C. H. M. Skinner: *Walt Whitman as an Editor*, the Atlantic Monthly, November, 1903, p. 680.

without his comment and advice."[1] Indeed it is well understood that in the offices of the Brooklyn Eagle the ironic legend has persisted of an amateur editor, who, to use a good popular expression, "took it easy." Already when he assumed similar functions on the Daily Aurora of New York, some years before, he was remarkable for the same absence of feverish haste. He left the memory of a rather fantastic editor-in-chief whose most serious occupation seemed to be, after a short appearance at his desk, between eleven and noon, to glance over the dailies, to go for a lounge of an hour or two under the trees of the Battery—studying the sea. And also at the Aurora, some divergence of views between the proprietor of the Journal and editor-in-chief resulted in the departure of the latter.

Without pretending to find an expression of the intimate man which is not there, it is interesting, nevertheless, to run through some of the articles produced by the Whitman of this period. What characterizes them is the good nature, the absence of pretence, and the go-as-you-please, which we find to-day in small provincial sheets. He comments on the doings of the day, and ingeniously delivers his impressions, revealing a candour and good sense, avoiding the oracular tone, and the inflamed period. His editorials have the quality of conversation, and are generally a bit trite. The man is not yet awakened: he is still the superficial, flowery young writer of the little stories which he printed on his return from Long Island. Nevertheless, from this confused mass, certain paragraphs emanate, in which, at least, one begins to suspect the real Walt. When he evokes such principles as are dear to him—generosity, humanity, liberty, honesty—his prose, ordinarily colourless, becomes animated. It is with real warmth that he combats capital punishment, treatment of Negroes (a courage which cost him his place on the Brooklyn Eagle), luxury of the churches, the authoritativeness of municipal power. Many times he gives counsel

---

[1] C. H. M. Skinner: *Walt Whitman as an Editor*, the Atlantic Monthly, November, 1903, p. 681.

of health to his readers, praises the bath, publishes receipts. He espouses always the cause of the individual against the law and is not breathless in praising his party. A success which he won during this time was to contribute— by conducting in his journal a vigorous campaign for it— to the transformation of old Fort Greene into a public park. For the welfare of the average man he had at heart, fully. Later, toward 1856, when he filled for a brief time the editorial chair of the Brooklyn Times, he supported vigorously an important project relative to some new hydraulic machines. Of his campaigns it was this that he still showed pride in, thirty years later, and he desired the memory of it preserved. The interest which he showed in the business of Brooklyn, the city of his childhood, appears in a very beautiful open letter to the City Council and Mayor, in which he adjures them to prove worthy of the great city which they administer, to be more comprehensive, larger in their rulings, more conformable to the individualistic spirit of the American community, reminding them in clear terms that they were the agents of the Master, that is to say, the Citizen. The noble and proud tone of this address, whose firm style is at times remarkable, surpasses the mere incident—the Sunday prohibitions—which motived it. In the particular inspiration which animates him one feels that a new man is in full awakening: it was, indeed, published by the Brooklyn Star in October, 1854,[1] at the eve of the capital event of the poet's life. Soon it is no longer his city, but the unknown world whose continents he is beginning to explore, which shall entreat him.

Until he was thirty and even a little beyond, his collaboration in journalistic work was varied and abundant. He had many friends on the press and could be sure of placing his articles. According to the words of his companion and first biographer, John Burroughs, he was the part "of the light battalion of publicists, who edit, with a facile pen,

---
[1] Reproduced in the *Conservator*, November, 1903, p. 135.

news, reviews, leading articles, no matter what, for pleasure, and to gain a living."[1] The big, cordial boy who was Whitman had won a place in the new literature and art of the city. He belonged for some years to a famous group to which one of his biographers, O. L. Triggs, has devoted an interesting page:

> While editor of The Freeman, he became one of the leading members of the group of New York Bohemians that met nightly at Pfaff's restaurant on Broadway to celebrate nationality in literature and art. . . Among the Pfaffian group were Fitz-James O'Brien, Fitzhugh Ludlow, Aldrich, Stedman, William Winter, Ned Wilkins, George Arnold, Gardette, "Artemus Ward," Ada Clare, the "Queen," and a score of others. The order had been established by Henry Clapp, who transplanted from Paris the moods and methods of Bohemia on the pattern of Henry Mürger's *Vie de Boheme*. Of this group Whitman was a recognized leader. Some of his stories were written at the hall of meeting. In one of his note-books in a rough sketch of a poem, beginning, "The vault at Pfaff's where the drinkers and laughers meet to eat and drink and carouse," and closing: "You phantoms! oft I pause, yearn to arrest some one of you! Oft I doubt your reality, suspect all is but a pageant." In an interview published in The Brooklyn Eagle in 1886, Whitman gives an account of the meetings: "I used to go to Pfaff's nearly every night. It used to be a pleasant place to go in the evening after finishing the work of the day. When it began to grow dark, Pfaff would invite everybody who happened to be sitting in the cave he had under the sidewalk to some other part of the restaurant. There was a long table extending the length of the cave; and as the Bohemians put in an appearance Henry Clapp would take a seat at the head of the table. I think there was as good talk around that table as took place anywhere in the world. Clapp was a very witty man. Fitz-James O'Brien was very bright. Ned Wilkins, who used to be the dramatic critic of The Herald, was another bright man. There were between twenty-five or thirty journalists, authors, artists, and actors who made up the company that took possession of the cave under the sidewalk.[2]

According to the recollections of an old "Bohemian," Whitman differed from the joyous band in one essential point, that is, he never became intoxicated. This unusual and singular affectation would suffice to give him, in the midst

---

[1] John Burroughs: *Notes*, pp. 80–81.
[2] O. L. Triggs: *Selections, Introduction*, pp. xxvi–xxvii.

of a frolic, a certain originality. He was content to empty
slowly his mug of beer, and in proportion as the company
became very "gay," his face became more passive and more
serious.[1] It is in Pfaff's cellar that some years later, in
August, 1860, the novelist, W. D. Howells, saw the poet for
the first time and thus recalls the meeting:

> I remember how he leaned back in his chair, and reached out his great
> hand to me, as if he were going to give it me for good and all. He had a
> fine head, with a cloud of Jovian hair upon it, and a branching beard and
> mustache, and gentle eyes that looked most kindly into mine, and seemed
> to wish the liking which I instantly gave him, though we hardly passed
> a word, and our acquaintance was summed up in that glance and the
> mighty fist upon my hand.[2]

A quarter of a century later, passing through New York,
Whitman, mindful of the fine moments of his youth, visited
his old friend, Pfaff, and the two, leisurely over a bottle of
champagne in honour of the old "Bohemia," evoked together
the jolly figures of former times, then dead or disappeared.[3]

At twenty-nine years, Walt as yet knew only New York
and his native island. It is true he had explored them thoroughly; but the immense continent, of which the metropolis
was then but the outpost, was unknown to him. The hazard
of a business engagement allowed him to penetrate the heart
of America, and to travel over a large part of his country.
It is not only for the enlargement of his vision that this journey is an important date in his life, but also because it agrees
with a romantic adventure, kept somewhat mysterious, but
of which we know enough to suspect that it had a serious
spiritual influence on the man. In fact, this journey was
doubly fecund and decisive. Walt had already lived and
absorbed much up to this time: but he returned, plowed
to the depth of his being, and bearing within him the embryo

---

[1] C. H. M. Skinner: *Walt Whitman as an Editor*, the Atlantic Monthly, November, 1903, p. 680.
[2] W. D. Howells: *Literary Friends and Acquaintances*, p. 74.
[3] *Complete Prose*, p. 181.

of a new soul. He acquired the consciousness of a continent and a consciousness of himself.

One evening at the beginning of 1848, while walking, between acts, in the lobby of the old Broadway Theatre, Walt made the acquaintance of a Southerner, who confided to him the project of founding a daily paper in New Orleans. He had much capital in the enterprise. The Louisianian had come to New York to buy material. They had a drink together, and after a quarter of an hour's conversation Walt was engaged as editor and received from the stranger two hundred dollars to bind the bargain and to pay travelling expenses.[1] As he had quit the Brooklyn Eagle and was out of a job, the enterprise was excellent. It appeared especially admirable, because it offered a providential opportunity —"to see the country" and a country curiously, entirely new, full of attraction for the Northerner which he was.

Two days after the interview he started. As the paper was not to appear for three weeks, he had plenty of leisure to travel by short stages, stopping according to his fancy to inspect what attracted him. His brother Jeff, then fifteen years old, was his companion. Of his family, he had a particular affection for this brother, founded on common tastes.

They travelled leisurely over Pennsylvania, and crossing the Alleghanies, embarked at Wheeling, on a merchant boat. From there they went slowly down the Ohio and the Mississippi, thus travelling through the Central States, land then newly opened. They reached New Orleans the twenty-fifth of February, 1848, and the first number of the Crescent appeared March 5. Walt worked as editor and Jeff as printer. Their stay was cut very short—they left toward the end of May—the climate being, it appears, unfavourable to the health of the younger brother.[2]

Walt nevertheless enjoyed himself to the full in Louisiana. To his avidity to know and to absorb the South presented

---

[1] *Complete Prose*, p. 188.
[2] *Camden Edition, Introduction*, p. xxxiv.

a choice pasture. Its atmosphere delighted him and he felt the accord between himself and what he saw. He learned that he was as much of the South as of the North. He reached there when everything was astir, just at the close of the victorious war with Mexico: he was just in time to meet General Taylor—future President of the United States— and his officers. As for his daily life, it was to all appearances the same as in New York. He mingled with everybody, loved the life of the pavement and the streets for itself; he idly went wherever there was something to be studied from life, and he profited by his sojourn by learning the raison d'être of Southern life. In a charming page of his memoirs, he tells us the impressions of these three months in the South:

> One of my choice amusements during my stay in New Orleans was going down to the old French Market, especially of a Sunday morning. The show was a varied and curious one; among the rest, the Indian and Negro hucksters with their wares. For there were always fine specimens of Indians, both men and women, young and old. I remember I nearly always on these occasions got a large cup of delicious coffee with a biscuit, for my breakfast, from the immense shining copper kettle of a great Creole mulatto woman (I believe she weigh'd 230 pounds). I never have had such coffee since. About nice drinks, anyhow, my recollection of the "cobblers" (with strawberries and snow on top of the large tumblers,) and also the exquisite wines, and the perfect and mild French brandy,—(temperance was already forgotten in 1848)—help the regretful reminiscence of my New Orleans experiences of those days. And what splendid and roomy and leisurely bar-rooms! . . . I used to wander a midday hour or two now and then for amusement on the crowded and bustling levees, on the banks of the river. The diagonally wedg'd-in boats, the stevedores, the piles of cotton and other merchandise, the carts, mules, Negroes, etc., afforded never-ending studies and sights to me. I made acquaintances among the captains, boatmen, or other characters, and often had long talks with them—sometimes finding a real rough diamond among my chance encounters. Sundays I sometimes went forenoons to the old Catholic Cathedral in the French quarter. I used to walk a good deal in this arrondissement; and I have deeply regretted since that I did not cultivate, while I had such a good opportunity, the chance of better knowledge of French and Spanish Creole New Orleans people (I have an idea that

there is much and of importance about the Latin race contributions to American nationality in the South and Southwest that will never be put with sympathetic understanding and tact on record).[1]

In his recollections of this journey Whitman remains wholly silent as to an event which was certainly the most important of his stay in Louisiana, one which strongly helped to print forever the image of the South on his memory and on his heart. An attempt to decipher this erased paragraph of his life—his relation with a Southern woman—compels us to note Walt's behaviour in the presence of women and to penetrate deeper into his character.

Walt was not a lady's man. As adolescent and youth, he was marked by his indifferent attitude toward girls. Those who knew him when he taught school in Long Island, and played games, went to village parties and reunions, tell, in recalling these, that women had no special attraction for this vigorous fellow, so ardent in enjoying his youth, so prodigal of care-free gaiety. No trace of a sweetheart, not the least of a love affair, appear in these twenty free years, at once wild and reflective, petulant and grave. The singular lad was made thus: the torment of love was absent from his heart. A woman in his presence was not a being essentially different from a man. And there is every probability that his youth had been chaste until his return to New York, at the age of twenty-two. And it remains certain that women and love in the habitual sense did not play in the life of Whitman the decisive and important part which they do in the life of the average man.

When he was plunged into the eddies of New York, he penetrated all its aspects. The testimony of his friends, and that of John Burroughs, for instance, is: "Throughout this period—from 1837 to 1848—without going into details, it is sufficient to say that his were all the experiences of life, with all their passions, their pleasures, their abandons. . . . Those

---

[1] *Complete Prose*, p. 440.

who have known the poet in these last years, and see in him only the calm, gray-bearded man of to-day must not forget, in reading his *Leaves*, that anterior and ardent phase of his life."[1] Or the word of Bucke that, "to use the simple and hearty old scriptural phrase, 'the love of women' has always been, and is in a legitimate sense, one of the main elementary passions."[2] What warranted certain people to say, for instance, that Walt appeared "to detest women,"[3] is probably his absolute ignorance of little attentions, of gallant speech, of cajoleries by which in all latitudes the amorous propensities of the civilized are translated. Walt never flirted, never sought feminine society, never armed himself to attract the favour of his interlocutresses, never published abroad the detail of his adventures. His discretion was such that he never pronounced nor let fall a word touching his relations with any sweetheart whatever. He thus deceived the unwary—the simple people of the type who sought to deduce from the fact that he never married the indisputable proof of his systematic indifference toward woman! Love stammering, bashful, interspersed by agony and sighs, it is plain that he scorned it with all the despotic indifference of the strong, realistic man—even to finding no trace of it in his poems. He was a lover, as a Walt Whitman could be a lover.

It is possible though that up to the time of his stay in New Orleans he had not perhaps yet experienced his real love. Nothing prevents the conjecture that the Louisiana capital held for him this surprise and this complementary shock. I say conjecture, for the known facts amount to almost nothing. They are contained in an avowal of the poet asserting his paternity. In a letter to his English friend and admirer, John Addington Symonds, dated August 19, 1890—and which was not published till 1902 by Edward Carpen-

---

[1] John Burroughs: *Notes*, p. 81.
[2] Bucke: *Walt Whitman*, p. 23.
[3] I. Hull Platt: *Walt Whitman*, p 12.

ter[1]—Walt wrote: "My life, young manhood, my mid-age, times South etc., have been jolly bodily, and doubtless open to criticism. Though unmarried, I have had six children. Two are dead—one living Southern grandchild, fine boy, writes me occasionally:—circumstances (connected with their fortune and benefit) have separated me from intimate relations with them." On his death bed, Walt expressed one evening to the two most intimate companions of his last years, Thomas Harned and Horace Traubel, the wish to dictate a kind of deposition, which they were to lay aside, in case if (unhappily) a public discussion should arise one day of this unknown event of his life, it could be met, facts in hand. His most precious wish, however, was that no one would broach this subject, the revealing of which would cause "surely a grave injury to someone." But the old man was then too feeble and could not realize his wish.[2] The secret was not revealed that evening and was soon carried with him to his grave.

In his last years Walt often alluded before his neighbours to this fact of his paternity. But he never went far. So open and so little accessible to prejudices as he proved, his discretion as to the incidents of his private life is unbelievable. It was discovered, after his death, that he had torn pages from his travel notebook, where may have been found written certain details of his adventure in New Orleans, so determined was he that this episode should remain in oblivion.[3] And this discretion, his intimate friends, and even his biographers, have religiously respected.

Mr. H. B. Binns in his book, so rich, so devout, so warm, is the first who has attempted to penetrate this mystery, which persists in the depth of a life fertile in surprises. The suggestive chapter treating of the romance of Walt in

---

[1]The Reformer, February, 1902 (reëdited with accompanying article in Ed. Carpenter: *Days with Walt Whitman*, pp. 137–152).
[2]H. B. Binns: *Life of Walt Whitman*, App. B., p. 349.
[3]*Id.:* p. 350.

Louisiana certainly opens new horizons and strongly presents plausible hypotheses. Nevertheless, I hesitate to admit all his conclusions. I believe especially that Mr. Binns has exaggerated the significance this romance had for the young man and his future development.[1]

A probable conjecture—even assurance—is that Walt Whitman when in New Orleans, in a sunny and languorous country, fell in love with a French Creole or Spaniard—a very attractive type of woman. The young journalist must have been, at twenty-nine, in the full flowering of his manly beauty and strength, splendid as a demi-god of primitive Hellas. Of exceptional beauty he was always, but at that time youth must have clothed him with irresistible masculine charm. What more natural than that a Southern woman, belonging to some noble family, on seeing him pass with such nonchalant and calm demeanour, should fall in love with him. It was perhaps the "old dear friend" with the charming face, whose portrait was seen on the mantel of his room forty years afterward, and of whom he was not inclined to speak, even to his relatives.[2] I am inclined to think that she was a French woman. "I walked much in that neighbourhood," he tells us in describing the French quarter—and that it was in her company that he learned the words borrowed from the language of France with which he has curiously sprinkled his writings. And perhaps the great lover was overcome, stirred to his very depth by this new complete love.

For he left undoubtedly to tear himself from the charm of sorcerer and the violence of this love. He was afraid of being caught in the net of a splendid and redoubtable passion, and fleeing the danger, he brusquely broke the bond and resumed his way North. In a poem, "Sailing the Mississippi at Midnight," written perhaps while on his return, there is a

---
[1] H. B. Binns: *Life of Walt Whitman*, pp. 52-3.
[2] H. Traubel: *With Walt Whitman in Camden*, p. 389.

stanza which reminds one of this possible experience of the young man:

> But when there comes a voluptuous languor,
> Soft the sunshine, silent the air,
> Bewitching your craft with safety and sweetness,
> Then, young pilot of life, beware.[1]

With his formidable individualism and his rabid passion for independence, Walt Whitman protected himself against a permanent attachment; he dreaded the yoke, the engrossment, the fixed habit, the restrictions imposed upon his personal and solitary manner of living, upon his tastes, his predilections. On this point, he frankly interprets himself, intimately;[2] he could not endure that a woman should hold a place in his life which might fatally lessen the domain of his liberty, where he determined to rule an absolute despot.

The instinct not to allow himself to be absorbed—even by a being dearest to him—was as strong as his passion for comrades and for crowds. It was less a rule of conduct dictated by experience than a natural repulsion to every fetter and intrusion: at all events, an essential matter with this singular and contradictory man. There was no advancing toward intimacy with him further than the limit set by himself. Whoever believed that he retained it saw that he had not crossed the impassable threshold of his individual self. There is no need to imagine romantic incidents and a whole secret drama to explain why he kept himself apart from the woman he loved. It would have sundered Walt from his own will. The only valid reason is doubtless that there is no reason.

> . . . I will certainly elude you,
> Even while you should think you had unquestionably caught me, behold!
> Already you see I have escaped from you.[3]

---

[1]*Complete Prose*, p. 374.
[2]Bucke: *In Re Walt Whitman*, p. 323; *Walt Whitman*, p. 60.
[3]*Leaves of Grass*, p. 98.

It is sheltered behind this rampart that he defends himself against external affairs and notably against the great affair of love. Walt Whitman uncrowned of his sovereign egotism would not be Walt Whitman. Perhaps without being conscious of it, he refused himself to a single one the better to be given in person, and later in a work, to all. Here we touch perhaps the heart of the prophet, the predestinate man, swayed by the demands of a mission, having to safeguard the unwritten rights of his individuality. Happily for this safeguard he possessed his overwhelming repose; after the possible intoxication of the hours passed with his beloved in the South, the astonishing sang-froid with which he was endowed must have returned to him. And do we not discover the purpose of his voluntary departure from New Orleans as an instinct of defence and of recovery of himself in these lines of a short poem of *Leaves of Grass*, in which it is difficult not to recognize a confessional value?

Once I pass'd through a populous city imprinting my brain for future use
    with its shows, architecture, customs, traditions,
Yet now of all that city I remember only a woman I casually met there
    who detain'd me for love of me,
I remember I say only that woman who passionately clung to me,
Again we wander, we love, we separate again,
Again she holds me by the hand, I must not go,
I see her close beside me with silent lips, sad and tremulous.[1]

Whatever may have been the adventures and their consequences, these three months in the South, as well as the journey going and coming, had a profound influence upon Walt of which his later work retains many traces. He had discovered a climate, manners, which he liked; and a temperament such as the sense of leisure, the coming and going, the capacity for joy, which marvellously corresponded to his own sensibility. The whole sensuous soul which this descendant of Quakers hid, vibrated under the vuluptuous and warm caress of Louisiana. This stay at the border of the Gulf

---
[1] *Leaves of Grass*, p. 94.

of Mexico was like the discovery of another civilization, rooted from afar, charged with the memory of ages. And in going and returning he proved the vastness of his country, the rich diversity of these States behind which other states came to mass themselves ceaselessly, almost without end, to the shores of the Pacific—the thirtieth exactly made its entrance into the Union at that precise moment and Mexico, an immense territory, was just conquered—these States which were being populated with marvellous rapidity, preparing the formidable federation of the western world. He returned with the soul of an American citizen, dilated to the country whose vast extent he did not know till then. He had observed, compared, seized the different peoples. New and altogether powerful emotions enriched the depths of his being, and he reached the North ripened, expanded, already transformed. Just as the abandoning of his work as village schoolmaster had marked the end of his adolescence, thus the young boy which he still was at his departure for the South was transformed into the man.

Walt had plunged into the heart of the continent and, undoubtedly, into the heart of woman.

The return was made slowly, and the brothers having some savings in pocket, profited by their good luck to penetrate still farther the vast interior of their country. Whitman has described for us briefly his itinerary, in his papers, a part of his travel notes and letters to his family which are in the hands of his testamentary executors. They reascended the Mississippi and saw its monotonous banks as far as St. Louis, where they passed many hours. Another boat, which reached Illinois, brought them to La Salle, then by canal they reached Chicago. They embarked upon Lake Michigan, visited Milwaukee, and Walt, who lost not a single detail of the landscape, was ecstatic at the smiling and prosperous appearance of the Wisconsin towns, where he would like well to have lived. After stopping at Mackinaw, where they visited the old fort, the brothers sailed on Lake Huron,

touched Detroit, passed to Lake Erie and inspected the
Canada shore, and after a short stop at Cleveland, debarked
at Buffalo, end of their long sail. The excursion to the neighbouring falls of Niagara was in order and they took the time
to examine them at leisure, like good tourists. Across the
rich and cultivated country sprinkled with towns and villages which form the centre of New York, they reached Albany, capital of the Empire State, and returned home by
way of the Hudson.[1]

The return voyage lasted nearly three weeks. For a man
like Walt, that was enough. He confronted the marvels
and carried within him the ineffaceable notion of the immense territory where floated the starry banner.

Again in Brooklyn with his family—his parents, four
brothers, still unmarried, and his younger sister lived then
under the same roof—he resumed his former life. Perhaps
he earned in the composing rooms the modest means which
supported him; the relative details of his life at this time
are more than meagre. In 1849 in Myrtle Avenue he had
a little print shop in front of which he sold some books. It
was there that he edited the Freeman, first as a weekly sheet
then a daily, where he defended radical principles which
forced him to break with the Democratic Party. The enterprise lasted almost a year.

Then came a new sudden turn in the career of this undisciplined man, who did not accept employment except on
condition of not being burdened by the yoke which it imposed, and avowed himself incapable of remaining long in the
same place.[2] He took up his father's business, carpentry
and construction. Walter Whitman, who was now over
sixty and in poor health, was no longer able to work.

Now the son took a hand. (It is not probable that he
had before this manipulated saw and hammer alone.) He
began to build small houses of two or three stories, for

---

[1]*Complete Prose*, pp. 441-42.
[2]Bucke: *Walt Whitman*, p. 25.

labouring men. When he finished one, he sold it and commenced another, not without enjoying in the interval studious leisure on the wild coast of his island. He built on his own account, doing all the work with his own hands. He left in the morning, like the workman, carrying in his little basket his luncheon, prepared by his mother, and came back in the evening, the day done.[1] There was at that time a great rise in property and building in Brooklyn and the occasion appeared propitious to pocket good profits. Even Walt, in spite of himself, made money. If he had continued to speculate in his houses, he would have realized a small fortune. At least any reasonable man, in his situation, would have profited by this providential and unique chance to hoard money. But Walt was not reasonable apparently. To the sad surprise of his family, who never understood this incorrigible, he relaxed, neglected his work, then in 1854 left it altogether, renouncing with gaiety of heart his most brilliant prospects. Perhaps he had had the vague fear of awaking rich some fine morning and that would have been for him the supreme humiliation. He had never done anything for money: this time he deliberately affirmed by his conduct the most beautiful silent scorn of it. Fortune and he had no common language. Walt did not wish her for a companion.

He had also another reason for abandoning his fruitful speculations, and this was irresistible and peremptory. It is that the careless boy with eyes open large upon life and so naïvely joyous of his magnificent health, the big boy, idler and dawdler, in love with the open air and direct contact with men, was big with an idea which came to be the axis of his entire existence. Already for many years a transformation was slowly operating in the depths of his being. Another Walt was about to be born. Something solicited all his strength, all his thought, all the instinct of his life: true, he did not know what it was, but it was surely something great.

---

[1] J. T. Trowbridge: *Reminiscences of Walt Whitman*, the Atlantic Monthly, February, 1902, p. 163.

To his intense gaze, the world appeared in a new light and he was absorbed in the contemplation of the marvels which now were being revealed to him. Since his thirtieth year, his inner life was lavishly enriched; the entire man was focussing his strength to direct it toward an end which he sought to formulate aright. Outwardly he was always the son of the carpenter, but in himself, he was no longer such. He had hours of gravity and of abstraction when one would have believed him transported upon a Tabor. And after ardent years passed in listening, in meditating, in accumulating, in surmising the result of the phenomenon to which he was a prey, he had to leave every other task to consecrate himself to this work. For now he knew. His task was given him exactly. He prepared himself to face the doing of it with the tranquil assurance with which he faced everything.

His brother George paints him for us at this epoch, living on Portland Avenue in a big house with his family. Walt appeared always the same simple man, affectionate and singular, who baffled his family by his absolute lack of practical sense. He passed his time in "writing a little, working a little, loafing a little, he got up late, began to write, then went out for the whole day; he wrote considerable, one knows not what." For a long time he had entirely stopped publishing the sleepy stories which he produced in his twenty-fifth year. Everybody in the house had regular work except him.[1] Sometimes he would go to the most solitary parts of Long Island on the shore in the woods and remain there entire weeks.[2] In 1853 New York saw a great Universal Exposition. Almost the whole year Walt passed numerous days and evenings in the vast brick and glass building, detailing all the marvels of art come from Europe which were exhibited there. This great onlooker entered into the thought and sentiment of

---
[1]Bucke: *In Re Walt Whitman*, p. 35.
[2]Bucke: *Walt Whitman*, p. 24.

the Old World, to learn what went on in the continent of his ancestors, and he profited eagerly by it. There was not only a rich collection of pictures, of sculptures (among them the colossal group of Thorwaldsen, Christ and the Twelve Apostles), pieces of jewellery, objects of art, but samples of wood, minerals, machines of all lands, "every sort of work, of product, of labour, coming from the workers of all nations,"[1] which offered him a subject of "inexhaustible study." At that moment when he was himself, a prey to inner travail, of fusion and of coördination, this inventory of the riches of the world and of human labour, with the sense of universality and unity revealed in it, particularly fascinated him. He felt the powerful pulse of the crowds of visitors under the great dome in an accumulation of marvels. With his miraculous power of absorbing and speculating, one may imagine what a world of knowledge and impressions he was able to acquire there.

That same year he had to take his sick father to Huntington. The old carpenter, feeling his decline, was drawn to his original home and wished to breathe again his native air. Walt was then among the scenes of his childhood. Now, the great crisis of his life was about to unfold. The time was near. Walt was about to reveal suddenly the reason of his coming, to justify his being, his race, and his time. The work, adequate to his personality, which he bore within him since he had listened to the inner call, arrived at maturity. All his life up to this had been but the prelude to the great enterprise, which henceforth shall be one with himself.

---
[1] *Complete Prose*, p. 505.

VII
"WALT WHITMAN, A COSMOS"

BEFORE the personality of Walt Whitman acquires a new meaning and moves about the central event of his life we shall halt a moment to consider the man face to face, such as he appeared about his thirtieth year. We shall discover in scrutinizing some of the intimate depths of his nature that the very core of himself seems to indefinitely expand, allowing glimpses of secret and subtle qualities which one feels but does not analyze.

In this glorious epoch of plenitude he virtually conceives his work without having yet planned, expressed, performed it. He presents himself as a marvellous type, unforgettable, the standard of a race; cell of the American Democracy and prototype of the world democracy, the stroller of New York, the "well engendered" son of the people, rich in correspondence with everything and everybody, who realizes a new aspect of humanity and marks an age of the world. However magnificent, however eternal may be for us his book, Walt, the man in the flesh who is about to put it forth, is at least its peer at this moment. He is, I repeat, at this period of brilliant and warm youth more than at any other, his book in life.

The perfect concordance between the interior Walt and his physical appearance is a genuine subject of astonishment. Nature had made him marvellously one. The man was very tall, broad shouldered, of massive frame, and admirably proportioned. His face, before acquiring that incomparable Olympian majesty old age was to impress upon it even in his portraits, still ravishes us with its rare beauty. His high-arched eyebrows marking a large forehead, eyes clear blue, nose very strong and absolutely straight, were framed in a perfect oval ruddy face, tanned by the open air, sun, and sea, and covered with a beard and a moustache which he never shaved. Before thirty—was it after his journey to New Orleans?—his black hair became gray, and the contrast of these silver threads with the appearance of extreme youth radiating from his face produced a very unusual impression. He was from head to foot a man who impressed one by his unusual proportions and the nobility of his carriage. In repose he evoked in the ensemble of his person and not by his face alone Greek beauty—not that of the decadence which fills our museums with its jaded type, but the strong, primitive, Hellenic type, that is to say, absolute harmony in rude power. In all his physiognomy, a certain primitive barbaric expression was prominent and marked him, among city-bred men, as a piece of natural rock in an artificial park.

Never, in the street, was he seen to hurry; though the natural grace of all of his movements was extreme, his walk was rather heavy and slow, and in moving forward he balanced his great body like a rhythm which was compared to the roll of an elephant. His voice, well modulated, charming, was one of his attractions. The eye was not large and his mild glance, little expressive of intelligence and vivacity, rather colourless, not piercing but absorbing, suggested that of the big mammals. The senses were with him of a remarkable perfection and acuteness; "he seemed to perceive sounds that others did not hear,"[1] avowed his brother George. His subtle sense of smell, which made him detect a particular odour at different hours of the day, approached that of the savage and the beast. Everything concurred to make the athletic and bearded boy who nonchalantly sauntered along the pavements of Broadway a specimen of splendid human animality, well equipped, perfectly poised, aplomb, free from the blemishes which come to the civilized in expiation of his

---
[1] Bucke: *In Re Walt Whitman*, p. 37.

moral refining. Never man issued more complete and more normal from a block of living stuff.

An invariable and radiant health to the time of his maturity, when he became an invalid, was like the flower of this rare organism. This health was his pride. "I doubt," he tells us, "if a heartier, stronger physique, more balanced upon itself, or more unconscious, more sound, ever lived, from 1835 to 1872 . . . (I considered myself invulnerable).[1] The physical joy which emanated from his person was to the verge of copious and excessive so that it was almost embarrassing, according to certain interlocutors.[2] His entire body aglow, of a ruddy super-abundance, seemed to elude the daily miseries of life. At a period when, after a long time, he knew only retrospectively these advantages, Walt thus described what he calls health: "In that condition the whole body is elevated to a state by others unknown —inwardly and outwardly illuminated, purified, made solid, strong yet buoyant. A singular charm, more than beauty, flickers out of, and over, the face—a curious transparency beams in the eyes, both in the iris and white—the temper partakes also. Nothing that happens—no event, rencontre, weather, etc.—but it is confronted—nothing but is subdued unto sustenance—such is the marvellous transformation from the old timorousness and the old process of causes and effects. Sorrows and disappointments cease—there is no more borrowing trouble in advance. A man realizes the venerable myth—he is a god walking the earth, he has a new eyesight and hearing. The play of the body in motion takes a previously unknown grace. Merely to move is then a happiness, a pleasure—to breathe, to see, is also. . . ."[3]

A more than ample frame bears the stamp of his origin and, from head to foot, Walt proves himself of the imperial race of manual workers, foundation and raison d'être of the

---

[1] *Complete Prose*, p. 522.
[2] John Burroughs: *Walt Whitman*, p. 52.
[3] *Complete Prose*, p. 502.

American democracy. Centuries of silent labour close to the earth and to the sea, centuries of robustness and open air, were necessary to prepare such a representative: it would have been impossible to cultivate any city-bred generations to produce this tan-skinned Bacchus, drunk with the wine of life. It is the truth which the famous portrait of the poet confides to us, the portrait which takes the place of the author's name in the first edition of his book, and which accompanies it in its transformation. This young man, in workman's dress, with an indifferent attitude, and at the same time firm, modest, and arrogant, with a calm, decided visage, whose glance, cast upon you, questions and follows you, appears to have arisen to justify his people, the men of the average, the silent heroes of the common people, the builders of cities, the modern Atlantes, arrived at the calm consciousness of sovereignty. The man in shirt sleeves who stands before you, his hand on his hip, his left hand in his pantaloons pocket, the felt hat tipped to the side, has the absolute attitude of a king. And he is, in effect, the individual-king. No court mantle could equal in majesty the insolent and natural looseness of his dress, the irreducible freedom of his whole figure. He comes as an ambassador of a new race, charged to promulgate his life throughout the world.

This portrait etched by McRae after a daguerreotype taken in July, 1854, is the document which shows us the physical aspect of the man at thirty-five, that is to say, at the very time when after years of searching and groping, he formulated the first songs of his poem. Dated from the same year, another daguerreotype has also come to us. It is a portrait bust, whose expression is strange. The face contains something of the faun and of the Christ at the same time. The epicurean lips which contrast with a certain thinness of feature and intense melancholy of glance give him an ambiguous expression not met with in another portrait. Whatever may be the beauty of this, I believe it will be necessary to consider it as rather exceptional: it is perhaps more suggestive than the full-length portrait, but certainly less true. Is it possible to recognize there the trace of the sorrow which the bringing forth of his book caused him, in the course of the years which preceded its coming?

There exists a kind of commentary on the first of these portraits, which, in the definite edition of his book, serves as a frontispiece to the *Song of Myself*, and it is to himself that we owe it. After the most ingenuous of immodesties, the poet took care to describe himself in the course of an anonymous article upon himself which he sent to the Brooklyn Times, when his poem and his personality were defenselessly exposed to lying interpretations. It is both the deep coloured sketch which we have of the man at this period and his signally veracious transmission to the future:

> Of American breed, of reckless health, his body perfect, free from taint from top to toe, free forever from headache and dyspepsia, full-blooded, six feet high, a good feeder, never once using medicine, drinking water only—a swimmer in the river or bay or by the seashore—of straight attitude and slow movement of foot—an indescribable style evincing indifference and disdain—ample limbed, thirty-six years (1855)—never dressed in black, always dressed freely and clean in strong clothes, neck open, shirt-collar flat and broad, countenance of swarthy transparent red, beard short and well mottled with white, hair like hay after it has been mowed in the field and lies tossed and streaked—face not refined or intellectual, but calm and wholesome—a face of an unaffected animal—a face that absorbs the sunshine and meets savage or gentleman on equal terms—a face of one who eats and drinks and is a brawny lover and embracer—a face of undying friendship and indulgence toward men and women, and of one who finds the same returned many fold—a face with two gray eyes where passion and hauteur sleep, and melancholy stands behind them—a spirit that mixes cheerfully with the world.[1]

Heir of two races which blended in him, Walt owed particularly to that of Holland one of the main traits of his temperament: his pyramidal phlegm, his equable humour,

---

[1] The Brooklyn Daily Times: September 29, 1855, Reproduced in Bucke's *Walt Whitman*, p. 195. This is but a transposition in prose of a fragment suppressed after the edition of 1860 of the "Song of the Broad Axe" (See Bucke: *Walt Whitman*, pp. 168–169).

his feeling for the concrete, his vast optimism, his strict propriety, his sensuousness, his propension to affectionate comradeship, all came to him by the channel of the Van Velsors. Surely the British stock would never have produced a being moving through life with that invincible, placid manner, nonchalant and idle, the immutable inner contentment, that appetite for things for their own sake, that perfect and smiling serenity. To his English ancestors, he is above all indebted for his excessive individuality, the terrible firmness of his moral structure. But that which one must admire supremely is the equilibrium which realized in his person the qualities of the two races which he fused in the crucible of one superior individuality. It strikes us as still more strongly evident when we examine as Bucke has done the results which the same combination came to in the poet's brothers.

Jesse, the oldest brother, was an incapable, who during his life could but do a hired man's work. The third son, Andrew, a feeble and mediocre man, disappeared at thirty-six. George, the fourth, represented the Whitman type in all its purity: virile, loyal, sincere, and righteous. He conducted himself heroically during the War of Secession and was made colonel. A magnificent character for a man of action, but devoid of all imagination and intuition. Jeff, the fifth—the favourite companion of Walt on many a jaunt—was, on the contrary, a tender, sensitive, divining character who, almost without instruction, became by sheer force of work a great engineer. He inherited the maternal qualities but not the robustness of the Whitmans. The last one, Edward, was an idiot. A total of three failures and two successes, each in one direction—which show us the trials, the gropings, the checks of nature in the work of preparing one superior type. Walt, alone, the second son, represents the perfect fusion of the two races, whose qualities acquire in combining in him a new power. This phenomenon of metachemistry Bucke has formulated in a page which clears not only the formation of the individuality of the poet, but the genesis of a representative man, of all time—thus, in truth, Walt Whitman not only possessed the qualities of the Whitman and Van Velsor, but these were all intensified in him to an almost superhuman degree; he was more a Whitman man than his father or his brother George, more a Van Velsor than his mother or his brother Jeff, and he possessed besides qualities unsuspected in his family to his time.[1]

Truly nature conducted herself royally toward the son of the carpenter of West Hills. She realized in him one of her absolute masterpieces. And genius, the intensifier par excellence, endowed him by a superaddition of creative force corresponding to his physical proportions.

With all this grandeur manifested in the setting of his personality as man, Walt practised a simplicity of attitude and of manner which did not distinguish him from the people, his daily company. One can imagine a youth radiating with strength and brilliant natural superiority going through life with a grave and distant air; he was a most commonplace everyday person exempt from any shade of pose, even the one of wishing to avoid it. Perfectly at ease with everyone, he certainly proved himself closer to the mother of a family on the way to market, or to a man handling a broom on a Broadway sidewalk, than to a philosopher, a lawyer, or a doctor. One has but to read the letters to his mother or to one of his uneducated friends to understand all the child-like ingenuousness in this great, full-grown, tranquil athlete. When he was not abandoned to his genius, Walt preferred the divine commonplaceness which made up the life of an ordinary man. He never abandons his place in the ranks of the "average," he belongs to this with all his fibre, proving it, yet is on the other hand the peer of the greatest interpreters of the race.

Conventions have so taught us to join the idea of individual superiority to distinction of intellect and of manners that we cannot suppress our surprise to see him so close to the

---

[1] Bucke: *Walt Whitman, Man and Poet*, Cosmopolis, June, 1898. p. 689.

common run of men, so genuine, conformable to the mass, so devoid of the life of comfort. He was endowed with all the elementary appetites, which the simplest people manifest, as "common" and little complex as the peasant or the woodpecker, who eats, drinks, and procreates, as free of manner as the docker at the harbour, or the mason at his work, as free of constraint and of prejudices as the tramp in the road.

He presents himself such as he is with his strong, healthy instincts of which he is not ashamed any more than he is of the fine body which he does not attempt to adorn. He affirms himself such as he is and rejoices in finding himself so elemental. Some have called him cynic for this, they who have not understood him. And according as he approaches maturity, this basic simplicity, whose roots reach far into the soil of the race, is but accentuated. "His only eccentricity is to be free from eccentricity."[1]

The picturesque rustic carelessness of his dress remains legendary. During the first years of his life in New York, the time when he published his "literature" in the popular reviews, Walt, returning from his island, thought well to sacrifice to the taste of the day in adopting a frock coat—a flower on the lapel—and a high hat.[2] Little by little this dress was simplified, and from the time when the idea of the work to be accomplished began to torment him, he was never seen except clad in an unchangeable suit of gray cloth or serge, never black, as he describes it for us. A big-brimmed felt hat, convenient for rain or sun, protected his head. More often his waistcoat was unbuttoned, and when it was very warm, he was seen coming along in his shirt sleeves with as much dignity as if he wore a fashionable coat. Despite this dress which a bourgeois would have called slouchy, he was remarkable for the invariable and scrupulous neatness of his linen, a corollary of his minute care of his body. He

[1] John Burroughs: *Notes*, p. 86.
[2] Bucke: *In Re Walt Whitman*, p. 34.

exhaled the good odour of the bath and of fresh linen. To
the eyes of certain people, who do not see how this dress corresponds to the whole man, this cool disdain of fashion is
often interpreted as a simple passion for advertising.

In matters of eating, he always preferred simple and substantial dishes. No masterpiece of the modern kitchen was
worth as much to him as a clam, which as a child he had
fished, and according to him the king of the shellfish of his
island. When he lived by himself he was seen every morning
to take his knife from his pocket, to cut large slices of bread
and butter them for his luncheon. He was an extremely
moderate drinker. He never smoked. To an advanced
age, he lived either with his relatives, where living was very
modest, or in a boarding house or in a bachelor's room. His
errant penates knew only the simple furnishing which a workman would easily have qualified as poor. His needs were
small in number and those which could be supplied anywhere; provided that he had a bed, washstand, a small
deal table and a chair, the rest was indifferent to him. A
luxurious interior would have seemed intolerable to him. He
had the aversion of a Quaker for anything that was ostenta-
tion and form.[1] One recognizes, nevertheless, in all his manners an ease and liberty entirely opposed to preoccupation
which rules the narrow and measured existence of a man well
groomed, shaven, dressed and cared for. He loved to show
himself barbarian, and he was one in all the force of spontane-
ity and independence of the word. A fierce instinct kept
him away from the unchangeable ways traced and followed
by mere convention. "Society" and its fantasticalities,
its pretty manners, gestures and speech, smelling of perfume,
would have nauseated him. Although no living being was
ever excluded from his sympathies, one sees that the
effeminate personage jaded and varnished, standing in
parlours, had upon him the effect of an emasculate, and that
with all the naïveté of the natural man he unmistakably

---

[1] O. L. Triggs: *Selections, Introduction*, p. xviii.

despised him. The sentiment of social hierarchy was null in him. He was a man among men, great and sweet toward all. In his daily life, although he did not live it as a real Bohemian, he showed himself an irregular, one careless of what other men cared for. When he lived with his parents in Brooklyn, it was rarely, according to his brother George, that he was at a meal on time. If a wish seized him to leave the house it mattered little to him that it was the hour that the family sat down to the table. He paid no attention to them and returned two hours later to sit down and eat. A mountain across the doorway would not have changed his resolution. He did everything in his own time, when he was ready.[1]

As in the time of his youth in which the epithet of idler was gratuitously bestowed upon him in his neighbourhood, people who judged him according to the ordinary standard were inclined to see in him one possessed to do nothing. His apparent nonchalance and his slowness baffled their judgment. In reality he was incessantly active; and when one reviews the work of his life, one is struck with the colossal task which he really performed. Indeed hard workers cannot show the equivalent of labour which the enormous quantity of documents, extracts, notes, commentaries, analyses, projects in every sense, found after his death, suggest but feebly. Let us add that this do-nothing not only would not depend upon any one while he was an invalid, and paid his board regularly when he lived under the family roof, but pecuniarily supported his family, his old mother, his feeble-minded brother, during a good part of his life, with the product of the labour of his hands.[2] But it was useless to demand of him feverish work, harsh and breathless. He had too much inner repose to break his back. He seemed to have all time and never moved except in his own way. While others gathered bank notes in their drawer, he ac-

---
[1] Bucke: *In Re Walt Whitman*, p. 36.
[2] Bucke: *Walt Whitman, Man and Poet*, Cosmopolis, June, '98, p. 690.

cumulated, without stopping, treasures of observation, of study, of impressions, of emotions, which he would render to the world after having imposed upon them the new stamp of his self. That was his raison d'être here below, as to others is assigned the alignment of figures in an office or the management of materials in a factory. With the obstinacy of his race, he follows an instinct in refusing to run with the dollar hunters. The riches which he coveted did not demand pursuits where one suffocated.

From idler to rake, the transition is natural, and after he had published the first songs of his poem, one of the most common accusations against him, very grave in America, was of being a man of dissolute morals. The appearances were at first glance against Walt, whose way of living and whose poetic affirmations were too unusual to escape reprobation. Nevertheless, just as in the case of his idleness, appearance was a liar. There is not anything in him to be praised or blamed, but all evidences established with certitude that he was a person of great reserve in conduct. In associating with women, we have mentioned his extreme discretion. He had perhaps a too exalted idea of the sex relation to corrupt it. Walt had a singular respect for himself. This very high conception of propriety included conversation and daily conduct. In his language and in his manners, a native distinction allied itself curiously with his perfect freedom; never, on his part, a word or a gesture of ribaldry. Among his comrades of the street, this behaviour added to his prestige because it was never accompanied with any arrogance, any hypocrisy. Walt was not a prude. He was simply, but fundamentally, a clean man in his choice of words as well as in his dress. Dirt for its own sake, literally or figuratively, was contrary to his instinct. And instinct guided the man entirely.

The strange boy possessed a power of attraction which the witnesses of his life, friendly or indifferent, are one in declaring exceptional and irresistible. It proceeded not only from the charm of his voice and the cordiality of his manners: the physical individual in repose attracted like a lover. This particular magnetism, the character and effects of which have a fundamental importance in the psychology of the poet and the comprehension of his work, prove more than the natural aroma of his magnificent physique abounding in health: it is like the sensible sign of his omnipotent individuality. No one knew how to define what he felt in his presence: it was something unspeakably great which did not depend upon his figure only, his height, or his carriage, but which flowed from his total personality. There is not a word to qualify this irradiation, which John Burroughs, who yielded as so many others, elect spirits as well as uncultivated natures, names a "new and mysterious bodily quality."[1] Every individual, by the sole fact that he lives, exercises an attraction, however feeble it may be. It is probable that, with Walt Whitman, this attribute was, by reason of his formidable individuality, carried to a hundredfold power. He attracts as a crowd attracts imperiously by the sole fact of living and of passing. In the street the simple passersby yielded to this fascination, which he did nothing to provoke. At every step, without any exterior reason, strangers turned their eye toward the man of elephantine movement and looked at him a moment for the unique pleasure of looking at him, sometimes with a smile of contentment and of silent amity. These yielded in spite of themselves to the mysterious sensation of an unusual presence. The obscure ones of whom he made habitual company in New York proved him to the utmost and the outcasts, we are told, were transformed by his contact. When he was the author of *Leaves of Grass*, visitors quitted him, after an interview with him, as if illumined, incapable of thinking of any other thing than of him, and the joy of finding themselves near him,

Orators, philosophers, poets, have exercised a spiritual

---
[1] John Burroughs: *Notes*, pp. 13-14.

charm their contemporaries are glad to witness: Emerson, for example, positively ravished his listeners. The magnetism of Walt's presence was of another kind. It was the outpouring, not only of an athletic man, but an athletic personality. To the visible superabundance of his vitality, his power as man, loving all, feeling all, equal to no matter what task, united in producing this mystery of nature. There was no other mystery than this of one colossal individuality such as the world knows but at long intervals. But it is above all as the possessor of this power that Walt appears so great, before even his work is shaped—his work in which he poured out the same magnetism beaming from himself.

It is easy to see that endowed with such strength of attraction, and, above all, tormented himself by the thirst of affection, the poet had throughout his life such attachments in number and diversity the like of which one rarely sees. He was passionately loved by the most frustrate beings as well as by noble souls: especially by the primitive and the vigorous. All along the road of his life he travelled surrounded by comrades whose absolute confidence responded to his own, kept alive about him to his last day the atmosphere of tenderness which his heart needed and which affected him, he said, as the natural phenomena, sun, wind, odour affected him. Of all the joys of his life, the supreme joy for Walt was perhaps to walk arm in arm with one of these labourers who was ignorant of his genius but who felt in his tiniest cells that he was a superb companion, that one could not but love him. Watch him pass with slow step, a sweet smile lighting his bearded face, in these juvenile and impudent lines where he himself pictures himself:

> Not a dilettant democrat—a man who is a double part with the common people, and with immediate life—who adores streets—loves docks—loves to talk free with men,—loves to be called by his given name and does not care that any one calls him Mister. Knows how to laugh with laughers—loves the rustic manner of workers—does not pose as a proper man, neither for knowledge or education—eats common food, loves the

strong smelling coffee of the coffee sellers in the market, at dawn—loves to eat oysters brought from the fisherman's boat—loves to be one of a party of sailors and workers—would quit no matter what time a party of elegant people to find the people who love noise, vagrants, to receive their caresses and their welcome, listen to their rows, their oaths, their ribaldry, their loquacity, their laughing, their replies—and knows perfectly how to preserve his personality among them and those of his kind.[1]

One of his cardinal attributes was what we shall call his catholicism, giving to this word its original meaning. He was all acceptation, neither debater nor calculator. Reprobation was no part of his nature, and dialectics glided over him without breaking through his singular indifference. At the time when he frequented the debating societies, he was interested in oratorical controversies; now as he deepened his new self, he put them from him absolutely. He was sensible only to the mute arguments suggested by things. Reasoning intelligence does not culminate in him: according to the famous saying, he was more open to truths which proved themselves than to truths to be proved. This may be judged as an anti-modern tendency if perspicacity of the first order which was his, and his amazing prophetic sense, had not largely compensated his dialectic poverty. Walt Whitman was intuition incarnate. "He seemed to be related, and as finely related with spiritual facts by his mentality"—we can say in reversing a judicious sentence of O. L. Triggs— "as he was related to Nature by his exquisite senses and physical constitution."[2] He possessed the key which gives access to the secret compartments of life, and concrete nature seemed to unroll before him like an open book. He heard it speak, as he heard his interlocutors. Reasoning would have been superfluous. Things themselves published their significations and justified their place. Walt was endowed to a marvellous degree with a primitive, ingenuous, total sense

---

[1] Another Version of the Article (cited above) of the Brooklyn Daily Times, September 29, '55—See *In Re Walt Whitman*, pp. 23, 24.
[2] O. L. Triggs:, *Selections, Introduction*, p. xxvii.

of the material. All that was purely intellectual was subordinated in him to the human and physical element.[1]

This silent absorption of the truth of life showed itself by the singular placidity diffused by his whole person. He was one who saturated himself slowly with powerful and primitive emotions, who enjoyed with a total inhalation sensuous and spiritual, with an intense but continent passion, and without the least frenzy. Among the dull, care-worn, contracted faces which the great city, noisome in its titanic labour, presented, Walt paraded his clean and restful figure, beaming with the smile of a child. That was the singular thing. This imperturbability, however intimately American he was, surely made him nearer to the Oriental than to a New Yorker of the nineteenth century. He seems to have come from another world than the eager city which he sang and exalted. He belonged to it with his whole being, yet he was like some sojourner from afar, astray on its populous pavements. Perhaps he was the prototype of a new kind of American. To the eyes of Europeans, the Yankee seems phlegmatic; but to his compatriots themselves the phlegm of Whitman was baffling. One might say that he partook of the immense indifference of Nature. Events appeared to affect him no more than pieces of inorganic matter, and in circumstances in which the least excitable of men would have lost his head, leaped with indignation, or burst with laughter, he never flinched. All idea of pose necessarily out of the question (it is enough to have considered Walt but a second to be persuaded that he had not an ounce of pose in his manners), was it the lack of nervosity or perfect stability? If we take into account the electric impressionability inhering in the pages of his work, we are inclined to believe that a miraculous equilibrium was the reason of this detachment of the "unaffected animal." If you deem the eye of the pachyderm stupid, perhaps you will find the look of Walt expressionless —even slow and sleepy. The eye of Walt contains a reflec-

---
[1] John Burroughs: *Walt Whitman*, p. 61.

tion of the inner cosmic peace, a little of the divine peace of eternity.

We therefore find ourselves before one of those numerous antimonies of which superior beings are made. If, by his invincible penchant toward indolent and dawdling absorption of life, Walt evokes rather the South, he displays a temperament truly of the North, by his absolute empire over himself. The same individual who vibrated in his very depths to imponderable psychic emotions, and who, in the evening of life thinking with a shuddering of heart and of the senses, confessed his "numerous tearing passions" was capable of Himalayan impassableness. The ardent curiosity which drew him toward all aspects of multitudinous life, the thrill of his vivid sensibility, all is resolved into that sovereign calmness which his friends loved. A man who has pushed his investigations in the spiritual domain as far as any one remains throughout by his attitude the brother of the ruminants and the hills. And we admire this unusual blending, in recognizing how much the world of emotions thus proclaims its affinities with the inorganic world. All the contrasts converged in his being to recompose a synthesis in which the universe appeared one in him. There are no more water-tight compartments; the material world and the spiritual world operate the supreme reconciliation in the body and soul of one individual, "Walt Whitman, a cosmos."

Walt's imperturbability is based on an absolute inner composure. Not less does the repose of his countenance bear the imprint of the life into which he was plunged than does this serenity belong to an epoch of restlessness, agitation, and conflict. It should be sufficient to assert that he bore within him something very old or very new. This elemental and invariable happiness, born of a perfect balance of his faculties, not of a heroic resolve to "see life en rose," he possessed to an astounding degree. It beamed upon him plentiful and spontaneous and evinced itself as the instinct of enjoying all his other instincts. His perfect equable temper was but its reverberation. However adverse fortune showed itself, he lost not a jot of his confidence. Nothing more easy than to be agreeable with him: never was he to be surprised into raising a discussion. Persons and things were adapted to him as if the great Artisan long before had prepared them for his use. His sweet, tranquil temper forced all misunderstanding and dissipated reserve. He had a clarifying presence. One immediately perceived, on meeting him, that all his physical majesty was accorded him that he might radiate goodness. Beneath this tolerance and this benignity there was no mawkishness: he had, one feels, a rock-like will, a terrible and unconquerable will, which was the foundation of the structure of his personality. When he so wished, he was capable of displaying a mute haughtiness, in which suddenly culminated all the giant infrangibility of his self. But these occasions are rare: the magnificent and warm simplicity of his greeting was the rule.

Any resolution which he had to take never made him seek counsel of any one, and he was slow in his decision. Before adopting it, he was inclined to examine, weigh, balance, for and against it, to allow the arguments to rest and ripen. Walt was not impulsive: circumspection was strong in him and came perhaps from his ancestors mingling with things of the soil. But once his resolution was taken, he would not yield, even if he knew that he was wrong. He had by heritage a strong dose of patience and stubbornness and followed always the "inner call," which his Quaker ancestors recognized as the supreme power in the world. His disregard of the opinion of another was total, and for him one may say a dead letter. Blame as well as praise left him perfectly indifferent. Touching his personal business, his reserve was extreme. He imparted his plans to no one and he had very decided notions as to what concerned himself alone. Toward certain indiscreet questioners—after he had published his poem—he had a manner of his own, not hard, but peremptory, to prove that he intended to remain the master of his house.

The entire man was marked with a great natural dignity. Vulgar familiarities did not belong to him. Without even taking into account the exclusive privacy of his life, of the feminine attachments of which no one intimate with him received the secret, this communal and fervent being who pushed freedom to the baring of himself in his poems, had a strong tendency to be secret. He did not permit certain locks to be opened.

Walt not only was not inclined to speak of himself but, in general, he spoke very little. His pleasure was to make his interlocutors talk, question, learn. Those close to him have shown the marvellous listener he was. The rôle of the person silent in conversation fitted him perfectly and that something large, open, and natural, which belonged peculiarly to him invited the confidence and provoked the effusion of others.

He cultivated a certain contempt for business—he had scarcely any aptitude for it, and he let it be known that no matter what business meant to his alert and enterprising compatriots, it did not concern him. When a transaction did not please him, he refused outright the most tempting offers. He ignored concessions. He worked all his life, as an amateur, just enough to earn money for his living and for that of his mother and infirm young brother, thus passing from one business to another, according to the innate instinct he had of changing pasture, breaking away, taking vacation whenever the desire took hold of him to be alone in some lost corner of his island, or to make an excursion on the sea where some pilot friend tempted him. The joy of life, the need of contact with life to feel it pass into him, kept him incessantly beyond too absorbing needs. He was closed to the notion of money, and he never had the idea, before he was fifty, of saving part of his salary. The gold fever which exactly at this time was drawing all seekers of adventure to California did not lure him from Brooklyn pavements. Another more serious search engrossed him. For his family, pecuniary care had all the importance which it holds in the families of the poor: for him none. To be sure he had to work that his mother might prepare the meal: but it was a natural thing, like breathing or walking, and he did not trouble to speak of it. The flowers of the field are not disturbed by the water which their celestial nourisher sends them every day. They wait, because they do not doubt. We have noted the one occasion offered him to make money and his regal disdain of it. He was truly for all men of "good sense," an incomprehensible youth. He was not stupid surely, but why so closed to human ambitions? . . . He had an idea in the back of his head, one knows not what, which he followed with a sweet, inflexible obstinacy. Is it not strange that a boy like this, without the shadow of patrimony, having only his two strong hands and his calm, heavy brain to live by, would not allow himself to be drawn by any hope of profit? "He had offers of literary work, good offers," says his brother, "and we thought that he had chances to make money. Yet, he would refuse to do anything except at his own notion—most likely when advised would say: 'We won't talk about that', or anything else to pass the matter off."[1] There was nothing but to let him alone; he was intractable.

Moreover, his family did not understand him, though his evident superiority forced itself upon them. He was so different. The father, who certainly never grasped the nobility of this great idler of a boy, was compelled like the others, after ineffectual ratings, to accept him as nature made him. His exquisite mother, bound to him by an infinite tenderness, failing in her humble mind to penetrate the singularities of the child whom she cherished simply with the divine indulgence of love, agreed that after all it was

[1] Bucke: *In Re Walt Whitman*, p. 33.

perhaps "poetry" the odd things which Walt wrote. For the entire household he was a mystery. But one sole thing could be affirmed, that he was the most affectionate of sons and of brothers, and that in some way impossible to define, he was superior to all of them. "Not only the family asked counsel of him," avows George, his brother, "even when he was a mere youth, but the neighbours also. All of us respected his judgment and had consideration for it. He was like us—and yet he was different from us. Strangers, the neighbours, felt that there was something in him out of the ordinary."[1]

The more we seek to define it the more conspicuous is the fundamental ingenuousness of the man. From the depth of him awakens the simple, candid, wondering soul of a child, come down for the first time on the road of life. He had need, like a baby, of tenderness and of caresses, he had need to watch the world pass, to know and absorb the slightest details. This enormous candour is perhaps, of all the traits of his character, that which justifies the most fully all the secret reasons of his individuality and of his work. His athletic proportions do not forbid us to see, even to his last day, the soul of a little child: and indeed curiously allied to his strong masculinity one feels in him something of the feminine and the maternal.[2] Everything existed to give him joy, someone said: indubitable sign of simple hearts. He never ceases to contemplate the pageant of the universe, and the joy of living persisted with Walt, just as new as on the day his eyes opened for the first time upon life. He seemed to pass his days enjoying emotions which men in maturity have outgrown, and to experience to ecstasy the Eden joy of the golden age. A soul of incredible youth and of infinite primitiveness was preserved fresh in him to the very grave.

In Brooklyn and on Broadway Walt became a familiar

---

[1] Bucke: *In Re Walt Whitman*, p. 38.
[2] John Burroughs: *Walt Whitman*, p. 49.

figure. In the street, the passersby recognized his high stature, his felt hat, his characteristic gait. Sometimes strangers would ask, on seeing him approach, so simple and so big, to what class, to what profession, to what earthly race, he could possibly belong. The gray of his beard and his hair made him appear older than his age, and the most varied conjectures were put forth. "Is he a retired sea captain?" asks one, "an actor, an officer, a clergyman? Was he once a brigand, or a Negro trader?" "To amuse Walt I frequently repeated these odd speculations upon him. He laughed until the tears ran when once I told him that a very confidential observer had assured me he was crazy."[1]

After all, what was he, this strange boy? Was he journalist, task master, printer, or some great personage disguised in a suit of serge and a big felt hat? One does not know what to say. He was Walt, and these four letters ensphere all that one can say of him and of other things besides. He was like a demigod of Hellas, again a semi-barbarian, which a miracle had projected at this time in the heart of an American city. It is of the poet alone that we must ask an explanation of himself contained in these verses of "Song of the Answerer":

Then the mechanics take him for a mechanic,
And the soldiers suppose him to be a soldier, and the sailors that he has
    follow'd the sea,
And the authors take him for an author, and the artists for an artist,
And the laborers perceive he could labor with them and love them,
No matter what the work is, that he is the one to follow it or has follow'd
    it,
No matter what the nation, that he might find his brothers and sisters
    there.

The English believe he comes of their English stock,
A Jew to the Jew he seems, a Russ to the Russ, usual and near, removed
    from none.[2]

---
[1] Bucke: *Walt Whitman*, p. 33.
[2] *Leaves of Grass*, p. 136.

For he had that in him which justified all conjectures. With everyone he awakened the sentiment of a close relationship. One hesitates to apply to him one epithet more fixed than the other because he had the title to nearly all of them. He was as exceptional as he was ordinary, and he proved the maximum power of the average man and by this he escaped all averages. One would say that his family extended from the man on the wharf to the President of the White House: his sole presence seemed to establish a bond between all and reveal universal relations.

We have stated, in examining his origins, how he was Dutch, how strongly he was a son of the Quakers. How much more he appears an American by these contrasts blended in the crucible of a young nationality which partakes of all the races of the Occident! But how much more still, infinitely more, he is man, a man-humanity!

Walt Whitman was an original product of the American soil, a native, an individuality "of new stamp, *sui generis*"[1] And it is not vain to recognize in him the prototype of a future humanity, prepared from the foundation of the centuries to flourish upon a virgin soil and to mark an era of the species.

>I am the credulous man of qualities, of ages, of races,[2]

speaks Walt Whitman somewhere in his poem. This character of universality is like the final touch which imprints his giant personality with a grandeur well nigh superhuman. At this point, despite his proximity, he appears to certain of his contemporaries like a legendary figure. William O'Connor, his friend, describes him a little later with the characteristics of a Voyager of the Ages, making a pilgrimage through the world, like Wotan of the Nibelungen.[3] The man was so vast, that still inhabiting the earth, he surpassed common proportions, and was clothed with immortality.

---
[1]Bucke: *In Re Walt Whitman*, p. 196.
[2]*Leaves of Grass*, p. 22.
[3]W. D. O'Connor: *The Carpenter*, Putnam's Magazine, January, 1868, p. 55.

PART THREE

"LEAVES OF GRASS"

BROOKLYN (1855-1862)

VIII

THE GREAT DESIGN

THE climax of this life is before us: it is between the age of thirty-five and forty-five that Walt Whitman reaches and passes the summit whose wondrous light lives in him and his work. Two events control the years of 1855–1865, one the publication of the first song of his poem, the other his participation in the Civil War: both, if not of equal importance as to his future, at least are fundamental in the history of his life. It is between these two dates that the man is full grown. We shall now try to elucidate the first one.

His thirtieth year having been passed, a great change was wrought in Walt. In appearance, he remains the same man or almost, and his characteristic traits, such as they already appeared when he taught school in Long Island, remain identical. Nevertheless, although the metamorphosis whence issues the new man who shall occupy us from now on was wholly inner, it is discoverable by certain details, attentively studied, and the more fruitful if the study keep close to him and even in his very setting. Walt of the storiettes, Walt the politician and journalist, who in living his nonchalant life tried to make his impression upon the world in traditional ways, has given place, by disappearing little by little, to a new Walt who is absorbed more and more in the contemplation of things and seeks to render more striking and more intimate his communion with life.

It was a little after his return from New Orleans that he experienced the first symptoms of this regeneration. The great journey which he had just made into the middle of the continent, the atmosphere of Louisiana, the love shock which he had undoubtedly experienced—all contributed to his fecundity. And he listened with a native fidelity to the inner call. True he did not know how to distinguish what the voice was murmuring. It was a new sensation. He would test it further. The spectacles about him which he knew so well all appeared to him in new light, and in himself a strange, subconscious power solicited him.

It was like a measureless expanding of his spiritual being, a prolongation of himself into the external world. He imagined himself drawn into a new cycle of existence. The people of the village landscape, all environmental things, were before him like an enormous book, which he had many a time read over, but whose pages appeared to him at present big with meanings heretofore not heeded. With reawakened eyes he set himself to read anew the old everyday book, and each of its paragraphs plunged him into astonishment.

> I remained like one absent and I listened to the splendid lessons of things and the reasons of things.
> They are so splendid that I nudge myself to listen.
> I do not know what that may be which I hear—I do not know how to say it to myself—it is all so marvelous.

Then a religious sense of life filters into him to the full. He must seize the suggestions which haunt him and wait in the expectation of the phenomenon at work within him. Although he perceives something entrancing, the final sensation was long confused. At the same time, an "imperious conviction" forced him to formulate everything which stirred within him. He perceived clearly an impulse. He felt himself called. He had something to do or to say; something must come forth. He was the interpreter of a revelation, he was called to a mission. As to that, no doubt! The powers imparted to him were such that he could not disobey, "as total and irresistible as those which make the sea flow or the globe revolve."[1] A revelation, a mission. . . .

---
[1] *Complete Prose*, p. 268.

But what? Under what form? There was the uncertainty. How express the inexpressible which was buzzing at his ears, the new passion which carried him away? By what words or by what acts interpret the whisper, powerful and sweet, of the thousand confused voices of this sea of impressions which was breaking over him? He had to listen, to see, to search. . . . The daïmon which had taken possession of his soul would not let him escape, it would show him the way to deliver his message.

In awaiting the sign which should be his destiny Walt plunges with still more entirety into the human tide, and into the realities about him. He does not draw aside, like the ascetics, to contemplate his new self. More and more he consorts with his friends, the people—stage-drivers, boatmen, travellers, men of the street. There is something intensified, more fervent, in the affection drawing him to them. He always had sympathy for the simple and the rude, but now he experiences near them a graver, more emotionalized feeling, a more complete abandon and communion. It was then that he definitely adopted the free and picturesque workman's garb which he had worn as a printer-apprentice, the garb which among idlers gave him a little celebrity. He felt himself troubled by an incessant need of camaraderie and companionship, which only plain people could fully satisfy. Heretofore it was rather the need of knowledge which had made him mingle with the world. To his thirtieth year he manifested himself the great bystander, the great inquirer, the great absorber. Now aspirations of fraternity dominate his sensibility, he needs to embrace, to breathe, to enjoy individuals, to be loved as he loves.

O the joy of my soul leaning pois'd on itself, receiving identity through
    materials and loving them, observing characters and absorbing them,
My soul vibrated back to me from them, from sight, hearing, touch,
    reason, articulation, comparison, memory, and the like.[1]

---

[1] *Leaves of Grass*, p. 146.

His outlook was not the same as that before 1848. It was like a total deepening of himself, in which the world, viewed from a different angle, participates. Little by little his life moves about one centre—the luminous sheaf of the new concordances which manifest themselves every day between his *me* and his not *me*—and he pencils innumerable notes in which are reflected the state of his soul and his transformed consciousness. His life, richly lived up to this, but without any other aim than to live, converges absolutely toward one great design whose accomplishment will occupy him to the very last day of his life.

After ten years of literary and journalistic Bohemia the man awakens, inundated by a faith whose expression he is searching. Various interpretations as to the nature of this crisis, the capital event of the poet's life, have been attempted by his biographers. We are not surprised that they are misleading: because there are no scales for a test so imponderable. The awaking of genius is a phenomenon which does not become clear by the aid of argument. For it was surely to the birth pangs of a genius that Walt was a prey from the time he had felt a total renewal of his consciousness.

According to Bucke, whose opinion we cite by reason of his authority as the "authorized" biographer of Whitman, at a precise epoch of his life which we do not know, but that it was toward his thirty-second or thirty-third year, a sudden illumination was bestowed upon him as upon the great prophets of history, Buddha, Paul, or Mahomet, by which he was endowed with a new and superhuman sense which Bucke calls "cosmic consciousness." Describing the phenomenon rigorously like a scientific fact, he comments upon certain passages of *Leaves of Grass* which appear to confirm his hypothesis.[1] Thus, in admitting this conjecture Walt had known positively his road to Damascus.

I confess that I feel within me an insurmountable anti-

---

[1] Bucke: *In Re Walt Whitman*, pp. 329-347.

THE GREAT DESIGN

pathy to this explanation of a fact, which we should accept as we accept the grass, the wave, or the pebble, without subjecting the mind to the torture of discovering first causes. Mr. Binns, who revived this recently in adapting it to his own temperament, has not more convinced me. It is indisputable that Walt was dowered with a "cosmic consciousness" to a degree which a very small number of men or supermen have attained, and I find particularly happy the formula of Bucke, which may stand. As to the explanation itself, in the simplest form of Bucke's statement, it seems to me almost puerile. To make a miracle intervene in such a life is it not to belittle it? All the greatness of the poet protests against such a postulate, and his formidable realism forbids any esoteric explanation. In the whole of his being and in the entirety of his life he presents himself to us in the brilliant light of humanity. Now genius, even that of a prodigious poet-prophet such as Walt Whitman appears, is not, I am sure, outside humanity. And every conjecture which tends to represent him with the features of someone Illuminated, even of a very Saint, is evidence of an incomprehension of the man.

How vain to found upon certain poetic affirmations the proof of a supernatural vision, which had from one moment to another transformed him!

I cannot be awakened, for nothing looks to me as it did before.
Or, else I am awake for the first time, and all before has been a mean sleep.[1]

Is it not clear that he is moved here by the illumination of genius? Why wish to fix a precise date for this transformation, when all that we know of the inner travail of Walt during the six or seven years which preceded the flowering of his book proves that it was not instantaneous, but slow and gradual. Why not hold to the simple truth of certain confessions of the poet, such as: "After continued personal ambition and effort, as a young fellow, to enter with the rest

[1] *Camden Edition*, III, p. 287.

into competition for the usual rewards, business, political, literary, etc.—to take part in the great *mêlée*, both for victory's prize itself and to do some good—after years of those aims and pursuits, I found myself remaining possessed, at the age of thirty-one to thirty-three, with a special desire and conviction. Or rather, to be quite exact, a desire that had been flitting through my previous life, or hovering on the flanks, mostly indefinite hitherto, had steadily advanced to the front, defined itself, and finally dominated everything else."[1]

Surely Walt sufficiently explains himself. The beginning of this metamorphosis seems to me simpler and greater than all the piled-up hypotheses. For fifteen years he was in the grip of life. He bathed himself in floods of impressions, of visions, of sounds, of joys. He lived as few beings on the earth have lived. He absorbed realities with the appetite of a young giant. In his imperturbable manner, he was gorged with emotions, he enjoyed through all his pores. For thirty years all the life with which he was satiated, all the accumulated joys, the thousand shows and assimilated experiences germinate in him, flower into a new consciousness by whose light the recesses of the universe, the secrets of the world of souls, the supreme "laws not written" were before him like the words of a book. Walt has been engrossed by facts, by men, by objects, by influences of nature. It was their prolonged contact, every day, free, which awakened, at a propitious moment, the powers sleeping in him. His new self was the natural fruit of his immense quest. The final explanation of the crisis is fully contained in this word of sublime candour, which he addresses to himself:

Walt, you contain enough, why don't you let it out then?[2]

Why be astonished at such a wonderful result, when determined by genius, the intensifier par excellence? He had

---
[1] *Leaves of Grass*, p. 426.
[2] *Id.*, p. 50.

met that amplitude by his extraordinary individuality. In this reacting to the world exercised upon him, in acknowledgment of the joyous confidence which he lavished upon it, his self remains the principal factor; and ancestral influences, races, environment, his previous life, all concur in preparing this result which astonishes.

He had a heart full of the substance of life and one drop sufficed to overflow it. And now he was inundated. An interior light appeared and grew, till its rays enveloped finally the entire horizon, placing in relief the smallest details of the landscape and their place in the divine ensemble. Through the identity of his being and of the world he perceives the unity of all, so that there flows into him the sense of the miracle of creation. To the extent that the pulsations of the external world echo within him, and that he himself is projected into this external world, the universal relation and the great consubstantiality of things, their monomultiplicity, become illumined with certitude. He arrives at the consciousness which supreme geniuses alone of the race have possessed, and it is not in his brain that it dwells only: his little finger is also penetrated with it. He is mastered by the power of a thing lived and felt, as one is by heat or cold. It is not a philosophic conviction, but a reality of every day which he will never weary in proving. When he contemplates himself, it is the radiant abyss of the whole he fathoms and when he casts his glance about him, it is his own being which he sees reflected in the face of things. Identity, identity! Law supreme! Walt slowly walks in a universe of wonders which his days are not long enough to count. For these new truths which he discovers everywhere are but confided to him that he may in his turn reveal them to the world. He is the man predestined to be the interpreter of a great Idea and, confident in his star, he obeyed and yielded himself to the impetus. . . .

That undoubtedly was the whole miracle, and the revelation which Walt received was akin to those which have given birth in the past to the marvellous legends of Sinai, of the road to Damascus, of the voice of the Maid, or the nymph Egeria. Only there was one difference: it is that perhaps such a revelation was never manifested to a man whose physical constitution, radiant and magnetic personality, attributes, character, marked him as king of his kind, before even he yielded to it. But between the Walt before and the Walt after the crisis there was no interruption. The second was superadded to the first, the new man sprang from the old one, as a flower from the stem, as the stem from the seed, after the strength of the soil had determined its germination.

For years the great Idea was incarnated under successive forms in proportion as it elucidated itself. It simmered a long time in him before arriving at the boiling point. He did not settle all at once on the medium by which he was to make himself heard, that is to say, of communicating his message to the world. Entirely self-absorbed in the contemplation of the great world, he revolved in his mind many projects.

Walt's metamorphosis took form in exalting in him the autochthonous and of increasing tenfold the innate passion which he possessed of his race, his soil, and his time. He was American in every fibre, and the previous revelation, which discovered to him both his own being and humanity about him, clarified the image of a heroic individual, the individual American, the democrat of the nineteenth century, and the magnificent Federation of States, in growth like an organism, expanding every day, beyond rivers and mountains and deserts to the limits of the sea-guarded continent. It was then in glorifying this new human type, and this collectivity united by new bonds, that Walt would fulfill his mission. He was come to justify his time and the labour of his people. He had made the trial of Democracy and he was about to publish his testimony. His deep knowledge of the crowd and of all the aspects of multitudinous humanity were a deposit within him of an enthusiastic faith;

upon this his new spiritual insight would enable him to erect the monument which he would dedicate to the exaltation of the modern times.

Among these projects, these embryos, these tentatives which he had in mind before coming to the definitive expression of himself, it is necessary to mention the *Primer*, recently discovered among his papers. We possess only the outlines of the book which he wished to give this singular title. It was, as a variant indicates, a "First Book of Words or A. B. C. for the use of young Americans, of Scholars, Orators, Professors, Musicians, Judges, Presidents, etc." (Notice the significant place which presidents occupy, the tail of the procession led by the individual, King of Democracy.) The note of the future poem already vibrates in this sketch. In developing his theme, which is to exalt the life of words, the evocative and representative power of words, which come to us charged with realities, which are realities, to affirm the importance of the voice, accent, to incite America to create boldly a rude speech, new, autochthonous, suggestive, full of idiomatic expressions, in touch with the time, the character of the people, instead of European expressions, anti-modern, which have no signification for the humanity of the new world—Walt proves himself already in possession of some of his fundamental motifs. The substance of *Leaves of Grass* was already formed at the time of the first editing of this outline, whose date remains uncertain. One merely knows that he worked on it till 1857 and that he made additions to it later. The *Primer*, in his original intention, was to be the subject of a lecture; but later he had the idea of making a book of it. But lecture and book were abandoned, and the *Primer* remained in its rudimentary form. It is that the sap circulating in these pages flowed into another project, the one definitive and actual, his poem; the form alone remained inchoate.[1]

During a sufficiently long period the idea of fulfilling his

---

[1] Walt Whitman: *An American Primer*, Edited by Horace Traubel.

mission in lecturing throughout the country preoccupied him. According to the colourful expression of his mother, he then wrote whole "barrels" full of subjects for lectures. Discourse appeared to him the mode the most direct and most effective of widely spreading the truths which he championed.

That was the cherished idea which he weighed, debated, looked at on all sides, with the slowness and the circumspection which he always showed in the elaboration of his plans; and to do this he was fully prepared since his adolescence. He devoted himself to a thorough study of the art of oratory, of gesture, of elocution, and of tonality, etc. . . . He was even drawn into debating clubs which he assiduously frequented and at the age when the first ardours of battle seethed within him. At one and twenty, when he was still at Long Island, he had discoursed abundantly, and not without success, in the meetings prepared for the election of Van Buren to the presidency.[1] His recitations of Shakespeare and Homer, alone near the sea, or to his friends, the coachmen and boatmen, likewise prepared him for the rôle of orator. He had in mind a vigorous, living, simple, and striking manner of expressing himself in public, as remote from the nasality of the preacher or the shouting of platform politicians, as from the parlour talker. He would try upon his auditors the effect of his personal magnetism and would establish such communion between them and him that they would take part, that is to say, in the action—in his discourse. He wishes "to hurry and plow up the soil of the hearer constantly dropping seed therein, to spring up and bear grain or fruit many hours afterward, perhaps weeks and years afterward."[2] The papers published after his death by his testamentary executors are scattered with fragments, sketches, and indexes relative to his platform project. He was so strongly attached to this, that in spite of the appear-

---

[1] H. B. Binns: *Life of Walt Whitman*, p. 33.
[2] *Camden Edition*, VIII, p. 251.

THE GREAT DESIGN   125

ance of his poem, he resumed it in 1857 and '58 and engaged all practical means to execute it. His plan was to travel through the country with a program of lectures, which he would deliver for a moderate price and of which he would himself sell advance printed copies.[1] They made "an integral part of his schemes for self-presentation."[2] Very early in his life the idea of presenting himself direct allured him. Such was his faith in the miracle of his own presence and the certitude that he had always had of the effluence of his personality physical and moral: nevertheless he made a speech, but once, the 31st of March, 1851, at the Artists Union of Brooklyn. The text of this address appeared in a daily[3] and he even kept some paragraphs in the selection of his juvenilia,[4] which show us that at this time the man already was passing through the first phase of his crisis. There is a notable passage where he strongly puts forth heroic beauty of conduct, that is to say beauty lived, as against the represented beauty by artists, which shows him big with his new consciousness.

This first intention of lecturing through the country, never completely abandoned, but unceasingly postponed, shows at least how from the beginning he felt the importance of his mission. We already clearly perceive that he was not concerned for himself, as are other geniuses, in the production of a literary work, verse or prose, in an artistic or an oratorical work, conceived for itself, but in an apostolate best adapted to his idea. He was to translate and to give himself, him, Walt Whitman, in the form the most appropriate to his time and his milieu.

He was stirred to put himself in touch with humanity. That had come to be the great ambition of his life and so remained: an ambition as immense as his share of human am-

---

[1]*Camden Edition, Introduction,* pp. liv–vii.
[2]*Id.,* IX, p. xvi.
[3]Brooklyn Daily Advertiser, April 3, 1851. See extracts in Bliss Perry's *Walt Whitman,* pp. 50–55.
[4]*Complete Prose,* p. 371.

bition was small. And now he perceived that his ten or fifteen previous years had been dominated by the idea of fulfilling a mission to humanity something greatly beyond the vain hopes of the candid and proud hours of adolescence. Perhaps he would realize it by these lectures. In the end fate was fulfilled in other ways. Whatever preparations he made for the rôle of lecturer and whatever was his prestige as a man, we easily understand why the great project should remain on paper. His temperament was too hostile to a manifestation of this kind. However free and natural had been his manner of addressing an audience, his profound aversion to all parade would have been an almost insurmountable obstacle. Every platform is a play in miniature and to every good orator certain gifts of the actor are indispensable. And Walt, although he adored it, was certainly not gifted for the theatre.

These shrouded preparatory years (1851–54) and these suggestive notes which have come to us can alone suggest the character, hint a period of internal effervescence and of labour, fervent, assiduous, persistent; Volume IX of the *Camden Edition*, padded with signs, with notations, with hints, preserves the reflection of this. Thought fuses from him in long jets, as though he were trying the mould into which to pour it. That which especially strikes one is that his diverse projects, during these ardent and meditative years in which the man is labouring to rid himself of his matrices, do not differ except in expression, still badly defined. Since he had listened to the clear call of his renewed consciousness, "the flush of his faith had been from the beginning one and the same character."

The moment comes in 1854 probably when these various plans which he had meditated had to be put away to make room for a work whose great lines, heretofore glimpsed, now impose themselves upon his mind. At the time he counted on resuming later his other projects: and the event disappointed him. It was in climbing the scaffolding of his houses, hammer and saw in hand, that the idea came to him of a poem which should be as the Gospel of the new spirit, such as his race and his time potentially contained, a great native Book for the use of the living of to-day; and during the intervals left him from the business of carpentry, slackened circumstantially, he revolved and matured it. It was the final realization of his great design, and all the essence of his previous sketches was accumulating for it, creating a new form whose contours, still indefinite, were to be after all very different from the primitive project. For if this was to be positively a poem, the raison d'être of the book as well as its proportions should be made a thing outré, strange, new, without precedent. . . . But the essential—it was that Walt was to be able to express himself. The gestation had been long. After five years of listening, ruminating his plans, taking notes almost everywhere, under the immediate dictation of impressions before the living model, at the Opera, on the pavements, on the ferries, near the sea, obedient to the inspiration of the moment which brought to birth sometimes some poetical lines, sometimes the paragraph of a lecture, he had come at last to master the bond which would make one whole of these particles; he had done with fragments. In the elaboration of his work he had advanced, as in life, without hurry or feverishness, in idling, in pausing, in repassing a number of times the same roads, waiting that the fruit be ripe to pluck it.

Walt then, compelled by his poetical call, quitted his carpentry and set to work. The task was difficult, and according to his own confession the writing of it did not come easily. He constructed a thing entirely new, and he had to endure the terrible struggle of great innovators with their material. He had especially great trouble in leaving out of his work "the stock 'poetical' touches" of which convention had filled the poetical arsenal—those he himself at one time used, and of which he was now eager to rid himself at one stroke. One time, we are told, pushed by desire for solitude and liberty, he retreated to a wild and desolate promontory to the east of Long Island where not a living being dwelt; there he wrote a first version, and dissatisfied with it, he threw it into the sea.[1] He loved to recite to himself, in pacing along some lonely shore, fragments of his work, as he had many times declaimed Homer and Shakespeare, to test their effect in the open air, accompanied by the deep bass of the ocean. He destroyed as many as five manuscripts before obtaining his definite text. Walt was obstinate like the old Quakers of his family and he wrestled hand to hand with the word till he had conquered it.

Early in the summer of 1855 the book was ready. Walt did not have the absurd idea of carrying his manuscript to a publisher, who would no doubt have asked if he were jesting with him. Walt was a printer and could say with Michelet: "Before writing books, I have actually *composed* them: I have put together the letters before putting together the ideas." Above all, it would have been expensive to have placed his leaflets in mercenary hands, and he was intensely eager that all the details of the make-up of the volume should be in his own hands. He had his own idea in the matter and was not indifferent to the book, for the manuscript was well prepared. He went then to his friends, Andrew Rome and his brother who kept a job printing office in Brooklyn, at the corner of Fulton and Cranberry streets, and arranged with them for the printing of the volume. He went himself every day before the case and composed with his own hands the greater part of it. .Walt duly preserved his self-possession and never allowed the movements of his intimate being to appear on his face of the "unaffected animal," at this decisive moment more than at any other; but one suspects the emotion which in spite of himself must have sometimes penetrated him while undisturbed he set his type. HIS BOOK, his BOOK! His Bible, for whose message he had searched during the years, to be formulating the paragraphs!

---

[1] O. L. Triggs: *Selections, Introduction*, p. xxiii.

The revelation which he was about to spread through the world, and which should re-echo beyond the centuries: it was there, between his fingers, he was handling syllables of fire. . . . The man with the ruddy face and grayish beard should have lived then grave and intense moments, enveloped in the mantle of his placidity. The poet revised his proofs slowly, sometimes carrying them to the seaside to reread again aloud and to verify the impression which his pages gave in nature's setting.

The volume appeared in the first days of July, 1855.

Walt realized his enterprise in secret. He confided to no one, and unless by certain fugitive symptoms, by his more frequent escapes, by the number of pages which he was writing, it is hardly possible that his family discerned the intense travail which was being wrought in him. His book had grown like seed sown, which spreads invisible and silent, beneath the soil. Who among his relatives and comrades would ever have suspected that this Walt, the idler, the friend of coachmen and of pilots, the frequenter of Broadway, the quiet and affectionate boy, so close to the heart of the simple, could cherish a design as mad, as unsuitable as that of being the singer of his Race and his Age? Without any preliminary advertisement, without ceasing a single instant to show himself the most everyday of men, this great phlegmatic being gave at one stroke his measure, and projected beyond him his real self, his formidable self, concealed from all. If Walt took the wisest precautions with a view of producing with his book the maximum of effect, he could not have succeeded more in amazing people than he did in announcing himself with this sudden positiveness and this terrible assurance. For the little household the event almost coincided with a bereavement. July 11th, some days after the bringing out of the enigmatic book, the old carpenter died. The last farmer of West Hills died at the very hour when his son proved to the world the virility of the blood from which he sprang. Walt, who loved him, accepted this loss with a fortitude with which he confronted all strokes of fate, and continued on his way.

The hour struck in his life: it was when after having absorbed all that the world offered to him of emotion, he gave himself as nurture, when, after having been fertilized, he became in his turn procreator. For Walt was not ungrateful to life; he returned to the great current all that he had received from it with his Personality superadded.

IX

THE FIRST SONG

ONE cannot resist an emotion when slowly fingering this small quarto, for which the bard of the New World himself set the type, and to whose pages he committed his great message. O the poor and fantastic volume, banal and touching—generations shall respectfully defile before it, perhaps, when it lies in the hall of honour of a great museum, not far from the first folio of Shakespeare. . . .

Bound in dark green cloth, very ordinary looking, a naïve decoration of flowers and leaves on the cover; in the middle sprawls, repeated on the other side, in gilt letters, now faded, this singular title, this enigmatic title, at once humble and haughty, this title which includes a whole program, itself a marvellous conception, simple and profound like all great things of genius: *Leaves of Grass*. To render it more eloquent the letters which compose it are extended a little awkwardly in tiny roots and leaves: these are not dead and rigid forms of the alphabet but living letters which germinate and imbibe their substance anywhere. . . . .

One hundred pages, printed in large type on ordinary paper, and the text, by its strange arrangement, gives, at first glance, the impression of a pell-mell of uneven verse sentences: that is all the volume. From the first page no light comes, for it contains only the title, *Leaves of Grass*, followed by these words: Brooklyn, New York, 1855. This singular *anonymat* suggests a blending of pride and of modesty: a name is read though, that of Walter Whitman, but concealed where, according to the American custom, is inscribed "All rights reserved." To make up for this, a portrait faces the title, the famous portrait which we have described, of a young man, in workman's garb, with a bearing at once firm and nonchalant, with the air of a sailor, a docker, or a cowboy. Walt signed his book with himself instead of his name. To some this singular likeness appeared a defiance, to others a pose. In reality, the author does not pose, he imposes with a cool assurance. The make-up of the book shows an inelegance, perhaps intentional, and suggests, outwardly a positive taste of the primitive.

The contents are more difficult to describe. However accustomed we may be to all the audacities of form and feeling, the strange man who did not wish to sign his name except with his likeness baffles still at first contact. After a preface of ten pages, printed in double columns, itself but a long poem in prose, where the author expounds and develops the essentials of his great Idea, follow a dozen lyric bits, without other titles than the volume. One of them, the first, fills more than half the quarto: it is the future *Song of Myself*—key of the entire work, such as we now have it. Are these then poems? We do not know. These verses have a rhythm as the wind and the sea have a rhythm—a rhythm which one does not perceive till one has closely scrutinized them; but any versification were it the most comprehensive—to lay aside rhyme, the very idea of which is remote—would not know how to justify them. The work of a fool or a mystifier, readers must think, even intelligent ones, of the year 1855; and we need not be much astonished that, to our own day even, *Leaves of Grass* appears to the mass a riddle.

These lyric pages repelled at once by their chaotic and barbaric expression. Their enormous novelty raised an obstacle between the generality of readers and the man who sings himself, him and his nation, distinct yet blended in one same embrace. They were like rude chants, filled with raucous accents of a new world where no literature has yet sprung, and they revealed a formidable exaltation of created things and of limitless life. One might believe the anonymous rhapsodist tried to force the entire onomatopœia of wild nature into his book. Since the age of the great bards of Greece and of India, the world had unlearned the sound of such a voice which resurged from the bosom of modern humanity with an accrued power, charged with new significance, bodying forth the aspirations of an Aboriginal of American cities. From these pages sprang a new Adam, resplendently nude, who shocks by his unwonted proportions and his disdain of all ornament, big, bearded, exhaling the wild odour of life. . . . In his preface, which is itself a manifesto, the new author explained his design: according to him the United States offered to a true and great poet the most splendid themes the ages and civilizations have known. These States conceal an enormous beauty which native bards not rhymers manipulating syllables and emotions imported from Europe, should justify by their songs, tallying them to the immensity of the continent, to the fecundity of its people, to the appetites of a proud race, fluent and free. And the portrait in the book seemed to say, accentuating as it were, the noble and calm confidence in himself from whom flowed the preface: "I, Walt Whitman, American of the people, I am come to show the way to these new bards, to sing America as she needs to be sung and thus reveal her to herself. As in former times, the portrait of kings in court costume was published, at the head of the chapter dedicated to their reign, I present me to you as the poetical representative of an age, as the one by whose mouth America is sung." And with a candid faith and an overwhelming audacity the man in the large felt hat, the friend of stage-drivers and of boatmen, celebrated himself, the delights of his body and the intoxications of his heart, with the shouts of a lover, returning in floods the bewildering joys which the world gave him. When you hold this book in your hands you forget that you touch a book: you touch a man who thrilled, rejoiced, was exalted, was diffused, in linking his people, his time, and yourself to his fervours, to his colossal faith, to his intoxicated joy. Walt introduced his personality into this book, and the book lives by the very rhythm of his life. He has not introduced only his great and throbbing heart, he has put there his body, the lineaments of his face, his voice, and even his dress. *Leaves of Grass,* it was a gift Walt Whitman made of himself to you, to me, to the nearest and the farthest, to the Crowd, the most authentic of his companions.

Eight hundred copies of the book were printed; these were put on sale in two or three bookstores in New York and Brooklyn. Walt at first fixed the price at two dollars; then not wishing that the price be an obstacle to its circulation, he reduced it one-half.[1] A free list was furnished to the journals, to the principal reviews, and to reputable writers. What welcome did the public give to the book into which Walt actually translated himself? At first it was silence. Without the name of the author, scarcely offered for sale, announced in only one or two friendly newspapers, the volume had nothing to call attention to it.

After a certain time, the booksellers, not seeing a single buyer come, asked that the unsold copies be taken away. As for the copies sent to the celebrities, many were returned to the author with insulting comment. It was the prelude to the tempest of abuse to which for long years the man and his work were subjected. Literary men of well-established reputation considered as an affront the sending of this book. Whittier, the great Whittier, threw, we are told, the book into the fire.[2] The Quaker poet disowned the son of Quakers. It is also known that in one editorial room *Leaves of Grass,* read aloud, furnished an hour of fun to a roomful of New York reporters, the worse for idleness.[3] And that was pretty much all. Laughter, gross words; there was Walt, with his message left and not paid for.

---

[1] H. B. Binns: *Life of Walt Whitman,* pp. 87–88.
[2] *Camden Edition, Introduction,* p. liii. Donaldson: *Walt Whitman, the Man,* p. 51.
[3] John Burroughs: *Notes,* p. 16.

THE FIRST SONG

Leaves of Grass was out about fifteen days when the author, one morning early, received the following letter, addressed to "Mr. Walter Whitman," a letter which he reread many times from heading to signature, before being sure he was not the sport of an illusion:

CONCORD, MASS., July 21, 1855.

DEAR SIR,—I am not blind to the worth of the wonderful gift of "Leaves of Grass." I find it the most extraordinary piece of wit and wisdom that America has yet contributed. I am very happy in reading it, as great power makes us happy. It meets the demand I am always making of what seems the sterile and stingy Nature, as if too much handiwork or too much lymph in the temperament were making our Western wits fat and mean. I give you joy of your free and brave thought. I have great joy in it. I find incomparable things, said incomparably well, as they must be. I find the courage of treatment which so delights us, and which large perception only can inspire.

I greet you at the beginning of a great career, which yet must have had a long foreground somewhere, for such a start. I rubbed my eyes a little to see if this sunbeam were no illusion; but the solid sense of the book is a sober certainty. It has the best merits, namely, of fortifying and encouraging.

I did not know, until I last night saw the book advertised in a newspaper, that I could trust the name as real and available for a post-office.

I wish to see my benefactor, and have felt much like striking my tasks, and visiting New York to pay you my respects.

R. W. EMERSON.

Thus the great Emerson, then at the height of his reputation, honoured in England as well as America, understood. Walt had read right: it was not a perfunctory acknowledgment which he had in his hands, but the warmest and freest acceptance which he could have hoped for his message. With his prophet eye, the sage of Concord pierced the rude envelope of his poem, and penetrated its inmost reality. And the man who incarnated the highest thought and the highest poesy of America saluted him as an equal, even as a master, and bowed before him. . . . This astonishing letter, this historic letter, which was—and which will always be—as much honour to one who wrote it as to the man who deserved it, was indeed a thunderbolt. Walt was able to foresee much, but he had not foreseen this. And however colossal was his assurance from the first, and clear the conviction of the bearing of his book, he felt possibly, at this very moment, that he had conquered, should he wait centuries. The opinion of Emerson, was it not worth the approbation of a thousand readers? And wholly indifferent as he proved to insults as to panegyrics, the comfort to him must have been immense.

Any other beginner—for, in the new way he had entered upon Walt could but begin—receiving such a letter would have been crazed. With nothing in his cool manner which would betray the emotion he was experiencing, Walt continued to receive the few reviews which here and there *Leaves of Grass* called forth. The scornful silence of the greater part of the critics and the indifference of the public appeared authoritative. At best from time to time some derisive judgments created diversion, in which the author was treated as a buffoon. The book was not opened except to create ridicule or exasperation. Walt, running through these appreciations, felt a warmth penetrate him in thinking of Emerson's letter, which was there, in his portfolio.

It was then that Walt, seeing his work misunderstood and vilified—he was not prepared for such an ignominious reception—and feeling alone with it, bethought himself of a great expedient. Since no one came to lift aloft his trampled banner, he would himself recover it and in combatting defend the assault. He had friends on the press—he had belonged to it himself for twelve years—and he would use both for his fight. This queer boy, who would not have lifted a finger for the winning of notoriety, and who, not once in his life, made an interested visit to an influential man, wrote three virulent and glowing articles on his book and on himself, which appeared, anonymously, in the Brooklyn Daily Times of September 29th, the Democratic Review of the same month and the Journal of Phrenology of Fowler and Wells, who accepted the agency of his book.[1] By their freedom, the bold and crude way in which the poet describes his personality, and defines the character of his work, these pleas *pro domo* present themselves as precious documents. A tropical individualism culminates and expands in them with an unmatched luxuriance. Some confessed themselves shocked by such a method of advertising. It was not that. As for the poet, he was not concerned with the success or failure of his book, because his vanity as an author was nothing: but the future of his Idea meant more to him than all the world. In his heart he believed in the revelation which *Leaves of Grass* announced, as in the movement of the stars. His day would come; but, wise man, he also knew that destiny helps them who help themselves.

Emerson was not satisfied to write to the author all the surprise and joy which the reading of his poems gave him. He spoke of them to his friends[2] and to visitors who made the Concord pilgrimage. When one of them, Moncure Conway, the historian of Thomas Paine, came, he presented to him the quarto with the foliage decorated cover, saying to him: "Americans who are abroad can now return: unto us a man is born."[3] "No man with eyes in his head," says Emerson again to Conway in lending him *Leaves of Grass*, "but could recognize a real poet in that book." And Conway was eager to go and see the one Emerson had spoken of in such words.[4] His expression of the power of Walt is unforgettable: "I went off to myself sleepless with thinking of this new acquaintance. . . . He has so magnetized me, so charged me, with something indefinable."

Walt, not having succeeded in selling his disdained book, was reduced to distributing it among his friends and relatives

---

[1] These three articles have been reprinted in *In Re Walt Whitman.*
[2] *Camden's Compliment to Walt Whitman*, p. 61.
[3] John Burroughs: *Walt Whitman*, p. 50.
[4] Moncure Conway's *Walt Whitman*, Fortnightly Review, October 15, 1866.

who probably did not understand it at all but who, through kindness or simple politeness, could not refuse it. The sale of the first edition was null: those of the eight hundred copies which were not gifts must have been thrown away or destroyed,[1] torn up or sold as old paper. It found, however, one buyer, the only one probably: a man stopped in front of a bookstore in Brooklyn, opened the volume, then paid for it. It was John Swinton, who became later a warm friend of Whitman.[2]

There was no doubt of it: it was a fiasco. In the general silence, broken only by insulting raillery, there was the magnificent letter of Emerson, and that was all. Walt, in thinking on the fate of his book, thought sometimes that that was enough. Two or three newspapers took the book seriously: The New York Tribune where later insults were not spared him, and Putnam's Magazine dedicated to him sympathetic paragraphs. The only really enthusiastic article which he read is the one of Everett Hale, published in the North American Review of January, 1856: "The book is worth going twice to the store to buy. . . . It does not contain a word intended to attract the reader by its grossness."[3] The advice was not followed; but the irony! The unique testimony, frankly eulogistic, which *Leaves of Grass* produced, was signed by a clergyman. . . . This unexpected precursor merits the homage of the future.

It would be wholly to misunderstand Walt to suppose that the frigidity of this reception made him lose a grain of his courage. From day to day, the plan of his enterprise was defined in his own mind. For it was not a complete and definitive book which he meant to offer: the dozen poems represent but the first stratum of a work to which his life was to be consecrated, and which was to grow, story by story, reaching proportions which he already saw; but life

---
[1] Bucke: *Walt Whitman*, p. 138. H. Traubel: *With Walt Whitman in Camden*, p. 92.
[2] H. Traubel: *With Walt Whitman in Camden*, p. 24.
[3] W. S. Kennedy: *Reminiscences of Walt Whitman*, p. 85.

alone in the successive phases of his individuality should determine its completion. As his friend Bucke indicated later, "a profound part of the plan of the work was the way by which many things in it were left free for future adjustment."[1]

Leaves of Grass came into the world at an epoch of turgescence and unrest in American letters. New aspirations, ideas, which corresponded with economic and political changes, disturbed the literary world. Among the confused notions which floated in the air which young writers seized, was that of an autochthonous literature, which should no longer be subject to European models. The American mind sought an expression of itself and deemed itself ripe for acquiring a poetical nationality. With these preoccupations, the lyrists borrowed their motifs from Indian legends—a method somewhat superficial of thus exalting, thus coming close to the origin, the truth of their race. In the salient work of the preceding years certain of these aspirations were visible. From 1848 to 1850 Whittier published *The Bridal of Pennacook*, the collection of *Voices of Liberty*, and the *Songs of Labour*. The *Bigelow Papers* of Lowell were of 1848, and the *Hiawatha* of Longfellow, an attempt at an indigenous epic, appeared some months after *Leaves of Grass*. The theme of these works was certainly American, but their spirit and form were scarcely so: those were of literature—sometimes excellent. A simple comparison between *Hiawatha* and *Leaves of Grass* suffices to show how wide apart were the two books appearing the same year. And Emerson was, moreover, among all, the one who most clearly formulated the ideal, and suggested, in his discourses, that there should be a real American poet. It was he who was truly the Precursor.

This transformation which was operating in American letters was accompanied by an effort of literary decentralization. For some time the activity monopolized by New

---
[1] Bucke: *Walt Whitman*, p. 137.

England spread to New York, before but little concerned with literature, and a stirring Bohemia of writers, journalists, poetasters, searching to find in the Metropolitan city the intellectual prestige which had not yet disquieted it. Walt was part of this for some years after he left his island with literary schemes, and the success of the Democratic Review, where he first published his stories, corresponded to this awakening. Some New York writers won celebrity, notably R. H. Stoddard and Bayard Taylor, around whom gravitated a whole coterie of versifiers and essayists, all working more or less at journalism for a living, and some of whom acquired a name. Walt did not belong to this coterie—and he was soon to make himself felt. In short the supremacy, till then uncontested, of the New England writers threatened to be cut into by the new group of New Yorkers.

Walt, with his book, seemed then to arrive exactly at the moment to fulfill the desire which suggested but did not define that something new and indigenous whose need was tormenting the American soul. But there: it was so new and so indigenous and *Leaves of Grass* incarnated the idea which was in the air in a fashion so rude, so adequate, and real, that no one consented to recognize it. The book was flouted by all or nearly all except the great Emerson, who never proved better than in this circumstance his power of prophet.

As is usual with fate, the conventional efforts answering to the new aspirations were accepted, and Walt's "barbaric yawp" which no one expected—and whose form and substance were both outlandish—was to be received by shouts and ridicule. There was the man, he whom all anticipated and called for, but as none had dreamed him so great he was passed by without a salute. After half a century America still fails to recognize him.

X

WALT INSULTED

NOT only was he not discouraged by his rebuff, but he was prepared to commit the same offense with a new daring. Far from exhausting his power, the first spurt of it accelerated its effusion and this time poems burst from him in full leafage, heavy and pithy, branching in rich verse. Walt had a cycle to encompass and he pursued at that moment one of his most decisive advances.

In the middle of the summer of 1856, just one year after his first attempt, he brought out a second edition. The book was considerably enlarged: it was 16 mo of 385 pages, containing twenty new poems, and this time each poem had a distinct title. The work, in growing, was distinguished as living beings are: more than that, the author was given, after his first bits, to a labour of correction and of revision, which he was to pursue faithfully to the verge of his death. Now the volume bore his name on the cover, also ornamented with leaves. The Preface to the edition of 1855 had disappeared, or rather was transmuted into poems, and the portrait, which made an integral part of the plan of *Leaves of Grass*, was retained. Walt did not have a publisher, but his friends, Fowler & Wells, the proprietors of the Phrenological Cabinet, on Broadway, were responsible for placing it on sale. Their name did not appear on the first page.

Profiting by his first experience, the poet took precaution that the book should not pass unnoticed. He showed the glorious letter of Emerson to his friend, Charles A. Dana, editor of the New York Sun, and Dana, who was also Emerson's friend, advised him outright to publish it: it was truly too decisive, too magnificent, to be kept in a portfolio. Walt then decided to append it to his poems, followed by a reply in a juvenile strain, one even somewhat rash in its inconsiderate pride, in which he reaffirms the need of a literature candidly autochthonous and manifests his audacious intention of satisfying it; the letter also contained a solemn homage to his dear "Friend and Master" Emerson, for having first signalled the shores of the "new continent of interior America." This reply, to speak true, was not very happy and, the day he wrote it, his usual discretion forsook him. Not only did he publish Emerson's letter after his poems, but with the splendid audacity of a beginner and in the very American spirit of an advertisement, he had printed in gold letters on the back of the cover this sentence: "I salute you at the commencement of a great career, R. W. Emerson," which flashed above the name of the author. "I regarded that letter as the chart of an emperor," Walt Whitman said later, to justify that audacity—for which he never sought to be excused, believing he did right. Since the great voice of Emerson, amid derision, was raised in his favour, he lifted his name like a standard. The appendix also contained the collection of reviews which his book had received for the year. These he placed impartially under the eye of the public. Naturally it was insult and ridicule which dominated these pages.

Leaves of Grass in this transitory phase of its development already startles by its tremendous beauty. Only the first story of the structure, whose completion he will work at all his life, was built, but such as it was then, it calls forth wonder. He is more master of his art later with his power disciplined; but never does he display so much passion, superabundance, torrential violence. The very titles have immensity, showing the poet in all the intoxication of his genius and of his idea. Listen to them rather: *A Poem of Women, Poem of Numbers in One, Poem of the Wonder of the Resurrection of the Wheat, Poem of Singers and of Words of*

Poems, Poems of Liberty for Asia, Africa, Europe, America, Australia, Cuba and the Archipelago, Poem of Absolute Miracles, A Poem of Propositions of Nudity, Poem of Speakers of Words of the Earth . . . . One seems listening to some First Man uttering in the morning of the world universal words which name things and encircle the earth. In them his arms reach the confines of the globe, his voice dilates beyond the seas. You are overcome by the bewildering and the boundless in these outbursts of an adorer of the total life. And it is not a hollow verbalism nor the cadence of periods which subdues you: you are possessed by these living words whose power is not of other books, but rather of real things.

Nevertheless the public did not better understand. The letter of Emerson, whose name shone like a beacon, forced attention, but could not open understandings. If, the first time, the effort of Walt was received with marked indifference, now it raised a storm of opprobrium and vituperation. A flood of insults, from full throats, rolled upon the 16 mo where were engraved these words in gold letters: "I salute you at the commencement of a great career, R. W. Emerson." After a half century has passed, one cannot, without smiling, turn over the leaves of the brochure[1] in which, four years later, Walt impassively published these testimonies—the most offensive as the most comic, the most furious as well as the most foolish. The vocabulary of insult is somewhat the same at all times and in all countries: but here truly the measure is more than full. The author of *Leaves of Grass* was more than a fool, he was a satyr: his book was not only a literary crime, but an insult to morals.

And while the bigots foamed, the "literary critics," the mob of scribblers dragged in the mire the would-be poet, ignorant of the first principle of the versifier's art. Walt was caught between two fires: he had to endure the malicious or rabid attack of the Boston Puritans or the rude clap-trap

---
[1] *Leaves of Grass Imprints.*

of his New York confrères. The literary coterie and the parlour flutists writhed in listening to this formidable bass. This bearded giant, with the manners of a docker, who thundered his raucous verses and aspired to the sacred title of bard! It was too droll. A man unshaven and vulgar, a buffoon, who knew nothing of rhyme, and who showed himself thoroughly ignorant of the niceties which make a real poet, such as salons and academies honour[1]. . . . This brute makes a sensational entrance into literature, with his slow, heavy tread, like the roll of the elephant. He should be returned to his zoölogical garden. . . .

Walt was especially the victim of venomous attacks of a clique of journalists and litterateurs, from whom he always kept aloof. All the coterie more or less conscientiously showed its malice in covering Walt with epigrams and jests. Walt Whitman was a vulgar advertiser, too mediocre to be distinguished in the usual ways of literature: he had published this extraordinary work merely to attract violent attention to himself. So that instead of being defended by the New York group, as prototype of a new literature, completely free of New England influence, the author of *Leaves of Grass* more than the insults of Boston had to meet the assault of these men who harassed him because he was not of them, and from the height of their pettiness, they had but contempt for this *rudes indigestaque moles*. . . . Walt on his part had but sorry esteem for the "New York scribblers."[2]

In a cursory review of this singular brochure of delirious pages of ineptitude and savage enmity, an admirable little monument erected among so many in all ages to human stupidity, one sees all that Walt had to endure these first years—and long afterward—the calvary which he had to climb, with no one near to support him except his own

---

[1] W. S. Kennedy: *Reminiscences of Walt Whitman*, pp. 97-98.
[2] H. Traubel: *With Walt Whitman in Camden*, pp. 55-61.

magnificent impassiveness, his own pride of the strong man. He was alone with his work and his immense optimism, and he listened to the insults. For the man himself as much as the book—the man whom he had put into his book was the victim of calumnies. We can understand their fierceness if we consider as a parallel instance what Émile Zola endured when he began. In the paragraphs of the dailies he is shown as a blend of the bully, the satyr, and the clown. Stories were hawked about in which he sometimes figured as an omnibus driver, who dismounted to prepare his poetical salmagundi, sometimes as a kind of Buffalo Bill in red shirt and boots prepared to fight the buffalo. By the vastness of his message he had sown the storm and he commenced to reap it. His capacity as a great innovator was justified by the fury which he encountered.

The need of quiet and the out-of-doors after the work of printing his book and the scandal which it called forth drove the poet to the wilds of his island. He needed to be alone with himself and nature, that nature in whose presence he had written some of his first pages; to be close to the sea which had revealed to him the rhythm of his poems, whose rude voice came to him again to justify the rudeness of his verses as when he reread them walking on the beach. . . . "When the book everywhere raised such a storm of anger and condemnation," he said to his friend, Bucke, "I went to the head of Long Island and remained there the end of the summer and the entire autumn—the happiest of my life— around Shelter Island and Peconic Bay. I went to New York later, confirmed in the resolution from which I have never been separated—to follow my poetical enterprise according to my own way, and to complete it the best I could."[1]

Fowler & Wells, his publishers, printed and bound an edition of a thousand copies; at least they made the plates, to be prepared for a large issue. In the face of the tempest

[1] Bucke: *Walt Whitman*, p. 26.

which *Leaves of Grass* raised they did not wish to compromise their business, then prosperous, and perhaps feared the lawsuits threatened by some: they suspended the sale. The number of copies sold could not be counted: it was not large, but there was some undeniable progress. Of the first edition, no more than one or two copies were asked for—some hundreds of this one were disposed of because of the sentence from Emerson in gold letters on the back, and the noise it made—enough to cover the expense of the publishers.

But the final result proved identical: after two trials at sea Walt's ship was forced to reënter port because of the violence of contrary winds. He had to wait the propitious moment. He waited four years.

Notwithstanding this, the second appearance of *Leaves of Grass* made a stir in the better literary circles. The work was provocative, it attacked prudery and literary prejudices. And out of all the controversy, a result, the most important of all, came: the battle began. The scandal roused by the bigots and snobs exercised the peril of complete indifference.

They were present at the first skirmishes of a battle which lasted during the poet's life, and which endures to-day, for or against *Leaves of Grass*. The first protesters were to be the surer builders of the final victory.

In the eyes of a few Walt became a personality—strange, detestable, or attractive—as he was, for ten years, among the crowd of his anonymous comrades of the people. The most interesting call which he received after the edition of 1856 was from Thoreau, who came to see him in Brooklyn one day in November. The author of *Walden*, another great book which appeared two years before, was accompanied by Bronson Alcott, the transcendentalist philosopher, who had already come to see Walt. Both were intimates of Emerson. If Alcott seemed to have admired Walt Whitman unreservedly, the latter made, upon "the young god Pan" as Emerson called his friend Thoreau, an impression curious and profound, which we find described with admirable sincerity in two of his letters to Harrison Blake.[1] The lover of nature and the anarchist dreamer found himself both attracted and repelled by the florid-faced giant and his unusual book, which won him by bewildering him. His instinct of the primitive and his artistic sensibility carried him forcefully toward the man who translated with such power the elemental emotions of life, but his savage misanthropy separated him from the passionate lover of crowds. Thoreau was truly much impressed—and did not conceal it—by the personality of Whitman not less than by his poetical message. His testimony has a singular value. He expected to be met by a loud-voiced boxer, with rowdyish manners, and he found himself before a good Colossus, gentle and calm, whose flushed face contrasted not less astonishingly with his gray beard, than his simple and courteous manners clashed with the picture made of him, from his poems. "He is apparently the greatest democrat which the world has seen," wrote Thoreau in recalling his visit. "He suggests sometimes something superhuman . . . he is a great type." Thoreau told Walt that *Leaves of Grass* reminded him of the great oriental poems and asked if he knew them. Walt answered, "No, tell me about them." One passage of their conversation was sufficient to flash the difference in their spiritual outlook. The Walden hermit expressed unreservedly all the contempt the crowd inspired in him, universal suffrage, politics, adding, "What is there in the people?" and Walt was shocked in his intimate feeling. It seemed to him that Thoreau insulted the good people of Brooklyn of whom he was proud, and his comrade workers.[2]

Here was a curious instance, enough to weaken all possible conjectures: alone, opposed by silence and execration, fine souls, men of letters like Emerson, Thoreau, Sanborn, Conway, whom education, mode of life, heredity, should have kept aloof from this poet, recognized the particular

---

[1] H. D. Thoreau: *Letters to Various Persons*, pp. 141-2, 146-8.
[2] H. H. Gilchrist: *Anne Gilchrist*, p. 237.

grandeur of the man and his book. From the first, it was only the Concord group who were aware that something out of the usual and truly new had sprung from the American soil—however serious may have been their reserve. "I feel that he is essentially foreign to me," wrote Thoreau after his visit to Brooklyn; "but his appearance captivates me. . . ." And as *Leaves of Grass* unchained the lightnings of Boston, the fortress of Puritanism, it transpires that Walt had, in Massachusetts, his first admirers and his most irreconcilable adversaries. The same year Emerson sent to Carlyle the volume which he was the first to salute, and with it this note: "One book, last summer, came out in New York, a nondescript monster, which yet had terrible eyes and buffalo strength, and was indisputably American—which I thought to send you; but the book throve so badly with the few to whom I showed it, and wanted good morals so much, that I never did. Yet I believe now, again, I shall. It is called 'Leaves of Grass,'—was written and printed by a journeyman printer in Brooklyn, New York, named Walter Whitman; and after you have looked into it, if you think, as you may, that it is only auctioneer's inventory of a warehouse, you can light your pipe with it."[1] Emerson spoke in the same way to another, with his sweet smile and his penetrating irony in which there was no malice, that *Leaves of Grass* affected him as a compound of *Bhagavad-Gita* and the *New York Herald*. Cleverness was respected at Concord and humour always had its rights. The speech circulated and was interpreted as an epigram without reflecting that always in the deep thought of Emerson there was perhaps something implied in that pleasantry.

So, for the second time, Walt did not succeed in delivering his message. A more serene season had undoubtedly come. In the interval, he reconsidered a favourite project which he had already had in mind, when he was seeking a means of expression, that of lecturing throughout the country. He

---
[1] *Correspondence of Carlyle and Emerson*, II, p. 251.

needed to be understood. For this he would have to induce others to understand. Perhaps if he were to explain himself face to face with the public, he would force a hearing, his living and magnetic word would penetrate the wall of misunderstanding which separated him from the world. He needed to create a "popular foretaste of himself"[1] which should prepare the way for his message. He even formulated his project in a note, found among his papers after his death.

> From now on, two concurrent expressions. They are to expand, amicable, coming from a common source, but each carrying its individual and distinct mark.
> First, the Poems, *Leaves of Grass* as of Intuitions, the Soul, the Body, (male or female) descending laws, social routine, creeds, literature, to celebrate the inherent, the red blood one man in himself and one woman in herself. Songs of thoughts and wants hitherto suppressed by writers. Or it may be avowed to give the personality of Walt Whitman, out and out evil and good whatever he is or thinks, that sharply set down in a book, the spirit commanding it.
> Second, Lectures, of Reasoning, comparisons, Politics, the intellectual, the aesthetic, the desire for knowledge, the sense of richness, from an American point of view. Also in Lectures, the meaning of Religion as statement, everything from an American point of view.[2]

He thus thought of fashioning for the United States two "athletic volumes," for his printed lectures would form another book, which should explain the first. He lingered a while about this project, finally to abandon it. He left the *Leaves* to battle alone for itself. People would understand when the time came.

In any case, the opinion of the outside world had no influence upon his real self. He lost nothing of his immanent optimism; he abided the moment to launch his bark a third time. He had time with him. . . . Those who carry in their breasts eternal things always have time. No—Walt was not hurried, and above all, he had no reason to abandon

---
[1] *Camden Edition, Introduction*, p. liv.
[2] *Id.*, pp. lv-lvi.

his destiny: "I am sure of one thing," writes Bucke, "and it is that the attitude and course of Walt Whitman these following years (the failure of the 1856 edition) form the most heroic part of all his career. He went on his way with the same enjoyment of life, the same ruddy countenance, the same free, elastic stride, through the tumult of sneers and hisses, as if he were surrounded by applause; not the slightest degree abashed or roused to resentment and opposition. The poems written directly after the collapse of this second edition are, if possible, more sympathetic, exultant, arrogant, and make larger claims than any."[1]

As to Walt's occupations during the four years following the second edition of *Leaves of Grass* no precise detail has come to us. He continued probably his favourite mode of life—moderate work—he gave six or seven hours a day to remunerative work[2]—interrupted by idling on the streets, on the ferries, hours passed with the frank lads of cordial manners, or in excursions on the bay or to the country. We only know, thanks to vistas on his life then, that they were sunny, communal years, when he lived, more freely than ever, the life of his poems. The intensity of his poetical labour at this time proves that the great part of it was given to the constructing his book, which grew a story every time it was returned to him.

Not only he reached then the age of his greatest creative power, but he is close to his fortieth year, quickly reached, quickly passed, when his individuality as man was supreme. His marvellous health was in full tide, and all his faculties, including the one which empowered him to look into the souls of men as into an open book, reached their complete flowering. A rough and royal beauty was wholly his, such as still strikes us in an admirable portrait, undated, but which must have been about 1860.[3] His contact with

---

[1] Bucke: *Walt Whitman*, pp. 141-142.
[2] *Id.*: p. 34.
[3] Reproduced in *Camden Edition*, I, p. 80.

everyday humanity was never more fervent, his need to absorb and to expand never more fully satisfied than then. It was between 1855 and 1861 that he passed a great number of hours with his friends, the pilots and stage drivers, and that he knitted in the world of workingmen the most solid bonds. Thomas Gae's testimony of Walt at this time is vivid—his gladiatorial frame, his tender solicitude toward a hard-handed band of men.[1]

It is evident also from his notes that an intense intellectual labour filled these years. He began to absorb history, geography, literature, by his own method, that is to say, without method, but abundantly. He was never in a hurry, and he appeared always to be idle: yet he had time for everything. It was believed that he united in himself many men's lives.

Above all, his poetical development absorbed him. He carries his poems in manuscript and reads them to right listeners. It was thus he read that superb lyric "Out of the Cradle Endlessly Rocking" to the Price family, his Brooklyn neighbours, and explained the incident which inspired it. Strange abstraction and exaltation marked his moods.[2]

---

[1] Bucke: *Walt Whitman*, pp. 32-34.
[2] *Id.*: pp. 25-31.

XI

EMERSON AND WHITMAN

Two or three years after the second edition, *Leaves of Grass* sprouted wonderfully; Walt had in manuscript a hundred new poems. The summer of his work was come. Thus, one fact was proved, that despite the violent rebuke to his previous efforts, he had succeeded in propagating a certain "advanced taste of himself." The Boston publishers, Thayer and Eldridge, open to new experiments, offered to arrange for a new edition of his book, which had been out of print since 1856.

Toward the close of the winter of 1860 Walt went to Boston to supervise the printing of a volume, a task which was and remained to the end, for a skilled workman like himself, minute, slow, and personal. He remained there the entire spring. The environment was new to him; he was as yet unacquainted with New England, so he studied at leisure the life of the street, the city, and its suburbs.

Some happy memories cling to this visit. Emerson put himself out many times to see Whitman, and it is in the course of these interviews that the two men had a conversation destined to be famous. "In Boston when people have to talk, they go to the Common; let us go there," said Emerson. That day, he wished to make himself thoroughly clear to his friend on a point which he had at heart; the matter was important, at the moment when Whitman was preparing a new edition of his poems. Some years later, when again in Boston, Walt summarized in these words the substance of this historic conversation:

I walk'd for two hours, of a bright sharp February mid-day twenty-one years ago, with Emerson, then in his prime, keen, physically and morally magnetic, arm'd at every point, and when he chose, wielding the emotional just as well as the intellectual. During those two hours he was the talker and I the listener. It was an argument-statement, reconnoitring, review, attack, and pressing home (like an army corps in order, artillery, cavalry, infantry), of all that could be said against that part (and a main part) in the construction of my poems, "Children of Adam." More precious than gold to me that dissertation—afforded me, ever after, this strange and paradoxical lesson; each point of E.'s statement was unanswerable, no judge's charge ever more complete or convincing, I could never hear the points better put—and then I felt down in my soul the clear and unmistakable conviction to disobey all, and pursue my own way. "What have you to say then to such things?" said E., pausing in conclusion. "Only that while I can't answer them at all, I feel more settled than ever to adhere to my own theory, and exemplify it," was my candid response. Whereupon we went and had a good dinner at the American House. And thenceforward I never waver'd or was touch'd with qualms (as I confess I had been two or three times before).[1]

Emerson appealed to him with a real and pressing affection of an elder brother, manifesting all the communicable fervour of a great soul; and Walt, with whom firm sweetness was stronger than his more decisive words, felt deeply touched by the warm sympathy which Emerson showed him that day. He did not reply; he had within him reasons which reason did not know.[2]

The whole relation between Walt Whitman and Ralph Waldo Emerson may be disposed of here.[3] It presents a double aspect: work to work and man to man. This petty problem might be judged futile: however, is it not well to determine the situation and reciprocal attitude of the most original thinker and of the greatest poet of the United States? An Emerson and a Whitman are of such importance to the world that nothing obscure should subsist between their renown.

Had Whitman read Emerson before 1855, date of the first edition of *Leaves of Grass*? Some, basing upon the evident

---
[1]*Complete Prose*, pp. 183–184.
[2]W. S. Kennedy: *Reminiscences of Walt Whitman*, p. 77.
[3]The order of this chapter is reversed. Tr.

analogy between such conceptions as are equally dear to the two writers, have been quick to see in the *Essays* the initial source and the determining cause of the first draught of *Leaves of Grass*. J. T. Trowbridge notably represents this opinion; it is amplified by George William Curtis in Putnam's Magazine about 1860, and often renewed since by those whom the overwhelming originality of Whitman offended.

Trowbridge, admiring *Leaves of Grass* only with reticence, declares nevertheless that nothing equal to *Song of Myself* had appeared in English since Shakespeare.[1] But for him the first part of the book reflects the influence of Emerson. This assertion Trowbridge supports by different facts, such as certain affirmations of Walt in his reply to Emerson, published in the Appendix to the Edition of 1856, and the sending of the copy of *Leaves of Grass* to the latter; but above all, on a declaration which Whitman made to himself in 1860 at Boston. While Walt was working at carpentry about 1854, he read one day, while taking his solitary mid-day meal, a volume of Emerson which he had put into his basket with his luncheon. It was a revelation. Filled just then with vague aspirations, this electric contact illuminated his very depths, and discovered him to himself. He formulated the event in these characteristic terms: "I was simmering, simmering, simmering; Emerson brought me to boil."[2]

Opposed to this statement, which Trowbridge energetically supports, there is an express statement of Whitman himself which contradicts it absolutely. Being frankly asked by his friend, W. S. Kennedy, as to the fact, Whitman declared, in a letter dated February 15, 1887, that he had not read Emerson before publishing his first edition.[3] Already another of Whitman's friends, John Burroughs, who wrote his *Notes on Walt Whitman* in 1867 from direct information from him, was careful to state this. It is after Emerson's

---

[1] W. S. Kennedy: *Reminiscences of Walt Whitman*, p. 79.

[2] J. T. Trowbridge: *Reminiscences of Walt Whitman*, the Atlantic Monthly, February, 1902, p. 163.

[3] W. S. Kennedy: *Reminiscences of Walt Whitman*, p. 76.

famous letter saluting *Leaves of Grass*, and his visit to Whitman in the summer of 1855, that the latter read *Nature and the Essays;* he remembers putting the volume in his little basket with his food and napkin one time, when, as usual, he went to pass the whole day on the then deserted beach of Coney Island to read, to bathe, to lie in the sun, and dream.[1] Walt declares, moreover, in this same letter, like many other young men, he had at one time "Emerson on the brain," also, he says, "that came late and affected only the surface." And he considers with satisfaction this crisis of his youth a stage habitual to "young men of eager minds."[2]

This is the debate. The contradiction looks flagrant. To resolve it and to show that it is but apparent, W. S. Kennedy has expended much erudition and eloquence. According to him, Walt knew the reputation of Emerson before 1855, and could and did read the reviews of his works and some articles on him in the Democratic Review, in which Whitman was, as we know, habitual collaborator between 1841 and 1847, and where many pages of copious citations appeared on the philosophy already known in intellectual America. In a word, according to W. S. Kennedy, Walt then knew Emerson without knowing him outright, which amply justifies the sending of a copy of *Leaves of Grass*.[3]

To our notion, the question should be envisaged from a point of view somewhat different. First of all, it is not necessary to accept literally, we believe, either the statement of Trowbridge or that of Whitman. To that of Whitman, especially, there is no reason to attach an absolute importance. It is not questioning his greatness to state his superb indifference to dates. All who have studied him before know this tendency to inaccuracy in the matter of figures, which was certainly characteristic, though illness and old

---

[1] John Burroughs: *Notes*, pp. 16–17.
[2] *Complete Prose*, p. 317.
[3] W. S. Kennedy: *Reminiscences of Walt Whitman*, pp. 79–83.

age may have aggravated it; and, even in the course of his reply to Kennedy, where he declares that he did not know Emerson before 1855, he deceives himself by ten years without knowing it. Besides, being endowed with the curiosity of an "omniverous reader" as was Walt in his youth, and his interest so keen for all manifestation of the thought of his time, it is indeed difficult to conceive that he had not been in contact with Emerson, then the most original thinker, of whom the press spoke, whose lectures and books aroused such enthusiasm and discussion between 1845 and '55. And having known and absorbed him—if only by fragments, his way of reading—he could not but be seized with his signification and with his greatness, not but feel the rapport—sure, intimate, and marvellous—between his idea, which he had not yet formulated, and the invigorating, new, refreshing conception of Emerson. In truth, he must have felt strengthened by a voice coming from a region entirely unlike his own. There, we believe, is found the sense and explanation of his open letter to his "dear Friend and Master" written in 1856, when he experienced by his own confession a crisis of Emersonism, and when, exhalting Individualism, "this new continent" of interior America, he added: "These shores, it is you who have discovered them. I say that it is you who have conducted the States, that it is you who have conducted me to them. . . ." There is, moreover, a hypothesis which seems to confirm—and to convert even into a quasi-certitude—a note from Whitman's hand recovered among his papers, one which accompanies a review article of May, 1847,[1] a note which establishes unmistakably that the thought of Emerson was familiar to him when he wrote it. It was not in the least necessary that he absorb a whole volume of Emerson; with his extraordinary intuition, some paragraphs were enough for him to penetrate the fundamental thought of the philosophy.

I avow that these affirmations appear to me superfluous:

---
[1] *Camden Edition*, IX, pp. 159-160.

to speak the truth, the fact is not to be doubted. Walt would not have been Walt if he had kept Emerson outside of his vast search into life and contemporary ideas. I am, therefore, disposed to charge to his faulty memory the statement in his letter to W. S. Kennedy. I also think, conscious as he was of his fundamental originality, of the perfect authenticity of his poem and of his message, he would show a certain momentary impatience in listening to his spiritual affinity with Emerson reasoned about—some small souls disposed to make him his "disciple." Whence the tone a little lively and very categorical of that letter, where he so vehemently and without restriction declares an independence.

Shall it be said that I accept in its rigour the verbal declaration which Trowbridge attributes to Whitman? By no means. Admitting that he had known fragments of Emerson in the years previous to his poem is not at all equivalent to claiming that the author of *Song of Myself* is indebted to him for his first inspiration. It is impossible not to see in this assertion a pure naïveté. What have such or such philosophy, such or such written pages, to do with the inspiration of Walt Whitman? *Leaves of Grass* has sprung directly from reality itself, from the heart of concrete things in contact with his personality. It is the very song of things, of beings, till then considered as improper to be translated into poetry, which takes flight from an individual. Things, beings, pageants, that living ensemble, these are responsible for this poem. Emerson, who evolved in a sphere totally opposed to that of Walt, could but give him a momentary support—perhaps precious, precisely because by all which differentiated them. We can easily admit that a certain chapter or theme from such a thinker affected him like a spur. But Emerson, most surely, was not for Whitman what East River pilots had been, harbour workers, actors at the Battery, Broadway coachmen, the spectacle of the Bay, Long Island shores, or the towns along the Mississippi or the

Great Lakes; these are what furnished the real stuff of a book which, according to the picturesque expression of Kennedy, juts up "as unique in character as the flora and fauna of a Galapagos Island emergent from the blue waters of the Pacific."[1] It is this multitudinous humanity and the largeness of nature which were the primitive source and continuance of his inspiration, which nothing written was capable of determining.

To say that Whitman is a differentiated product of Emerson's philosophy is to declare that under another climate the elephant could spring from the deer, or the bison from the peacock. Emerson and Whitman belonged to different species. Thus in a certain sense the poet was fully right when he wrote to his friend: "It is of no importance whether I read Emerson before starting or not."[2] The originality of this book is the most absolute perhaps which has ever been manifested in literature.

It would be equally obtuse not to see the concordances which actually exist between the two men. Emphatically opposed to their heredity, their education, their temperament, their spiritual tendency, yet upon certain points their parallelism is undeniable. Why would he not joyously salute *Leaves of Grass* at its birth, he who seven years before traced among others the prophetic lines of *Man Thinking*,[3] which stir us with an electric thrill when, in reading them, we think of Walt Whitman? And what more natural than these concordances? We have remarked that from 1845 to '50, an intense period of renewal of the literature and the soul of America, certain ideas were in the air, which all contemporaries were absorbing more or less. Some common aspirations, felt by Emerson and by Whitman some years apart, were formulated by them in their vastly different work.

Whitman could not cast a shadow on the suave and won-

---

[1] W. S. Kennedy: *Reminiscences of Walt Whitman*, p. 79.
[2] *Id.*: p. 76.
[3] The author must refer to *The American Scholar* of Emerson. Tr.

derful Emerson. To exalt the first is not to diminish the second. They are two great priests of Individualism and Optimism: one issues from the sphere of intellect, the other from the sphere of life lived. Each, in his way, occupies a supreme place, though Walt Whitman, from the more universal point of view, immensely surpasses Emerson.

What were, on the other hand, the personal relations of the two men? What, above all, was Emerson's intimate opinion of Whitman? The question is not worth stopping for, except that by reason of it Whitman was subjected to certain base calumnies. We have Emerson's enthusiastic inspired letter, written under the impulse of his admiration and his emotion, when he received *Leaves of Grass;* the real Emerson is discovered there. When Walt, universally reviled, published it as his defense and fixed a phrase of it in gold letters on the back of the second edition, Emerson was for a moment vexed;[1] but he remained outwardly calm. He saw immediately all the embarrassment which that untimely publication was bound to bring him as a patron of Whitman. Emerson was not deceived; there was tumult enough, and some printed in full-length letters that he was crazy. This hue-and-cry was annoying to a man thoroughly peaceable, accustomed to the quiet of his closet. Then when four years later the third edition of *Leaves of Grass* appeared, Emerson strongly regretted seeing the pages retained which in their conversation in Boston Common he had begged Walt to suppress. Side by side with the radical Emerson, who is one of the most exalted minds, the most advanced, the most admirable of the age, there was another Emerson of university education, philosophic, clerical, bookish, formal, descendant of an ecclesiastical line, the eminent respectable citizen of literary and bourgeois Concord, slave of incredible prejudices, the Emerson, for example, who said to a young girl visiting him on Sunday who wished to play the piano:

---

[1] Bliss Perry: *Walt Whitman,* p. 115.

"No, no, I pray you . . . to-day is Sunday."[1] The Emerson of life and the Emerson of the book were not always identical, as was Whitman. To that Emerson, whom we no longer know, but who, at that time, was as real as the other, some rudeness of the artisan-poet, as well as his vivacity of language, was not acceptable. But there were first of all Emerson's family and his immediate neighbours to whom the personality of the "rough" of Brooklyn was rather odious, and who looked upon Emerson's admiration for his book as a regrettable weakness. These friends, people bigoted and narrow, were pleased, because of the calumnies and tittle-tattle, to exaggerate the annoyance of Emerson at the time of the stormy publication of his letter, to mar some innocent pleasantries he let fall, and to transform into positive proof against the man, the antipathy which Emerson experienced toward the most coloured passages of *Leaves of Grass*. Indeed, later Woodbury made himself the interpreter of this mischievous enmity, in attributing to Emerson various perversities intended for Whitman.[2]

These calumnies, bigoted and "respectable," do not bear investigation. The truth remains that the great and loyal Emerson never retracted the enthusiastic words of his letter, nor withdrew his friendship. There is only needed, to prove it, certain private letters, which peremptorily establish this and which some day will surely be published:[3] the attitude of Emerson leaves no doubt as to his sentiments. When overseeing the printing of his book it was Emerson who many times came from Concord to see him.[4] Would he have done this if he was seriously angry at the publication of his letter? And, in general, in his personal relations with Walt, it was always he who made advances, who sought him, attracted by that enormous power which he felt but could not define because it surpassed him. Walt, it seems, when in-

---
[1] H. H. Gilchrist: *Anne Gilchrist*, pp. 233-234.
[2] Woodbury: *Talks with Emerson*.
[3] I. Hull Platt: *Walt Whitman*, p. 31; H. Traubel: *With Walt Whitman in Camden*, Vol. I, p. 180.
[4] John Burroughs: *Walt Whitman*, pp. 66-67.

vited by Emerson to come to Concord declined the invitation, true to an instinctive dislike of a purely literary company, which he would be sure to meet there. It was inevitably noticed that in preparing his collection of poems for *Parnassus*, in 1875, Emerson did not include a single fragment of Whitman. The reason for this very probably is that he thought *Leaves of Grass* rather as rhythmic prose or some other new form than as poetry properly so called. Emerson did not by that disclaim Whitman; and in various circumstances he knew how to offer the poet some evidence of his personal attachment and his consideration.

Walt, on his part, showed a deep affection for Emerson. He showed this to the man as well as to his writings. "From the first visit which he made at Brooklyn in 1855 and the two hours which we passed together, I experienced an affection, and a singular attachment for him, by his contact, conversation, company, magnetism . . . we probably had a dozen (perhaps twenty) of these interviews, conversations, promenades, etc.,—five or six times (sometimes in New York, sometimes in Boston) we had good long dinners together. I was very happy—I do not think, nevertheless, that I was entirely at my ease with him: it was always he who did the talking and I am sure that he was equally happy[1]. . . ."

By the tone of certain pages which Walt has written of Emerson, it is easily seen how much he revered the man. The insistence of Emerson during their famous conversation in Boston Common, in wishing to make him suppress the passages in *Leaves of Grass*, not only left no unpleasant trace in Walt's mind, but he considered it as a proof of genuine affection, "which I felt then, and feel to this hour, the gratitude and reverence of my life could never repay."[2] Walt Whitman judged with clairvoyance the writer and thinker, perceiving nicely the "darkness" and

---
[1] W. S. Kennedy: *Reminiscences of Walt Whitman*, pp. 76–77.
[2] *Id.:* p. 77.

"sunny expanses" of his work. He accorded him the first place among the poetical initiators of the New World, and gave him rank with Washington, Lincoln, and Grant.[1] "Emerson is not far from being our greatest man," he declared in 1890, to an English visitor, "in fact, I believe him to be our very greatest man." But above all, the solemn, touching lines, which he wrote near the new-made grave of Emerson, remain the supreme salutation of Whitman to Emerson: "A just man, poised on himself, all-loving, all-enclosing, and sane and clear as the sun. . . . It is not we who come to consecrate the dead, we reverently come to receive, if so it may be, some consecration for ourselves and our daily work."[2]

Those who yielding to bigoted and formalist prejudices wished to change the relations of these men have but tried to tarnish one of the splendid pages of the literary history of the United States. It is vain, however; for the last echo of these calumnies is vanished, posterity hears only the joyous accents of Emerson, saluting *Leaves of Grass* at its birth and the solemn farewell words of Walt Whitman before the coffin of the great precursor.

During his stay in Boston Walt knitted literary friendships which for a short time were to influence the destiny of his book. Again this curious anomaly was proved: it was in the Puritan city to whose temperament all the liberal instincts of the man and poet were opposed that he found comprehensive sympathy. He met in Charles Eldridge, his publisher, a real comrade, not less than an admirer. It was also during this visit that he made the acquaintance of John Townsend Trowbridge.[3] The first edition of *Leaves of Grass* won him instantly, and despite the numerous re-

---
[1] Bucke: *In Re Walt Whitman*, p. 111.
[2] *Complete Prose*, p. 189.
[3] The account of this meeting—*Reminiscences of Walt Whitman*, the Atlantic Monthly, February, 1902. The extract is omitted. It is one of the many pen portraits of Whitman, and another testimony to the power of his personality.

serves of his rather formalist character, he did not hesitate to reverence the genius of the man whom he met in the first hours of his struggle.

Other interesting memories attach to these months when, far from Manhattan, Walt corrected the proofs of his new *Leaves*. It was at this time that he heard Father Taylor, pastor of the church for poor sailors, whom some friend, Emerson perhaps, had pointed out. He who kept strictly away from oratory finds himself more at ease, and nearer the infinite in the great cathedral of the world, and was deeply stirred by the extraordinary words of the old sailor, as much as his parents, in his childhood, had been by the sermons of Elias Hicks, the Quaker preacher, "with black eyes which sparkled at times like meteors."

> Quiet Sunday forenoons, I liked to go down early to the quaint ship cabin looking church, where the old man ministered. . . . Father Taylor was a moderate-sized man, indeed almost small (reminded me of old Booth, the great actor, and my favorite of those and preceding days,) well advanced in years, but alert, with mild blue or gray eyes, and good presence and voice. Soon as he open'd his mouth I ceas'd to pay any attention to church or audience, or pictures or lights and shades; a far more potent charm entirely sway'd me. . . . I remember I felt the deepest impression from the old man's prayers, which invariably affected me to tears. . . . For when Father Taylor preach'd or pray'd the rhetoric and art, the mere words (which usually play such a big part), seem'd altogether to disappear, and the live feeling advanced upon you and seized you with a power before unknown. Everybody felt this marvelous and awful influence. One young sailor, a Rhode Islander, (who came every Sunday, and I got acquainted with, and talk'd to once or twice as we went away,) told me, "that must be the Holy Ghost we read of in the Testament."[1]

In June or July the book at last appeared. It was a very beautiful 12mo, incomparably superior in appearance to the other two editions: it is evident in running over these 456 pages, printed on choice paper, that a serious firm met the expense of the volume. Nevertheless, certain unusual arrangements preserved its particular stamp. The title on

---
[1] *Complete Prose*, p. 386.

the first page spreads in letters naïvely written and ornamented, and above the date, "1860-61," inscribed at the foot of the page, one may read: "year '85 of the States." On the cover appeared various primitive emblems, and also throughout the volume: a sunrise on the sea, a globe in space, a butterfly poised on a hand. Walt did not like the volume at all, simple product of confection: he held that the exterior should carry the imprint of a personality. The characteristic likeness which accompanied the first two editions—and appeared to the sixth, to accompany ever after the volume through its evolution—was replaced by a reproduction of a portrait in oil painted by Charles Hine in 1859, in which Walt looks like an old sea captain.

One hundred and twenty-four new poems were added to the thirty-three original pieces. The volume was completely changed. Not only had it formidably grown, but its fragmentary aspect had disappeared. For the first time it was presented as an organic whole with a prelude and a finale; and the author in it pronounced already the essential word that his book is not a mere book, but a man who comes to speak and to offer himself to you; is Procreator who would engender a new and haughtier race of men for America and for the world, the numberless family of children of the New Adam. The poems were distributed in four groups: *Democratic Songs*, *Leaves of Grass*, *Children of Adam*, *Calamus*, followed by some others bearing an individual title. Obedient to a Quaker impulse, he numbered the months as they are in the calendar of Friends: first month, second month, etc., instead of January, February, etc. Walt was of his time, but he was also of his family; and in everything he remained faithful to the interior call. In the fourth part, *Calamus*, he published the thirst for impassioned comradeship, of the close affection of man to man, which tormented him to the verge of sorrow, and was indeed with him insatiable.

Although it has been abolished by later manipulations,

this edition is the most highly coloured, the most challenging, the most audacious of the editions of *Leaves of Grass*. The Walt Whitman of his fortieth year is there revealed in the wild, with all his ardent virility. And despite the successive rearrangements, and of the author's incessant labour on his poems, it contains the bulk of the first half of the book, as we have it to-day. Between the edition of 1855, the finishing touch, that of 1860 marks a decisive advance, in which the poems begin to be definitely reduced to order. The principal contours of the future edifice are already to be found there.

This time, Whitman was sailing under happy auspices. For a serious edition he had the support of a worthy house, with its means of publicity, and the vessel with its new rigging, with its hold reënforced, was big enough to resist the gale. The adventure, too, was different. The ship did not immediately gain the high sea; it tacked, profiting by favourable winds, but making little by little its path. And Walt watched his banner float in the rear in the morning sun.

The book had a moderate but sure sale. Two or three thousand copies were issued, and was not this a success for such a work? For five years, because of the fierce opposition which Walt's "barbaric yawp" raised, curiosity was awakened. One wished to see what was at the bottom of this terrible man, whom legend made alternately a clown or a satyr. He was not in any case an ordinary man. He who had advanced, unhurt by this hooting, roused the interest of thinking men: and some studied this phenomenon in the pages of his book. The extravagances and excesses which at first provoked laughter or fury, shocked less this time. The public made, in a word, the first step, not toward acceptance, but toward inquiry.

The sale of the volume was one sign and the publishers, who had faith in their poet, were firm in their determination to support him. From time to time a sympathetic review appeared, and Walt, according to his custom, himself came to the rescue by sending to friendly papers anonymous articles. But the most important point was that a weekly publication defended him with great warmth.[1] The New York Saturday Press was an aggressive organ, where young writers exalted every boldness, they sent sharp arrows at the mandarins of literature, and particularly at the majestic Philistines of Boston: its editor, Henry Clapp, was a frequenter of Pfaff's German restaurant, where the "Bohemians," of whom Walt was one, met, and where W. D. Howells was introduced to him in August of the same year. More than all, the Atlantic Monthly, the Boston literary review which Lowell edited, had shown some consideration for him in publishing a poem in the April number.[2] Thayer and Eldridge published also *Leaves of Grass Imprints*.[3]

There is then ground for hope; the dawn of attention seems to be breaking. Perhaps in the end Walt will succeed in fulfilling his mission. But it was ordained that the audacious enterprise was to meet disaster. For the greater glory of the poet, perhaps, adverse fate was not immediately vanquished, and the number of obstacles kept pace with the formidable advance of the book on its time.

The ship of Walt, set out this time in fairer weather, was stranded on a bank which no pilot could have avoided. It was the eve of the Secession War, the vast event which absorbs everything, swallowing all which is written or published of the poems or of the attention given them. When it burst, the publishing house was ruined. The firm, Thayer and Eldridge, whose receipts were not forthcoming, failed, dragging *Leaves of Grass* in its fall. And all the hopes founded on this edition were suddenly and pitiably mowed down.

Then bad luck pursued Walt for six years. The book a

---

[1] John Burroughs: *Notes*, p. 1.
[2] Bliss Perry: *Walt Whitman*, p. 127.
[3] Bucke: *Walt Whitman*, pp. 199–200.

third time disappeared. But what could not disappear again, what was the shelter from all storms, and what was infinitely more important than the success or failure of one particular edition, is that some people in the world—very few indeed, but by the inherent value of the work, its infallible power of contagion, that was enough—a few people acquired a taste for the book. And it was never to be torn from the heart of them. Walt had been heard by perhaps a dozen elect souls, who would never let his message perish, but who would exalt and transmit it. His tree had taken root. It was the commencement of everything, the prelude of future victories. *Leaves of Grass* would never from now on be without defense against the champions of "poesy" and "morality."

This edition of 1860 notably won two men who lead a company of great companions, two men who are not only to be dear and faithful friends, but champions of his work before the world: John Burroughs, future poet and naturalist, and William Douglas O'Connor. Walt met O'Connor one day in the office of Eldridge, his publisher, who was bringing out a novel of his. He was a journalist who, like Thoreau, lost his place for having ardently espoused the cause of John Brown.[1]

He was a young man of twenty-eight, enthusiastic, generous, good looking, one of the noblest natures, the completest, the most attractive which it was possible to meet, and Walt was immediately drawn to him. He merely saw him then: presently circumstances brought about a close association. Besides, a new soil was prepared in which the seed sowed by the poet should germinate. Some copies of the two previous editions reached England without provoking any other emotion than rare and obscure attacks. But that of 1860, accepted by some young men, was destined, in a few years, to win for Walt fervent admiration.

In the hall, until then empty, where the bard of the New

---
[1] H. B. Binns: *Life of Walt Whitman*, p. 190.

World put forth his strange verses, some listeners entered very softly. And they heard that powerful and tender voice, stirred in spite of themselves; and the impassive man pursued his recital, as before the limitless audience of the humanity of the future, whose judgment he seems to foresee.

PART FOUR
THE WOUND DRESSER
WASHINGTON (1862–1865)

XII
AT THE BEDSIDE OF THE DYING

However surfeited this life may already appear, a sudden event is about to penetrate and fill it, which, without breaking its unity, is its dividing line. Between the man such as we know him and the man after the war one sees the passing of a profound emotion; and of the numerous breaks in his life this is the most violent. Walt for many years finds himself torn from his home, from himself, from his work; he is plunged into a feverish, tragic atmosphere, charged with pain and poison, all in the accomplishment of a sad and radiant duty whence will issue at once the helplessness of his old age and the perfection of his personality. We are now at the threshold of a unique experience, some aspects of which envelop a sacred mystery of humanity: this much-alive man gives to it the unsuspected limit of his strength, showing through it all the legendary and superhuman individual which he had introduced in his poems and whose reality was thus to be proved. Walt, after having offered himself to everyone in his poems, is about to give himself in person to thousands of human beings athirst for him.

The storm clouds were gathering when he returned to New York. The nomination of Abraham Lincoln to the presidency precipitated the crisis; the Union was threatened, and some of the slave states formed themselves into a confederation to maintain at any cost the privilege on which their prosperity was built. It was the eve of the Civil War, in which North and South were about to engage in a prolonged, bloody struggle.

Whitman, who since his youth had followed with attentive eye the inner politics of his country, and who knew its hidden springs, was passionately interested in the crisis at hand. He had foreseen it and he knew that a grave and decisive hour had come. Under his immense exterior apathy he vibrated intensely to all that convulsed the national life. He was super-American. And to him it mattered more than to all the world that America, bearer of the modern idea, the democratic idea, *his* idea, should come victorious from the crisis. The Civil War was the great shock of his life.

In some lines of touching simplicity, he noted the first moment of the redoubtable conflict.[1] Walt lived through the beginning of the war in the atmosphere of the street, sharing the emotion of the crowd and the stupor following the first defeat. His whole being was seized: the feverish reading of telegrams, the noise of passing convoys in the street, the marching of troops, all pushed into the background the normal preoccupations of his life. And at the sight of the great city which was arming for war, impassioned odes to the banner of the Union, the Union in peril, burst from his heart like a cry of love.

Forty years had I in my city seen soldiers parading,
Forty years as a pageant, till unawares the lady of this teeming and turbulent city,
Sleepless amid her ships, her houses, her incalculable wealth,
With her million children around her, suddenly,
At dead of night, at news from the south,
Incens'd struck with clinch'd hand the pavement.

A shock electric, the night sustained it,
Till with ominous hum our hive at daybreak pour'd out its myriads.
From the houses then and the workshops, and through all the doorways,
Leapt they tumultuous, and lo! Manhattan arming. . . .
War! an arm'd race is advancing! the welcome for battle, no turning away;
War! be it weeks, months, or years, an arm'd race is advancing to welcome it.[2]

---

[1] *Complete Prose*, p. 16.
[2] *Leaves of Grass*, pp. 219–221.

In New York men were enlisting *en masse;* his brother George, one of the first. He himself was not enrolled among the combatants; the inner call, which he followed in everything, did not bid him go. He watched, listened passionately, leaving to circumstances the responsibility of deciding his part in the drama. He knew the South and was far from hating it, but his fervent sympathy was now with the Northern cause. Victory for the North meant salvation for the Union. Not a doubt as to this, and any other opinion to him was impious.

Presently the interior call was heard in an unexpected manner. While running through the daily lists of the wounded in the terrible battle of Fredericksburg (December 13, 1862) he read the name of his brother George, who had made the entire campaign with the 51st Regiment of the volunteers of New York, a simple soldier who was already a captain; he was described as struck in the face by the bursting of a shell, and seriously wounded. Walt left instantly. He would nurse his brother and send back news to his anxious family. After three days of suffering and fatigue, having been sent in the confusion of camps and hospitals from one to another, he reached his brother George at Rappahannock.

He found himself suddenly thrown amidst the cruel realities of the aftermath of a battle, face to face with the wounded, the dying, the dead. One of the first sights he met in camp was a heap of amputated feet, legs, arms, hands, at the foot of a tree within ten yards of the house, a full load for a one-horse cart.[1] He had gluttonously fed of life till then, and he now was satiated not with death alone, but with the unbearable horrors attending a battle-field. The captain's wound was not serious; he already was recovering, and Walt was free to visit the camp, especially the field hospital, where the wounded, without care, were heaped in disorder, still clad in their blood-stained uniforms. He went among

---

[1] *Complete Prose,* p. 20.

these sufferers and spoke to them. He was without means and bitterly realized his helplessness.

He wrote letters under their dictation to parents; he went among the hospital tents of the army of the Potomac—the miserable tents where lay thousands of wounded, and some dying. He familiarized himself with the sights of the field. He looked, studied, identified himself with all. In his brother's regiment he discovered Brooklyn friends. On December 28th he left Falmouth to convoy the wounded and ill, many of them his own townsmen, to Washington. He had no precise plan at the time. It is under the sole stress of events that he began the extraordinary task which was about to absorb him, body and soul, for the following years. Now that he found himself among the great army of the mutilated and feverish who were filling the capital, an imperious force held him. He had touched suffering, and was under its magnetic attraction. He was wholly fascinated.

Walt followed his instinct faithfully. And his instinct bade him attach himself to these panting, bleeding men who had need of a hand to dress their wounds, to remain near these poor, tortured hearts, suffering for the look or the word which would inspire them with courage. This time the call was heeded.

And it is then that naturally, without being tied to any program by the sole strength of the bond which united him to his wounded, he undertook little by little the rôle which he was to fill during the war, that of "volunteer nurse." He was far from suspecting, that moment, that the 16th of December, 1862, he had quitted Brooklyn never to return again except as a visitor.

It is in January, 1863, that he commenced his daily visits to the sick and wounded in that vast lazar-house which Washington then was, encircled by improvised villages, where sometimes fifty, sixty, seventy thousand sufferers were cared for. In proportion as he came in contact with this crowd of the helpless, an experience little by little came to him. He realized his inability to lift himself to the grandeur and extent of their suffering; he was not, however, as helpless as in the first days. His large instinct of humanity trained by the weeks passed at the bedside of the sick suggested to him now a hundred little devices—so great in results—by which the anguish of the hospital and physical pain might be mitigated. He regulated his ministry by a method all his own.

Thanks to his *Notes of the War*, his letters to his mother, and his articles to newspapers, we know what constituted his hospital service. It is strongly stamped with his personality and is marginally vouched for by the nurse, the sanitary inspector, as well as the ordinary charitable visitor. Walt in the hospitals was the unique, the great and good Walt, a real man who, among the stricken soldiers, found, in his ample heart at once manly and maternal, all the original ways of helping them.

It was his custom to pass through one or many wards of a hospital, stop a moment before each bed, offer the patient a trifle, a biscuit, an orange, a sheet of writing paper, a stamped envelope, tobacco, a bit of money, or, if he had nothing more to offer, simply a smile, a word of friendship, a nod of the head, neglecting no one. He was sure to notice, among the rows of young men, those who needed particularly his care, the downcast, the prostrate, whom the feeling of their abandon and the dismal atmosphere of the hospital plunged into a black stupor. These needed comfort and solace more than medicine: their recovery depended upon it. One of his customary tasks was to sit at the bedside of the weak and sick, and write letters to their mothers, brothers, sisters, sweethearts, who for months were without news of their soldier. He also brought to them history texts, illustrated reviews and the daily papers which passed from hand to hand. He kept in a notebook the need, the wish, the pain of each one, the trifle which he was to bring in his next visit to arouse pleasure and consequently health.

Nothing was petty or useless when it served to soothe some poor languishing fellow. He knew that the odour of lemon in the hand caused joy to a feverish patient. He knew a man's delight in tobacco, in hearing him read, recite a poem, or conduct a guessing game. The wounded Rebels and the blacks received from him the same attention as the Union soldiers. The man of crowds thus practised his invariable method, which was to keep in touch with individuals; but how much more at this tragic hour, at the bedside of the anguished and dying, in the distress and foulness of a hospital in war time!

Whatever was the catholicity of his sympathy, Walt devoted much of his time to those whom he called his "special cases." In the hospitals the number of very young men, from sixteen to twenty, the greater number coming from the country, was considerable. It was to some of these boys, enfeebled by fever or wounds, weakened by homesickness, upon whom his patient tenderness was exercised and wrought miracles. Here is one, for instance, among so many others:

June 18th.—In one of the hospitals I find Thomas Haley, Company M, 4th, New York cavalry—a regular Irish boy, a fine specimen of youthful physical manliness—shot through the lungs—inevitably dying—came over to this country from Ireland to enlist—has not a single friend or acquaintance here—is sleeping soundly at this moment, (but it is the sleep of death)—has a bullet-hole straight through the lung. I saw Tom when first brought here, three days since, and didn't suppose he could live twelve hours—(yet he looks well enough in the face to a casual observer). He lies there a fine-built man, the tan not yet bleach'd from his cheeks and neck. Poor youth, so handsome, athletic, with profuse beautiful shining hair. One time as I sat looking at him while he lay asleep, he suddenly, without the least start, awaken'd, open'd his eyes, gave me a long steady look, turning his face very slightly to gaze easier—one long, clear, silent look—a slight sigh—then turned back and went into his doze again. Little he knew, poor death-stricken boy, the heart of the stranger that hover'd near.[1]

---

[1] *Complete Prose*, p. 31.

AT THE BEDSIDE OF THE DYING

This silent and tender vigil at the bedside of the dying evokes the stanza in which the poet is pictured on the battle-field, a whole night, near the body of a combatant:

Vigil strange I kept on the field one night;
When you my son and my comrade dropt at my side that day,
One look I but gave which your dear eyes return'd with a look I shall never forget,
One touch of your hand to mine O boy, reach'd up as you lay on the ground,
Then onward I sped in the battle, the even-contested battle,
Till late in the night reliev'd to the place at last again I made my way,
Found you in death so cold dear comrade, found your body son of responding kisses, (never again on earth responding,)
Bared your face in the starlight, curious the scene, cool blew the moderate night-wind,
Long there and then in vigil I stood, dimly around me the battle-field spreading,
Vigil wondrous and vigil sweet there in the fragrant silent night,
But not a tear fell, not even a long-drawn sigh, long, long I gazed,
Then on the earth partially reclining sat by your side leaning my chin in my hands,
Passing sweet hours, immortal and mystic hours with you dearest comrade —not a tear, not a word,
Vigil of silence, love and death, vigil for you my son and my soldier.[1]

Most of the youths, lying for weeks in the hospital, were friendless, poor, far from home. The feeling of loneliness, together with the peculiar general misery permeating a hospital, profoundly depressed them. Surgeons, nurses particularly, did their duty, many with great devotion and even heroism. But the number of victims increased, the service was bound to become routine, indifferent, even cold. "Oh, I wish that you, or rather women having the same qualities as you and Mat" [his sister], he wrote to his mother— "were here in crowds to be placed as matrons before the unhappy soldiers sick and wounded. Your presence alone would be enough. Oh, what good that would do." And again: "Mothers full of maternal love, however untrained

---
[1] *Leaves of Grass*, p. 238.

they might be, but carrying with them the memory of the home and the magnetic touch of hand, are the true nurses."[1] And something in the character of Walt fitted him for this healing power; with his obtrusive masculinity he had for them a reserve of latent femininity and the tenderness of a good mother. He was himself like the good odour of home to young boys, eager for soothing love. None would have known as he did how to unlock closed hearts, how to make them open at the caress of his hand and his voice. He was the mother to the sick youth, as well as the comrade, with a world of tenderness for the young Americans stricken by sickness and wounds.

It is during these years that he truly won this magnificent title, at the head of one of his poems (its aureole to remain forever about his name)—Wound Dresser—of wounds spiritual as well as physical.

Returning, resuming, I thread my way through the hospitals,
The hurt and wounded I pacify with soothing hand,
I sit by the restless all the dark night, some are so young,
Some suffer so much, I recall the experience sweet and sad,
(Many a soldier's loving arms about this neck have cross'd and rested,
Many a soldier's kiss dwells on these bearded lips).[2]

---

[1] *The Wound Dresser*, p. 42.
[2] *Leaves of Grass*, pp. 243-4.

XIII

THE WOUND

IN PRACTISING this priesthood of humanity Walt belonged absolutely to no one. He was called "his own missionary." To work in complete independence apart from paid employes, simply to prove himself a man well disposed and affectionate among the sick men to whom he gave his overflowing strength was the whole secret of his mission. He was thus alone, left to the suggestion of his instinct and to his own resources.

Since the first weeks of his arrival in Washington he had to organize a little his material life, to find some modest income for himself and his dear wounded. Toward the close of 1863 a friend came to visit him, in a poor bare little room, the cheapest he could find, in the third story of an old building; it was literally a garret, containing scarcely any furniture but a bed, a deal table, and a little sheet-iron stove. "I found him preparing his luncheon . . . cutting bread with a pocket knife preparing to toast it; all his utensils were of the simplest."[1]

He was lucky in meeting, as soon as he reached the capital, a friend whose acquaintance he had made in Boston two years and a half before. And such a friend! The most generous heart, the noblest, the completest which fate could throw in his way. . . . It was Douglas O'Connor, who left his city and his profession for a position in the Lighthouse Bureau. He and his wife welcomed Walt as one of their own children—though old, he was always a big child; and for six months he not only had his place at their table, but he had all the little attentions which his mother and his sister were

[1] J. T. Trowbridge: *Reminiscences of Walt Whitman*, Atlantic Monthly, November 2, 1902, p. 163.

wont to give him in Brooklyn. Walt found in the O'Connor home hearts of his own calibre; never did he leave the house without a promise to return; and he was soon to find in O'Connor his most ardent champion. Major Hapgood procured him work in the office of military paymaster. He kept accounts for a few hours every day, and received enough pay for his daily needs. Occasionally he sent to New York and Brooklyn newspapers hospital notes and was liberally paid for them. Long afterward, when he collected his *Notes of the War*, he utilized these letters some of which, very long, are living pictures, where the lamentable army of victims are seen in their misery and their multiple suffering.[1]

He did what he could himself, out of his scant means to supply his numerous little presents to the wounded; he had scruples about making outside appeal, even for such a purpose. For a long time he thought of giving lectures throughout the country to collect money needed for the sick. Once in February, 1863, he wrote to a faithful friend in Boston, James Redpath, that a little money would be a great help for his work, and his friend responded to the appeal. Mr. Redpath, with Walt's touching letter, sought the help of Emerson, who had rich and generous friends, and Emerson himself was wholeheartedly in favour of the work of his friend Whitman. Little by little good souls, men and women interested in his work, sent him subscriptions as well as confidence, relying on him entirely to distribute the money wisely to the soldiers. Then he could distribute oranges, cakes, cream, pieces of silver—this with great devotion. The desolating impotence of the first days was over.[2]

In October, 1863, he returned to Brooklyn for a month. John Hay, who was a friend of O'Connor, procured him a pass.[3] Then he came back to his post a few days before he

---

[1] Three of these articles have been reprinted by Bucke with the title *The Wound Dresser*, a collection of letters of Whitman to his mother during the war.

[2] *Complete Prose*, p. 51.

[3] Bliss Perry: *Walt Whitman*, pp. 141–142.

received news of the death of his brother Andrew. His mother was very lonely but the hospitals were now part of his life. He would not quit the wards full of pale youths except to help in the landing of new boatloads of wounded, hurried from the battle-fields, or perhaps for a brief sojourn to the army among the tent-hospitals of the camp, where distress was still more frightful.

In a hospital at Armory Square, close to the wharf, where were crowded those unable to be carried farther—the worst cases—was his most arduous labour. Walt was himself astonished at his extraordinary self-possession so close to unnamable horrors. It was when outside the hospital in his room or out walking, that he thought of the bloody scenes; when he was near some poor devil whose flesh was eaten by corruption, he would feel a sudden convulsion pull at his heart and tremble from head to foot.[1] Or perhaps pierced by an emotion which brought him to tears, he would take from his pocket a notebook, pencil a few lines: the embryo of a future poem.[2] The astonishing quietude of his nature served him marvellously in these circumstances; he could control his emotion and assist with the exterior impassiveness of a man of science at all the sights of the hospital. The smiling face, the sweet humour in the presence of the sick concealed a soul in grief. He writes to his old mother: "How miserable appear all the petty pride and vanity of this world in the midst of scenes like this—these tragedies of soul and body. To see such things and not to be able to prevent them is terrible. I am almost ashamed to be so well and free from all sickness." In seeing so many innocent victims, thousands of men and boys formed for a splendid and fecund life mowed down, he experienced the colossal horror of the war, though he recognized proudly the need successfully to finish the struggle in which the destiny of the country was at stake. He himself would enlist un-

---
[1] *The Wound Dresser*, pp. 123–124.
[2] Bucke: *Walt Whitman*, p. 171.

hesitatingly if his presence was more needed in the ranks than in the hospitals.

With all his absorbing care of the sick, his increasingly awakened curiosity would not allow him to neglect a study of the aspects of Washington in war time, and all the details of the life of the soldier, on the march in camp, at rest, receiving pay, or in the aftermath of battles. He looked not only at the slow, interminable procession through the streets of ambulances carrying the wounded to the hospitals, at the dreary squads of captured deserters, but when a regiment marching to the front halted in the street, he mingled with the men, listened, asked questions. The vigorous beauty of the native Americans, from field and factory, was to him a continual subject of wonder. Were they not the justification of that enthusiastic faith in America which he had expressed in his poems? His emotional and impulsive nature, sensitive to the electric thrill of the crowd, responded intensely to the starry banner, Yankee Doodle, the rhythmic tread of a regiment of cavalry, all the trumpets, drums, cymbals, the march of an armed regiment. He was seized with the same emotion as the man in the street. He had never experienced the like before. He was stirred most by the manœuvring ground. The special reality of troops in the field, with tragic suggestion they roused after battle, in which sixty thousand men were left on the ground, gave to these frequent shows a terrible beauty which penetrated his very heart.

With an attentive ear he listened to the reports of battles from the sick and convalescent who had fought in them; their story of the skirmishes, the action, the battle-field, details of which the daily papers, with their colourless and free summary, said nothing. Thus he penetrated these innermost aspects of the reality of the war, learned history at its very sources, the history which never gets into books. One day he visited a camp of black troops and noticed how fine they looked. *Some War Memoranda* published later abound

THE WOUND

in impressionistic vignettes of the life of the soldier in the field —such as the astonishing picture of the wounded on a moonlight night—part of the battle of Chancellorsville.[1] He used to go to the Capitol during stormy sessions rejoicing in the sumptuous building and noting the mediocre orators. He loved to stride through the empty corridors or to see the sun set on the Genius of Liberty crowning the structure. But all of these were but crumbs of his life at that time; his work in the hospitals kept him by the power of fate. Early in 1864, evoking the coming years, he saw no other prospect than to be consecrated to the sick and wounded so long as they needed him.

The call was heard: he obeyed.

It was the spring of the year 1864 that the terrible battles of the Desert and of Spottsylvania took place. The crowd of wounded brought into Washington was enormous. In May the appalling flood still kept growing. The greater part of the newcomers remained long in the army uncared for; their wounds, hastily dressed or not at all, were inflamed and putrid from exposure. Quick amputations were in progress. Many lost their minds. Since the war began the hospitals had not offered such a horrible sight. Walt redoubled his work in the effort to be equal to the superhuman task. The result was that at the end of May he fell ill. This time human endurance reached its limit, the worst was come. He braced himself to the task; he neither could nor would leave his wounded at this critical moment. But he soon had to yield and to remain for days from the hospitals sending someone else in his place. The good giant was wounded for the first time in his life and for life.

He did not lack warning, but his faith in his own strength was boundless and his health was proof against everything. The summer preceding he suffered from dizziness, deafness, sore throat. Several times the doctor told him to refrain from this too-constant contact with the poisoned air of the

---
[1] *Complete Prose*, pp. 28–30.

wards. He, however, so sure of his phenomenal health, paid no attention, entirely absorbed in his duty.

Added to all this, in the height of the summer while assisting at an amputation of a gangrenous limb, he gashed his right hand; it happened with one of the "special cases"—a Rebel. The inflammation reached the arm, which began to swell. It healed rapidly and he gave little attention to the trifling accident which one day was to be of grave consequence. He wrote as usual to his mother of his perfect health, his weight, his appearance. But at the beginning of June, 1864, as a result of his enormous labour in the crowded hospitals, and of the extreme heat, the symptoms of the preceding summer reappeared, but with quickened strength. "It is probable," he wrote his mother, "that the poison of the hospital has affected my system and I see it is more than I supposed. Some days I believe I am better, and I feel revived, but, some hours after, I have a new attack."[1] He did not get better.

He had too long absorbed the poison from wounds and at last the corruption reached him. More than malaria, the repeated shocks and anguish of these frightful years, the torture of his loving heart before the hecatombs, the perpetual effort to preserve his self-possession in the presence of the suffering and the dying, the enormous strength expended in heartening the distressed boys ended in sapping his athletic constitution. He had suffered too much in seeing suffering; his was moral illness as well as physical. And after having lifted so many of the prostrate, he himself was prostrated.

The doctors ordered an immediate change of air and in July he left for Brooklyn, where he intended to remain the weeks needed to recuperate. He had to remain six months. He had been heroic and loving; now he was exposed to peril; his physical perfection was at stake—one day or another, if not to-day, surely later—the heavy ransom of the lives

---

[1] *The Wound Dresser*, p. 197.

he saved—he, so proud of his vigour and his untouched vitality, he who knew no illness, and who by these terrible years, at the age of forty-six, at the very climax of his power, was transformed at one stroke into an old man. A respite in Brooklyn and New York gave him new aplomb and he returned to Washington. Nevertheless, something remained, some unknown fatal germ which, slyly hiding, would one day smite him. The war marked him, also, as one of its victims.

XIV

THE COMRADE HEART

To any one dying, thither I speed and twist the knob of the door,
Turn the bed-clothes toward the foot of the bed,
Let the physician and the priest go home.

I seize the descending man and raise him with resistless will,
O despairer, here is my neck,
By God, you shall not go down! hang your whole weight upon me.

I dilate you with tremendous breath, I buoy you up,
Every room of the house do I fill with an arm'd force,
Lovers of me, bafflers of graves.[1]

HAD he not justified, in the course of these years, this proud affirmation of his poem? By the power of his tenderness and his personal magnetism he many a time had saved lives pledged to the grave. He had offered his neck to the weak, and spent his resistless will like the Walt Whitman who sang himself in *Leaves of Grass*. He had accomplished work forbidden to the doctor and the priest.

This mission of Walt in the hospital represents the time when "the mysterious bodily quality,"[2] which always won him the silent homage of glances in the street and untold sympathy, reached its highest power. It was then that his magnetism radiated with an intensity commensurate with the suffering everywhere visible. It would be difficult to suggest the effect of the presence of the man on the wounded if eye-witnesses had not pictured it for us: we know that his very presence was powerful enough to change the at-

---
[1] *Leaves of Grass*, p. 66.
[2] John Burroughs: *Notes*, pp. 13-14.

THE COMRADE HEART

mosphere of an entire ward. He was rich with the whole of humanity which he had already absorbed. His giant individuality operated as a tonic. He was more than a medicine to the prostrated boys. In some cases where science was impotent the doctors would say: "Turn him over to Whitman. Perhaps he will save him."[1]

Walt never boasted of the immense service he rendered. Yet his labour, when it is considered, staggers the imagination. He estimated that he individually visited from eighty to a hundred thousand wounded and ill; as for the number of lives saved, that remains the secret of love. Close friends who every day saw him pass or went with him alone knew the truth aside from the attendants of the hospitals. O'Connor recalls a picture of him unforgettably beautiful when on a midnight visit to his home. He came to ask for supper, his coat on his arm, his cuffs turned up, shod in great regiment slippers, very straight and tall, appearance rude and majestic; he was returning from a convoy of wounded. O'Connor later, in flaming words, charged America to remember what this simple man, without other reason than his heart, had done for her sons.[2] And Bucke inscribed this homage in his book: "Those who joined the ranks and fought the battles of the Republic did well; but when the world knows, as it begins to-day to know it, of the way this man—with no encouragement, without the least obligation, with simplicity, without drum-beating nor any approving voices—went into these immense lazar-houses, and consecrated his days and nights, his heart and his soul, and finally his health and his life to the sick and wounded sons of America, it will say that he did better."[3]

Great was the spiritual effort of the Wound Dresser in this persistent task. Great also was the moral effect which these years produced in him. He left the hospitals with the deep

---
[1] *Camden Edition, Introduction*, p. lxi.
[2] W. O'Connor: *The Good Gray Poet* in Bucke's *Walt Whitman*, pp. 123–128.
[3] *The Wound Dresser*, pp. 199–200.

conviction of having lived sacred moments which no word was able to convey; this is why he loved to keep silent about his experience. "Those three years I consider the greatest privilege and satisfaction (with all their feverish excitement and physical deprivations and lamentable sights), and, of course, the most profound lesson of my life. . . . It aroused and brought out and decided undreamed-of depth of emotion in me."[1] The emotion was so intense and prolonged it broke him at last.

This mission always remained to him of a character quasi-religious, so much was it a fervour. He was bound to the victims of the war by an unspeakable union. His great mother-like heart bled for the sons of his race, sacrificed in full force, for all the robust boys, from field and shop, "intelligent, independent, tender in feeling, accustomed to a life free and healthful." He believed that men never loved one another as he and some of the poor wounded boys, dying and loving one another. In his confession to his mother and to his friend, Mrs. Price, he speaks of the profound tenderness of the young soldiers, how marvellously they respond to affection.[2] Many a time the holy mystery of suffering and love was for him so rich that he could well say that he received more than he gave in that exchange of tenderness. One of the few times he broke silence on this subject, so intimate and moving, was in the presence of his friend Sidney Morse, the sculptor who made a bust of the poet toward the close of his life. He said:

> The most precious time of my life, my love for my mother and my love for those dear boys, Secessionists and Unionists. . . . It seemed to me, during all this time, that I was not far away caring for strangers but absolutely at home with my own flesh and blood. . . . I do not know why I speak of this but I want to show you the little note books with blood spots. . . .[3]

---

[1] *Complete Prose*, p. 72.
[2] Both letters are in *The Wound Dresser*, pp. 128-129.
[3] Bucke: *In Re Walt Whitman*, p. 391.

Oh, the little notebooks made of leaves folded and fastened with a pin, the dozen little notebooks, yellow, blotched with blood, filled with notes at the bedside of patients, watching the dead, or at the clinic, the notebooks where the comrade wrote the name, cases, wants of the invalid, accounts from the field of battle from the mouth of the wounded, and which he tenderly kept—for himself alone, full as they were of memories impossible to be "said or sung."[1] They were like a tabernacle where a thousand sorrows were kept, a thousand tearing emotions, a thousand untranslatable secrets. A depth of human tenderness dwells in their pages.

Beyond this tragic and soothing experience, which stirred the depths of his being, unique lessons from the war came to Walt Whitman. Not only new songs jetted from him by this taking up arms for the great cause of the Union, but in all his later poetry, enriched by impressions and emotions, the reflection of the war was extended, of a war enlarged to the confines of the world and deepened by a spiritual meaning. He went so far as to say that, without the capital event of the years 1861-1865 and his hospital life, *Leaves of Grass* would not have existed. Although three editions appeared before the war, this apparent paradox is true. The poet meant to say that without the war his book would have remained unfinished and that it came, in unexpected and compulsory collaboration, to perfect the work begun, and to give it its plenary signification. One of the great results of the struggle is that it allowed him to confront his country and his race, to acquire the definitive consciousness of all the reality and the grandeur of the States, united by a stronger than the federal bond. "I never knew what young Americans were," he wrote, "till I had been in the hospitals."[2]

More than any other he was able to appreciate in the hospitals where "the marrow of the tragedy concentrated"[3]

---
[1] *Complete Prose*, p. 1.
[2] *The Wound Dresser*, p. 116.
[3] *Complete Prose*, p. 74.

the courage of the fighters, the native strength of the race, the character of the men. He was close to those from all the regions of the vast continent, from New England, from Virginia, from New York, and Pennsylvania and from the West, the volunteers from the centre and the Great Lakes. He communicated with his country entire represented by thousands of fallen youth. And the feeling of the unity of his land through the multiplicity of its types and territories seized him as if he had been transported to the top of a mountain from whence his look could encompass total America. "It may have been odd," he remarked when he saw troops filing by him at night, "but I never before so realized the majesty and reality of the American people *en masse*. It fell upon me like a great awe."[1] A great light came to him, he discovered "authentic America" as he loved to repeat. His aboriginal faith issued from this period of blood and of horror, tempered, justified, tenfold enlarged.

And the supreme lesson of this contact with America one and undivided was that he could verify the concrete reality of one of his ideas, perhaps the dearest of all his ideas, the one at all events which radiates with the most brilliancy about his work and his personality. Walt at the same time that he made proof of America made proof of comradeship. Rather, comradeship was the key to his gospel, such as he understood it; by the light of his communal instinct and such as certain periods of his life illustrate, it established itself as something immense and new, the highest and most essential of human emotions. In every soul he perceived the germ of deep and tender feeling which awakens at the contact of another soul, and this natural attraction, at once physical and moral, which draws man to man is according to him, at the base even of social solidarity, more real than bonds formed by interest and rewards. And the frontiers of a nation do not stop the flight of this pure manly emotion of

---
[1] *Complete Prose*, p. 43.

friendship, which after having penetrated the whole continent projects through the whole world its millions of threads, invisible, woven inextricable. Comradeship is the woof of a world democracy as well as American democracy. Walt knew this better than any one, this sentiment exquisite and strong. It entered into his life, surrounded by companions, and the most natural symbol of him is his arm about the neck of a friend. It was there in the hospitals, according to the happy expression of Triggs, that "he perceived the new chivalry arising, the chivalry of comradeship. He saw that love lay latent in all hearts, and that a practical comradeship already existed among men."[1]

An immense peace filled Walt now that he saw the triumph of his Idea. His great dream of Democrat and modern Apostle was not vain, since reality took pains to confirm it. He was right, and his book, which was himself, was also right; and that book would perhaps be right one day before the world as it was right for him.

He had also other lessons from the experiences of this short and sublime period. A daily witness of physical pain and agony, he passed in every sense the limits of life and death. If he had studied before the source and secret of life, he had now heaped observations on the mystery of death. He derived a great lesson, one he verified a thousand thousand times: death, in reality, is not surrounded by the terror which our imagination, filled with fantasies, conjures when we are close to it. And Walt would never forget it, as the second part of *Leaves of Grass* proves where he sings the divine peace of death without terror, death the other form of life, and sings with the serene certitude and even joy of a soul who knew it for a good neighbour and was untormented by the enigma of the beyond.

If the poet—without knowing it—carried within him a poison germ from all the wounded his fervent comrade soul

---

[1] O. L. Triggs: *Selections, Introduction*, p. xxxiii.

impelled him to bend over, he also went from the hospitals—and of that he was clearly conscious—with the blessed memory of these years of tenderness and of sorrow, as fruitful for him, the individual, as for the nation itself, renewed in its depths.

XV

HYMNS OF THE WAR AND OF LINCOLN

IN JANUARY, 1865, he again filled his post in Washington; his mission was not to be abandoned. The hospitals with their fascinating reality remained; and as long as they sheltered the sick of body and soul, Walt continued his visits. He gained, in his good Brooklyn, a new supply of vigour and felt himself strong as before. However, it was no longer "the same unconscious and perfect health," which had abounded in him up to this time; and he confessed that it was his first appearance in the character of a man not entirely well, but that would go over in due time.[1]

His material condition, on the other hand, was changed. His career was shaping itself to a new sudden turning, perhaps the most unexpected: Walt, the dreamer, Walt, the incorrigible "amateur," the follower of his own instinct, became a clerk in the service of the Government. He lacked then a few years of fifty, and the close care of the wounded had for a moment lulled his old passion for roving and change; more than that he had a fair income, and he saw, in a fixed monthly wage, the opportunity for more regular and more generous distribution in the hospitals. Thus it was with pleasure that some months after his return to Washington he received work in the Department of the Interior, in the Bureau of Indian Affairs.

Some friends, interested in his mission, found employment for the Wound Dresser. Before obtaining it, one of them, J. T. Trowbridge, had failed in an attempt in March, 1863, with the Secretary of the Treasury, S. P. Chase. Although

---

[1] Bliss Perry: *Walt Whitman*, pp. 152-153.

he had presented in favour of his protégé, a letter of recommendation from Emerson, Chase would not admit the author of *Leaves of Grass* as one of his assistants.[1] The Secretary of the Interior this time did not have the same scruples as his colleague of the Treasury; perhaps he was ignorant of the poetic personality of his employe. But no matter, Walt was provided for. He received honourable pay for work but little absorbing. Never had he earned so much money— except perhaps at the time when his building enterprise put him for a moment on the road to fortune, which he was careful to put from him with prudent haste.

This money allowed liberality without changing anything in his manner of living. He remained at his desk during the day and devoted his Sundays and sometimes his evenings to the wounded. They remained his steady preoccupation. The war was not finished; and even after the victory and the disbanding of the armies, there was ample work still in the hospitals. The final battles, March, April, before Richmond, were sanguinary ones and the last victims had to lie for months awaiting almost hopeless recovery. Walt did not forget these sufferers; they were still its victims. Every Sunday he loaded and shouldered his haversack and journeyed to these who needed the strength of him. All the year 1865 and a great part of 1866 he continued his Sunday visits. Burroughs who sometimes went with him writes: "Words are poor and feeble things in an affair of this kind. . . . His magnetism was unbelievable and inexhaustible. Dim eyes became bright at his approach. . . . A fortifying air filled the ward and neutralized its bad odours.[2] One after another of the hospitals closed; soon there was but one, Harewood Hospital, secluded in a wood northeast of the city, last resort of the incurably wounded, those obstinately ill, and the unfortunate without house or home. Four or five wards were still full of their sad occupants; and Walt kept on,

---

[1] J. T. Trowbridge: *Reminiscences of Walt Whitman*. Atlantic Monthly, February, 1902, p. 163.
[2] John Burroughs: *Notes*, pp. 12-13.

HYMNS OF THE WAR AND OF LINCOLN

trying "if he could do something" for these veterans of sorrow. This was seen when years later, passing their immense army in review for the last time, he addressed to all the dead in the war the solemn adieu of one who ever kept their memory sacred.[1]

At the very moment when the struggle was near its end, he was preparing to unveil the monument more enduring still, which he had built in secret for them. During the years of feverish commotion all poetry apparently disappeared in the gulf that yawned at the nation's feet: but from this very gulf it had arisen, and in the soul of the Wound Dresser, steeped in profound emotions, new poems burst forth. His book was not swallowed up in the storm; it had silently grown a story.

In the first days of the war the shock which he suffered on seeing his city and America take arms was translated into flaming odes which seemed penetrated with the holy fire of the Prophets. Under the daily inspiration of the enrollment *en masse*, of telegrams read aloud of the passing of troops through the streets of New York, he wrote the larger part of his *Drum Taps*. He left the manuscript at home when he went to care for his brother George. Bye and bye, his personal experience in the hospitals and camp, the tragedies he had seen, the unspeakable emotion experienced among the wounded, gave birth to other poems in feeling still more intense. The collection took shape toward the end of 1863. When he was spending a month in Brooklyn with his mother, in November of the same year, he wrote to his friend Eldridge: "I must be continually bringing out poems—now is the hey day—I shall range along the high plateau of my life and capacity for a few years now, and then swiftly descend."[2] On his return to Washington, one day a friend came and found him in his garret; he took the manuscript from his trunk and read fragments of it with strength and feeling and

---

[1] *The Million Dead, Too, Summed Up. Complete Prose*, p. 72.
[2] Bliss Perry: *Walt Whitman*, p. 143.

with a voice of rich but not resounding tone.[1] He revised the poems the following year and put the finishing touch to them during the six months' enforced vacation in Brooklyn. Now the volume was ready and he intended to "move Heaven and earth" to have it appear.[2] It was the old, old difficulty. The Boston publishers, when pressed, refused to be responsible for *Drum Taps*. Now that Walt had employment and a salary, he could resort to his favourite method. He was his own publisher, as he had been and would be. For years he had worked as a printer, he thoroughly knew the business, and he kept in touch with the pressmen of New York. It was there he gave his manuscript to be printed early in 1865.

The book was ready at the beginning of April. The poet happened to be in Brooklyn, came perhaps to revise the last proofs, when a fresh thunderbolt shook the country: Abraham Lincoln was assassinated! In the existing circumstances, after the surrender of Lee, the war scarcely over, such an event could but stupify and crush the whole nation prostrate before him in whom was incarnated the cause of the Union in the period of suffering, the greatest citizen and the greatest president. Walt was struck to the heart. "We heard the news very early in the morning," he wrote in *Specimen Days*, "Mother was getting breakfast, and the other meals later, as usual; but the whole day not one of us ate a single mouthful. We each drank a half cup of coffee; that was all. We spoke little. We bought all the morning and evening papers and then a number of special editions, and we passed them silently one to another.[3]

Lincoln had more than Whitman's deep love. He had studied him at close range, and the one-time raftsman from the West who, with a firm and prudent hand, had guided the Union during the tempestuous years, was in his eyes the

---

[1] J. T. Trowbridge: *Reminiscences of Walt Whitman*, Atlantic Monthly, February, 1902, p. 163.
[2] Bliss Perry: *Walt Whitman*, p. 149.
[3] *Complete Prose*, p. 20.

highest type of democracy. He was a man and a type after his own heart who justified his faith and his philosophy. The first time that he saw him was in Brooklyn, in February, 1861, the day when the new president made that singular entrance into New York, the event Whitman describes with the hand of a master. From the top of an omnibus blocked by the crowd, Walt leisurely studied and noted "his look and gait—his perfect composure and coolness—his unusual and uncouth height, his dress of complete black, stove pipe hat pushed back on his head, his dark brown complexion, seamed and wrinkled yet canny-looking face, black curly head of hair, disproportionately long neck, and his hands held behind as he stood observing the people."[1] He saw Lincoln again in Washington, where he became to him a familiar figure. In the streets he often met the President's carriage and in summer every evening, on his way to his lodging out of town, he passed by Walt's home. Sometimes Walt mingled with the enormous and picturesque crowd which on reception days besieged the White House. And he did not fail to see the canny shrewdness of that face, even the plainness with the "deep latent sadness"[2] which the vast responsibilities of the times had imprinted there but where the "old goodness and tenderness"[3] remained. The face of Lincoln exercised on the great reader of souls a powerful attraction: beneath the deep-cut lines he saw a "subtle and indirect expression"[4] which no portrait could reproduce. That "something else" was surely the personality of this man, extraordinary and at the same time common; and the poet of personality sought to decipher its puzzle. Later he became intimate with John Hay, the future Secretary of State, then private secretary to Lincoln. Walt knew in a confidential way some aspects of the real man.

---

[1] *Complete Prose*, p. 303.
[2] *Id.*, p. 37.
[3] *Id.*, p. 57.
[4] *Id.*, p. 38.

The poet and the President because they frequently met came to bow and smile when they passed on the street. Perhaps there was something else in the greeting than the conventional courtesy on the President's part, and he mixed with it a certain sympathetic, almost conscious curiosity. Walt's imposing figure, which had become familiar to passersby on Pennsylvania Avenue, may also have intrigued him. Once in the winter of 1864, the President was talking near the window of the White House to a member of Congress and his friend; he held a letter in his hand ready to read, and, while reflecting, turned his glance toward the window. At that moment Walt was coming toward the White House on Pennsylvania Avenue, with his slow and balanced step, his big felt hat on, hands in front pockets of his overcoat, his head high, radiating that Olympian simplicity which always attracted passersby; the President wished to know who he was, and when he was told, said nothing but he followed the man with his eye insistently until he was out of sight. Then as if speaking to himself, Abraham Lincoln, with a peculiar tone and strongly emphasizing his words, made this remark: "Well, he looks like a *man*."[1] In the difficulties of every kind which came upon the Union and in spite of the reproach of dilatoriness and inertia which the ignorant and saloon politicians did not spare the President, Walt respected and trusted him. The country, by the enthusiastic reëlection of Lincoln in 1864, gave him ground for this trust. And it was this man who was stupidly murdered by a madman in the midst of the boundless joy which hailed the victory of the Union. . . . The memory of the hour of grief would never leave the heart of the poet, which bled with all, more than all. With the years, his fervent admiration for the "mighty Westerner"[2] came to be a kind of religion. In his old age, when April 14th returned with the perfume of the lilacs, he did not fail, on every occasion possible, to

---
[1] John Burroughs: *Notes*, p. 122.
[2] *Complete Prose*, p. 436.

renew publicly his solemn commemoration of Abraham Lincoln.

Before that death, Walt laid aside his nearly completed volume. There was a gap in his book now, the enormous gap of that freshly made grave. His *Drum Taps* would not be brought out thus: the sudden emotion with which fate had finished the war must be expressed anew. And little by little it grew into the being of Walt in rhythmic accents of sorrow. To the dead hero he would consecrate a hymn. It then happened that the collection, supplemented by the last poems composed under the direct impression of the murder of April 14th, did not appear till two or three months later, that is, about the middle of 1865. The little volume of a hundred pages with its appendix (*Drum Taps* bearing the imprint: "New York, 1865" and the *Sequel to Drum Taps* that of "Washington, 1865-66," the two series bound together) did not display below its title the parental support of any publishing firm. It entered all alone into the world, having no name except the author's as a guarantee. We do not know exactly what welcome it received, but there is every reason to suppose the sale was very small and that the volume passed unnoticed. *Leaves of Grass* had raised a certain commotion because of its vast, open, insolent novelty: there was no such reason this time why *Drum Taps* should rouse the attention of the public.

It was nevertheless the same Walt who purposed that these new Songs should as the first ones issue from him in contact with reality. Just as before, at the Opera, listening to Alboni, or in the noise of Broadway, or the moan of the waves on the Long Island shore, his *Leaves* sprouted from him—it was viewing the proud pageants or the blood of the *real* war, not the imaginary, that he set the measures of his *Taps*. Perhaps if he had sung brilliant exploits of conquering generals in a dithyrambic and pompous manner dear to poets of patriotism he would have met approval from those in whom mediocrity is awakened by mediocrity. But these were poems of war which of all the world Walt could conceive. How wonderful, how strange, how authoritative they came from the heart of the Wound Dresser alternately transported and tortured. It was like an inner, emotional mystic epic of the war, in the two chief aspects—the extraordinary national uprising of the beginning, the boundless devotion to the cause of democracy—then the immense sacrifice of young lives which he who loved them so pathetically, celebrated with strains of passionate sadness. The poet put all his immense, heart-broken tenderness in the "psalm of the dead" honouring friend and foe, sacrificial offering to the cause. And what gives an incomparable significance to this book inspired of honour and love is the vision of final reconciliation which rises above the combatants.

My enemy is dead, a man divine as myself is dead,
I look where he lies white-faced and still in the coffin—I draw near,
Bend down and touch lightly with my lips the white face in the coffin.[1]

Then, mournful and splendid crown of these verses inspired by the war are the hymns to the memory of Lincoln—those deathless chants: *When Lilacs Last in the Door Yard Bloomed* and *O Captain, My Captain* which may be compared in power of emotion to Siegfried's funeral march in Nibelungenlied and which are sufficient one day to make Whitman recognized as the poet who sings the American nation, the Homer and Pindar of the United States. In *Drum Taps* the death of Lincoln appeared as an event, one with the war. The drama by this reached its epilogue in an emotion of consecrated terror and of superb fate. The poet incarnated, in unforgettable poetry, the sorrow of a people; he was the heart of America in tears, gathered at the grave of her great son.

Such was the poetical fruit which the war ripened in Walt Whitman. Later, when he reissues these poems, he can

---
[1] *Leaves of Grass*, p. 251. This poem was translated into Provençal by Charles Bonaparte Wyse. Tr.

annex them, then integrate them with his *Leaves;* they will make a new unit in the completion of the whole. The world may indeed disdain them; it is none the less true that he immortalized the purest and most intimate emotion of the Civil War and of all war.

XVI

O'CONNOR'S LASH

WHILE he was composing the glorious funeral hymn of Lincoln, Walt filled his place daily at his desk in the Department of the Interior. He rigidly performed his new duties and was even promoted in the department. For six months he had devoted the leisure of a calmer life to the wounded remaining in the hospitals, when the portfolio of the Interior passed into the hands of honourable James Harlan of Iowa. Lincoln had appointed him much against his will but finally yielded because of Harlan's Methodist support, a sect which had loyally supported the Government during the war. Harlan himself had been a Methodist clergyman, then lawyer, senator, and president of a college.[1]

One day a notice from Boston revealed to the new minister that one of his subordinates—the punctual and pacific employe with the white beard in the Bureau of Indian Affairs—was the author of a much-disputed book. Harlan to investigate the case betook himself one evening to Walt's desk and searched it, and, discovering a book covered with annotations in ink and coloured pencil which to him was suspicious, carried it away to examine it.[2] It was a copy of *Leaves of Grass* which Walt in his leisure moments was revising in view of a new edition. In the privacy of his office Harlan searched out the cause of the denunciations: the case was judged without the preliminary of a hearing. The morning after, the book was cleverly replaced in Walt's desk and he immediately notified that the department no longer needed

---

[1] *Complete Prose*, pp. 445-446.
[2] H. Traubel: *With Walt Whitman in Camden*, pp. 470-476.

his services. The Wound Dresser was shown the door without explanation.

The blow was sudden. Walt, astonished for a moment, received it with his customary philosophy. His stupefied and indignant friends protested. J. Hubley Ashton, who had a position with the Attorney General, went the following day to the Secretary of the Interior and demanded an explanation. O'Connor besought him to do this. Did Mr. Whitman neglect his duties or was he unable to fill them? No, he was a good employe, by the acknowledgment of the Secretary. The only reason for his dismissal was that he had written a book which he had discovered "by chance" in the department. Ashton, uselessly of course, tried to explain to the honourable inquisitor what *Leaves of Grass* was, its fundamental idea, etc. Harlan shook his head. And Ashton insisted. He knew Whitman thoroughly and he could testify what his life had been; he told of his splendid work in the hospitals, his immense service to the victims of the war. The Secretary listened without flinching. The friend pursued his plea; the worthy Secretary interrupted him; he would not keep in his department the author of *Leaves of Grass* not even if the President himself ordered it. He would rather abandon his portfolio than recall his decision. There was nothing more to do and Ashton bowed himself out.[1]

His friend did not stop there. Walt left the Department of the Interior on June 30th, and in July he received from the Attorney General, James Speed, employment equivalent to that which he left. It was the first rap for Harlan. In this miserable little conspiracy against Whitman, the real victim as we shall see was none other finally than the executer himself. It was the first of three public attacks to which the poet had to submit. If ever an adequate revenge was drawn from an insult, it was the one being now prepared. He who was most indignant at the ignorant and odious

---

[1]Bucke: *Walt Whitman*, pp. 41–42.

hypocrisy of the Secretary of the Interior was the generous friend, the noble and impetuous O'Connor, at whose home Walt passed the first months of his Washington life. Not only did he influence Hubley Ashton to intercede for the poet but he interpreted Harlan's procedure as a crime against the liberty of literature. This crime he would avenge. And in the flame of his wrath, the writer in him was roused. Two months after discharge appeared a pamphlet entitled *The Good Gray Poet: A Defense*. It was a name suited to his appearance which people on the streets of Washington probably had given him, on seeing him pass by.

O'Connor wonderfully directed his sling, and the honourable Harlan was to be marked forever. It is difficult to analyze the scintillating pages of this philippic: in verbal power, sinew, movement, flash of image, satiric verve, it is allied to the most colourful and the most eloquent pieces of French prose, from Courier to Hugo. It translates not only the limitless enthusiasm and the burning sincerity of an admirer, but the sure taste of an artist, absolute master of language. O'Connor proved in it, in choosing examples in literature of all ages and all races, with unusual erudition, that the great work of the past—the great Hindoo poems as well as Moses and Ezekiel, Shakespeare as well as Dante, Rabelais as well as Cervantes—contained some of what the Harlans objected to—a part without which they would not be complete. O'Connor thus made in the New World the eternal plea for the indefeasible law of literature. Then, widening the controversy, he pleaded the whole cause of the poet, disposed of all the blots laid upon him from the beginning and reduced them to nothing. To the royally human character of his friend he offered a brilliant public tribute in laying bare his character, in recounting his mission in the hospitals, in making known the big meaning of his work. O'Connor did not mince his words. He spoke imperative challenging terms, showing what sovereign spirit of purity had dictated the poem which had roused the anger of all the

Harlans. He flayed with a ferocious irony the disease of shame which corrupted rather than corrected morals. And the man and his work, thus exalted, justified, projected into full light, were put in the rank of absolute genius. He was not far from demanding for him, as compensation for the stupidity and outrage, the prytaneum as an honour to this other Socrates. ". . . The man who realized the sublime thing, an authentic book; who wrote to make his country greater, her citizens better, her race nobler; who has thrown into living verse a philosophy designed to exalt life to a higher level of sincerity, reality, religion."[1]

O'Connor, with all the eloquence, the audacity, and brilliant mind of the Celt inflicted upon Harlan the most appropriate chastisement. He conferred upon him the immortality of ridicule: the name of Harlan was now saved from oblivion. The good friend went to battle like a crusader. It was not the first time that the vehemence of his conviction and the ardour of his intransigeance made him the champion of an unpopular cause; as journalist in Boston, he was discharged for having sustained without restriction the anti-slavery cause. And, in defending Walt, he was not stopped for a moment by the thought that this conflict with the Secretary of the Interior might cause him serious trouble, being himself an employe of the Government. Not only he accomplished a magnificent task, but he left a work, beyond the occasion which called it forth, and which has a place in American literature, where it is, of its kind, without a parallel.

In completing his pages, O'Connor called the republic of letters to the defense of one of its insulted representatives. He was not content with this collective appeal, but sent his pamphlet to a number of men of letters in America and England, asking them by letter to rally to the cause of the poet.[2] The panegyric itself obtained slow recognition among the philistines; but, as an act of courage and justice is never

---
[1] W. D. O'Connor, *The Good Gray Poet*, in Bucke: *Walt Whitman*, pp. 124-125.
[2] Bliss Perry: *Walt Whitman*, p. 171.

lost, the plea had some effect on opinion, and in certain circles created a current in favour of the poet. Some writers who moderately admired *Leaves of Grass* were forced to admit that Harlan's act was ignominious and many people not interested in literature did not conceal their disapproval. O'Connor did not perform in vain his gallant exploit. Scornful of insults, he took up again a subject which he had taken to heart, in publishing the story in which the great figure of his friend appears encircled by the aureole of legend, like some pilgrim of eternity[1]—and which helps to interpret later the engraving of Herbert Gilchrist, an admirable portrait in which one does not forget, after having once studied it, the look bathed in tenderness and its unspeakable expression.[2] And eighteen years later, in a long open letter to Bucke he fought the old fight for his friend of former days, with the same freshness of enthusiasm.[3] Always the noble O'Connor was at Walt's side, through all time the figure of loyalty, ardent faith, and unreserved admiration. This philippic, whose words still vibrate as when first written, marked a famous date in the history of *Leaves of Grass*. It was the first lance broken in public in honour of Walt. Among the sanctions which he received up to that time none justified him so amply. This time a magnificent, clarion-like, haughty voice was lifted in his defense, an avenger armed with compelling words against long-enduring calumny. Since Emerson's letter, ten years before, nothing as comforting was offered him on his way. "Thrice blessed be his memory" Walt piously pronounced at the grave of O'Connor, remembering what he had been to him in the lonely, desolate days of his beginning.[4]

---

[1] W. D. O'Connor, *The Carpenter*, Putnam, N. Y., January, 1865.
[2] Bucke: *Walt Whitman* (frontispiece).
[3] *Id.*: pp. 73-79.
[4] *Complete Prose*, p. 513. Tr.

PART FIVE
THE GOOD GRAY POET
WASHINGTON (1865-1873)

XVII

THE GREAT COMPANIONS; PETER DOYLE, THE CONDUCTOR

THE little tempest was over; Walt was now approaching a serene period of life. At his new post in the Department of Justice, the Good Gray Poet remained seven or eight happy years; he is left to the joyous absorption of life and of things as before in New York, but with the fulness of his fiftieth year approaching. No outward event marks these equable quiet years, following the enormous expense of strength which his work in the war had demanded, unless it was the slow but decisive forward advance of his book. Fate allowed him this interval that he might plentifully enjoy the life he adored before the dread shattering of his health.

When he accepted his post, Walt did not give up his independence. He interpreted his duties as department employe somewhat as before he had his trade as a printer. Some hours of work at a desk left him free to be himself. Walt fell in admirably with his new life and even felt its charm. From a large office window of the department he enjoyed a fine landscape; he never tired of the view which stretched eight or ten miles toward the south, of the panorama of the river, the surrounding heights, the green of the gardens. He had great freedom in his work: he was on friendly terms with his chief, the Attorney General, and the Assistant Attorney Hubley Ashton was a comrade. With his colleagues, too, his relations were pleasant. Walt in his way appreciated the comfort of his office; he who was used to garrets and the bareness of his own home often came in his free hours happy as a boy to find a good easy-chair, a fire, and a good light. On winter evenings especially he liked to come there to pass many hours in reading books in the office library.

The poet thus lived a relaxed, less crowded, less exuberant phase of his many-sided life. There was no fear, however, that he was static: in spite of his regular and prudent habits he remained always the impenitent Bohemian whom his friends knew to the last hour. Walt was too great not to remain himself, Walt the clerk the same as Walt the carpenter, or the printer. He remained the great lover of pavements that he was in New York, and on the avenues of Washington the passersby knew well his rolling and nonchalant gait and his big hat. Never were the ampleness of his figure, his massiveness, and his manner more attractive. His florid face seamed by life, his flowing hair and fleecy beard; the man near fifty was stamped with a new majesty which we see in his portraits.[1] The unobtrusive authority of his least gesture, his natural dignity of manner, the "simple power," the easy assurance of his step, suggested the idea of a Commencer of an Adamic, as Burroughs says. Morning and evening it was easy to distinguish him, on Pennsylvania Avenue or in the Capitol, head high, throat bare, hands often in the front pockets of his coat, casting his absorbing glance at the crowd, stopping, listening, chatting a bit with policemen, pedlars, porters, drivers, slipping an alms into the hand of a cripple or smiling at a child. Walt travelled his kingdom and counted its marvels every day.

Walt knew at this time elect companions, whose strong and generous friendship contributed much to the happiness of these years. Without them, now that his fascinating hospital mission was done, these years would have been monotonous: Washington, a nest of office-holders and functionaries, was not at all like New York, and was more or less an exile for Whitman, deprived of the pageant, the odour,

---

[1] H. B. Binns: *Life of Walt Whitman*, p. 227.

the contact of the sea near which he was born and reared. They were three government employes, like himself: O'Connor, whom we know; Charles W. Eldridge, former publisher of *Leaves of Grass*, with whom side by side Walt had worked during the war in the Treasurer's office; and John Burroughs, who was employed in Finance. Burroughs who came to have a considerable share in Whitman's life, before becoming himself a famous writer, was a farmer's son whose preoccupations drew him early toward literature. He was strongly influenced by Emerson, and published, very young, in a Boston review an unsigned essay which was easily attributed to the master: later he had been a school teacher and a journalist. When the war was in full swing, he came to Washington, without a definite aim, thinking perhaps to enlist: and a little later he entered the Finance office. *Leaves of Grass*, which he read by chance, a little after the edition of 1860, produced upon him an extraordinary impression, such as he received from no other book. From that time on, the young man never failed, every Sunday, to carry with him in his solitary walks the strange volume. He was compelled to penetrate its full meaning, which grew vaster with every fresh reading. One of his first thoughts, on arriving at Washington, was to seek the acquaintance of the poet. And from the day when he met him making his way through the wood to one of the hospitals, his haversack on his shoulder, they became intimate companions.[1]

There were also Hubley Ashton, Trowbridge, E. C. Stedman: these were congenial spirits. The hospitable O'Connor house was the usual meeting place of the group. Walt, when he was not going to the hospitals (which he visited till the spring of 1867 and where, the Christmas of 1866, he gave a fine dinner to the last of the wounded soldiers),[2] often came there to pass Sunday afternoon, after he

---

[1] John Burroughs: *Notes*, pp. 9-13.
[2] *Camden Edition*, VIII, p. 193.

had breakfasted with the Burroughs family,[1] where he regularly arrived late. These choice spirits discussed among themselves political events, the books, the personalities of the day, and sometimes hot discussions arose. O'Connor proved himself a marvellous talker, and it was his flaming words which especially enlivened these conversations: like a true Celt, he adored controversy and indulged his delight of battle. Between Walt and himself there were sometimes Homeric word tourneys, in which Walt, led in spite of himself by this fever of eloquence, threw off his habitual reserve to swell the loud concert: for the two men, despite their affectionate harmony, differed strongly on certain points. On the question of slavery, notably, O'Connor was intractable. When in the height of the war, the Wound Dresser returning from the hospitals, death in his soul, letting escape from the depth of his bruised heart this exclamation: "This war must end!" O'Connor, leaping up, would cry: "As long as slavery lasts, the war must go on."[2] Walt made a mistake in surrendering his Dutch placidity and in not leaving his friend to his own fury, for one day a bad turn came. The two friends were discussing the question of suffrage rights for the blacks, which was then being agitated in the Senate; O'Connor defended ardently the principle of obligatory emancipation, his hobby. Walt who, in real clairvoyance, was not the dupe of theory and was not ignorant what "unchained brutes" the blacks admitted to citizenship would show themselves, wanted them gradually enfranchised That was not democracy: it could only be based upon conscious and worthy individuals. At a certain moment, the intractable O'Connor was furious, and Walt answered him violently—violence was very rare with him, but all the more terrible. They might resort to their fists, but this time they were too far apart. They parted in a quarrel. It was in

---

[1] *Camden Edition*, VIII, p. 220.
[2] Kennedy: *Reminiscences of Walt Whitman*, pp. 34-35.

vain that their friends tried to reconcile the two men.[1] This happened in 1871.[2] During these years, they kept apart till the day when everything was forgotten and when an affection was reborn as fervent as before. Walt had had the intuition, from the first moment of their meeting in Boston, that some day the rabid doctrinarianism of his friend would separate them.[3]

However intense and confiding they were, these friendships were nevertheless insufficient to fill the entire need of tenderness which, far from weakening, was rather intensified in Walt's heart now that he was far from his city, far from his family, far from his old comrades. He was irresistibly drawn to primitive and tender people, ignorant of literature, unmindful of the high problems which fire men like O'Connor: he found in them people of his own type, and in the delight of proving himself one of them experienced in their company pure, peaceful joy. It was surely when with them that he passed the most delicious moments—arm in arm with some friend, who was ignorant of his authorship of *Leaves of Grass*, or at least cared nothing about it, he proved the intimacy of companionship. In his many years in Washington he became familiar with its streets and its people. He renewed especially the old camaraderie of former years with omnibus drivers and conductors. John Burroughs, who lived then in daily intimacy with him, has left a vivid little picture of the poet, photographed in his favourite place, on the platform, near the conductor of whom we are to speak:

. . . . A bearded, florid-faced man, elderly but agile, resting against the dash, by the side of the young conductor. . . . The man wears a broad brim hat. . . . A strong, fat, fretful babe of fifteen months is worrying its mother in the crowded car: the white-hatted man reaches inside and takes the babe from the mother out in the air . . . in less than a minute it is sound asleep and the conductor gets off for his first meal . . .

---

[1] H. B. Binns: *Life of Walt Whitman*, p. 236.
[2] Ellen Calder: *Personal Recollections of Walt Whitman*, Atlantic Monthly, June, 1907.
[3] *Complete Prose*, p. 512.

and now the white-hatted man, holding the slumbering child, also acts as conductor the rest of the distance. He makes a good conductor, too, pulling the bell to stop or go on as needed.[1]

When he spent his vacation in New York Walt did not forget his friends of the line. One of them especially, the very one who figures in the account now to be given, filled in his heart and his life a place so exceptional that it must be mentioned by itself. One evening in 1865, Walt, returning from Burroughs's house, entered a Pennsylvania Avenue omnibus, and as the weather was bad he took a seat inside; a great cloak thrown over his shoulder gave him the appearance of an old sea wolf. He was the only passenger at that late hour and in such weather. After a time, the young fellow, who was keeping his melancholy place on the platform, entered without knowing why, drawn by a secret sympathy for the bearded man, and they joined in conversation. From the first there was mutual attraction and in a quarter of an hour they were talking as familiarly as two friends. Walt, instead of getting out at the end of the trip, continued the whole way and back again with his friend.[2] The conductor, Peter Doyle, was a young Irishman of nineteen, a blacksmith's son, whose parents had emigrated to Virginia when he was a baby. At the outbreak of war he enlisted in the Southern ranks, and took part in the fighting. He was wounded and made prisoner: after leaving the hospital, he found this work as conductor. He was alone in life.

From that evening they became inseparable companions. Doyle, when his work was done, would wait for the poet at his office, and they went together for long walks in the suburbs of Washington, happy release after the motionless, confining hours in the department. The two simple fellows were real adventurers when following the banks of the Potomac or one of the great highways encircling the capital, walking six to twelve miles and back again. Walt was a

[1] John Burroughs: *Birds and Poets*, p. 224.
[2] *Calamus*, p. 23.

tireless walker and wore out the legs of his young friend. All along the road he sang, whistled, recited from Shakespeare, shouted in passing through the woods, like a boy expanding all his young soul. He named the constellations for the young man and when he spoke of the stars his voice became eloquent and grave. Sometimes other friends were of the party. The poet thus enjoyed the happiest hours of all and, to his last day, he preserved the keen memory of these delicious, aimless strolls in the evening by moonlight, or on fair Sundays. They were happy years from 1866 to 1872. The road, the open air, the comrades, no joy of life was comparable to this, when one has, like Walt, a heart athirst for nature, tenderness, and freedom. The sadness was not to be able to live forever and ever, anywhere, in the fields or on the shore, with the half dozen truly dear friends gathered in the course of life, loved because they have given you what is most precious. When Walt was free, and the little Irishman was at work, he mounted the omnibus and made many trips on the platform beside him. In the evening, he waited till the conductor had "swept," when they would go together and sit in a café on Washington Avenue. Sometimes the young man, worn by work, fell asleep at the table while the older one was talking; then Walt, respecting the sleep of youth, stayed there without saying a word to awake him till the place was ready to close.[1] The poet, a lover of music, used to take his "boy" to the navy concert, and it was always he who led him into some adventure; sometimes they went walking, bought a melon of a farmer's wife, and sat down in a doorway, in the open street, to enjoy it. Passersby glanced at them, and smiled at their appearance.

Walt wished to introduce his companion to the great business of his life, his poems, to explain what was his intention, his effort, his idea. Doyle listened without in the least understanding what he was driving at. With the patient tenderness of an older brother, the poet tried to

[1] *Calamus*, pp. 24–25.

awaken in the virgin mind the comprehension of things which is the theme of his book. He did not expect much in the way of result: he wanted but the unreserved affection of the youth. One day he made him a present of *Drum Taps* in manuscript, which Doyle, who had no idea of its value, mislaid.[1] When the conductor, out of work, found himself short of money,. Walt loaned him some freely. In time of weariness or discouragement, the word of the great older man, who might have been the father and who wished only to be the tender friend, used to comfort the young lad, forbade him to be cast down, preached to him contentment and good humour, indispensable weapons in the daily struggle, he said.

We are able to see the limitless affection which united two beings so dissimilar, thanks to the letters which Walt wrote, when he spent his annual vacation in New York, and later, after he had quitted Washington for good, to the young man whose absence was to him then a bereavement. These letters to his "dear little Peter, his darling son, his young and dear brother, his dear beloved comrade," breathe a purity, a constance, a large tenderness, in which the man appears more truly than in the most perfect analyses of his commentators. It is to this source we must go to discover the great heart of love of the Good Gray Poet. It is also there, as in the letters to his mother, written from Washington, during and after the war, that is revealed this soul of a little child, this soul divinely close to the simple ones, which he knew how to keep till his last day.

What makes the singular attraction of this open-hearted correspondence full of commonplaces, incorrect, free from the least suspicion of literature, is that it lets us see the positive and the concrete in the life of the poet, it translates the infinite candour which is the base of his character. It shows us another aspect of the man who wrote *Leaves of Grass*, not by the reverse of his genius, but the common soil

---

[1] *Calamus*, p. 30.

in which this genius had root. Walt was bound by all his fibres to average humanity, and he could not have come close to simple souls, except he proved himself one of them. It is indeed authentically he, the good rosy-cheeked giant, whom we hear in the tender and naïve prattle of his letters to Peter Doyle and to his old mother—these letters where he loved to gossip of the thousand nothings of his bachelor life, in which he speaks of his shirts and a new vest with as much seriousness as of a session of Congress; where he rejoices like a youngster at a gratuity given to employes which will allow him greater liberality to his family; where he celebrates in ecstatic terms the excellent coffee and the savory buckwheat cakes which his mother prepared for him for his morning meal. She is suffering from rheumatism in the wrist, as a result of household work, which she performed all her life; he begs her to find a woman to do the washing and the heavy work. The older the mother became—she was seventy at the close of the war—the more tender his solicitude toward her. He asks constantly news of his brother George, who speculated in building like his father, and who, luckier than he, was making money. He sends them or marks for them articles which appear about himself, announcement of his volumes, knowing that they will mean little, but thinking they may give them pleasure. . . . In this poor chatter, we feel, however, a grandeur, the human grandeur, of Walt Whitman: and finding him so ordinary, so mediocre, so commonplace, so far from all arrogance and all pretention, it seems to us that we grasp better the amplitude of his personality, and that we are better prepared to understand his extraordinary book. These letters, without art and so touching, create an astonishment which resolves into joy—joy of meeting a being ample enough to comprehend at once the appetites, the preoccupations, the content of the mass, and the most sublime transport which the human soul could commit to words. They must be read to know all the good nature, simple heartiness, ingenuous joy, concealed in the heart of a sovereign poet-prophet; in them we see the summits and likewise the intimacies of the valley.

Is it not strangely characteristic that the same man who wrote *Song of Myself* should write this letter among a hundred similar ones to an omnibus conductor?

Brooklyn, October, '68.

Dear Lewy,

 I wrote you but a few lines that you may know that I have not forgotten you. . . . Duffy is here conducting an omnibus on Broadway and Fifth Avenue. He is the same old Duffy. I hear that William Sydner is in bed sick. Tell Johnny Miller that there are still traces of the old Broadway drivers, Balky Bill, Fred Kelly, Charles McLaughlin, Tom Riley, Etc.

 The chief characteristic of Whitman's letters to the young Irishman is the confident tenderness which they breathe, the absence of all suggestion of superiority; Walt was Walt and he was the older, but in the interchange of affection they were equals. Never, through absence, trials, and old age, did their friendship fail, despite the long interval of their letters. And to all the more emphasize the exceptional place which Peter Doyle filled in his life, Walt inscribed his name twice in his prose works, in evoking their long, joyful walks and their pleasure parties.[1] Doyle on his part always kept after his friend departed a tender, lasting memory of the dear old man, of the "affectionate father and comrade," of the cordial and gentle giant, by whose side, arm in arm, he many times tramped the avenues and highways. In the sanctuary of his simple and faithful heart Walt continued to live, as in the old days. And on hearing Doyle speak of his Washington companion, the impression is that he was more intimately close to him than to any one.[2]

 This companionship of Peter Doyle and Walt, which fills one period of his life, is the most vivid illustration which we know of the impassioned sympathy which impelled him

---

[1] *Complete Prose*, pp. 70 and 446.
[2] *Calamus*, pp. 21-33.

to young men of the common people. It was one of the propensities very significant of the man, and by his own admission, the most fundamental. He once said in the presence of his friends: "Men of letters and artists seem to fly from companionship: to me it is exhilarating, affects me in the same way the light or the storm does." Walt sought especially for friends primitive and cordial natures, beings who gave themselves unreservedly; and it was with the uneducated, with young artisans, that he found the touch of humanity without alloy. He was irresistibly drawn to them, and his magnetism of the strong man attracted them with the same power. As O. L. Triggs has written: "He fed upon people as bees upon flowers."[1] The extreme need of loving which tormented his heart overflowed in such affections as these. He had lived them with awful intensity, during the war, at bedsides where thousands of youths suffered; and at the approach of fifty, without a home as he was, because of his inviolable desire for independence, his thirst for intimacy and tenderness was intensified. Thus "dear son, my little Peter" was at once his child and comrade.

This imperious penchant for intimate comradeship which led him to choose his brothers from the anonymous crowd, was manifested in him with an entirety and a fervour which made it an emotion almost new in humanity. It was in all the strength of the word a passion, from which he extracted a joy which approaches close to a penetrating sorrow.

I am he that aches with love.[2]

He has sung it, this great hunger, in the poems which are grouped under the title *Calamus:* in their moving and mysterious verses are found repeated the secret thrills of his heart, and it was not without fear of being misunderstood, that he thus reveals himself, so intimate and more sacred

---
[1] O. L. Triggs: *Selections, Introduction,* p. xl.
[2] *Leaves of Grass,* p. 93.

seemed to him the strange sentiment which unites him to certain beings. To hold in his hand the hand of a friend, to feel the touch of his shoulder, to place his bearded lips on his cheek, flooded Walt with a happiness whose sweetness the world did not know. More than that, it appears, that in the love which he had known and enjoyed all his warm and sensuous soul was lifted into virile friendships, to which clings, for this great Lover of the human individual, a perfume more subtle, a significance more remote. For Walt Whitman what he calls "manly attachment" or "binding affection" as opposed to "love of man and woman," had an immense importance and spread from the individual to the collective, to humanity.

Resolved to sing no songs to-day but those of manly attachment,
Projecting them along that substantial life,
Bequeathing hence types of athletic love,
Afternoon this delicious Ninth month in my forty-first year,
I proceed for all who are or have been young men,
To tell the secret of my nights and days,
To celebrate the need of comrades.[1]

The unusual and impassioned character of these attachments of man to man naturally provoked the surprise of some commentators and incite special writers to place the poet as a sexual anomaly. The novelist, Johannes Schlaf, has definitely replied to the more recent and copious of these psychopaths.[2] It is not less certain that the fervour of these attachments shows a singular phenomenon, which opens unknown perspectives in a life fecund in surprises. However ordinary, however close, Walt shows himself he is not less proved, on the other hand, an exceptional, because of the formidable personality which was his: and like exceptional beings, unique, he was a law unto himself. In his work as in his life, are strange and novel things, which will long remain unexplained. In any case, it is not the searchers

[1] *Leaves of Grass*, p. 96.
[2] Johannes Schlaf: *Walt Whitman*.

for anomalies who will ever find the key. Perhaps he who shall describe the exact nature of the attachment which united the Apostle of Galilee to his disciple John will be able to clear the mystery of love which is concealed in the tender comradeships of the Good Gray Poet.

XVIII

THE FIRST VICTORIES OF "LEAVES OF GRASS"

There was a curious something in the destiny of Walt Whitman. When his incomparable prestige sufficed to assure him wherever he lived, a kind of celebrity, his fame as a poet remained almost nul. Aside from his little group of friends and passionate partisans who were fully aware of his importance as prophet, scarcely any one in Washington suspected that he was author of *Leaves of Grass*. *Drum Taps* had not been read. Some were curious as to the truth of the man in the big hat whom they met in the street, who was maybe a sea captain, a Virginia planter, or an old pirate; but no one supposed that he was a poet. So much did Walt, with illumined features and his flourishing health, appear remote from the conventional type of poet.

Yet, *Leaves of Grass*, relegated to the background of his preoccupation during the ardent years of the war, was not forgotten; from the time of his employment in the Interior, he utilized the leisure of his official life to revise slowly and minutely, in view of a new edition, the volume of 1860, lost in the wreck of the firm of Thayer and Eldridge. This work was in progress when Secretary Harlan took to his office to test it better the erased and annotated copy in which Walt indicated the changes which he wished to make in his text. He carried on slowly, according to his wont, this labour which he was to renew unwearied during his whole life, persuaded each time that he was preparing the completed edition of his work: but life was the stronger, and in proportion as Walt pressed the sap, the *Leaves* grew. During the summer of 1866 he came to New York, to busy himself in the printing of the book.

Since the close of 1862, when he left for the battle-fields of Virginia, Walt forsook Manhattan: but he did not lose all contact with the dear city whose every pavement reminded him of the history of his wonderful youth. As long as he was employed in the Department of Justice, he took rather long vacations every summer—sometimes for three months—which he used to spend in Brooklyn with his mother.

In revisiting New York, he found, each time, the big city more beautiful than before and wondered at it with the words and the ecstasy of a child. In a note to a Washington friend is found described, in the impressionistic manner usual in his intimate letters, that fascination which the city exercised upon him:

> Harry, you would much enjoy going round N. Y. with me, if it were possible, and then how much I should like having you with me. This great city, with all its crowds and splendor, and Broadway fashion and women, and amusements, and the river and bay, and shipping, and the many magnificent new buildings, and Central Park and 5th Avenue, and the endless processions of private vehicles and the finest teams I ever saw, for miles long of a fine afternoon—altogether, they make up a show that I can richly spend a month in enjoying—for a change from my Washington life. I sometimes think that I am the particular man who enjoys the show of all these things in N. Y. more than any other mortal—as if it was all got up just for me to observe and study.[1]

The ocean, above all, of which he was deprived at Washington, to see it again, to sniff anew its odour, he was as a man intoxicated. Here again he subjects himself to the great enchantment, is filled with the great plaint of eternity, which had soothed him in his youth:

> BY THE SEA-SHORE, CONEY ISLAND,
> SUNDAY 3 P. M.
>
> DEAR PETE: I will write you a few lines as I sit here, on a clump of sand by the sea shore—having some paper in my haversack, and an hour or two yet before I start back. Pete, I wish you were with me the few hours past,—I have just had a splendid swim and souse in the surf—the waves

---

[1] *Calamus,* p. 19.

are slowly rolling in, with hoarse roar that is music to my ears—the breeze blows pretty brisk from southwest, and the sun is partially clouded—from where I sit I look out on the bay and down the Narrows, vessels sailing in every direction in the distance—a great big black long ocean steamship streaking it up toward New York—and the lines of hills and mountains, far, far away on the Jersey coast, a little veiled with blue vapor—here around me, as I sit it is nothing but barren sand—but I don't know how long I could sit here, to that soothing, rumbling murmuring of the waves—and then the salt breeze.[1]

Walt also used his vacation profitably to issue his book. Again he had no publisher. By his salary as clerk happily he could support the expense of the coming volume. This fourth edition appeared about November, 1866.[2] It bore only for a title: *Leaves of Grass*, New York, 1867, and did not contain the portrait. Again is found the contents of the edition of 1860, but redistributed according to the demands of a total revision. Not only were the titles changed, but the grouping was not the same, and the sections of long pieces appeared numbered. The work continued to be arranged conformably to its definitive editing: it became more and more organic. Above all, Walt who six years before was deaf to the entreaties of his friends, among them Emerson, determined of his own will to suppress some of the crude words and too vivid images which had created a great furore. It was not in the least to be conformed to the public taste that he made this suppression. There was only this, that having been through the war and its horrors and having lived to be forty-seven, the author gained a new light, and that in rereading *Leaves of Grass*, he judged the present time little in touch with the general tone of his poem. To compensate, some verses inspired by the war, source of so much emotion for him, were placed here and there among the old poems.

A little later—probably the following year—the author

---

[1] *Calamus*, p. 84.
[2] *Camden Edition*, VIII, p. 186.

FIRST VICTORIES OF "LEAVES OF GRASS" 225

desiring to add to his book *Drum Taps*, which appeared separately in 1865, bound the whole in one volume, whose three hundred and seventy pages comprehended the mass of his poetical work up to that time. The additions, *Drum Taps*, *Sequel to Drum Taps*, and *Songs of Parting*, remained with their independent pagination: it was the first stage of the definite incorporation with *Leaves of Grass* of the war poems. The edition thus completed amounted to two hundred and thirty-six poems, of which only eight were new.

Nothing especial appears to have characterized the fate of this edition. It was little or not at all displayed, Walt being his own publisher. It had certainly a small sale, for he wrote to Peter Doyle, in the fall of 1868, that there remained in his hands but two hundred and thirty copies,[1] which was the proof that some twenty persons in the world were interested then in the new poet. The "critics" also were interested, in their own way. They were ambushed in the dailies and profited by it to republish their old lampoons. Walt, whom these attacks of waggery, sometimes acrimonious, did not the least disturb, told Doyle what resistance the sale of his book met: "New York, October 14, '68. There is a pretty strong enmity here toward me and *Leaves of Grass* among certain classes—not only that it is a great mess of crazy talk and hard words all tangled up, without sense or meaning (which, by the by, is, I believe, your judgment about it)—but others sincerely think that it is a bad book, improper, and ought to be denounced and put down, and its author along with it. There are some venomous but laughable squibs occasionally in the papers. One said that I had received 25 guineas for a piece in an English magazine, but that it was worth all that for any one to read it. Another, the World, said: 'Walt Whitman was in town yesterday carrying the blue cotton umbrella of the future' (it had been a drizzly forenoon) so they go it. When they get off a good squib, however, I laugh at it just as much as

---
[1] *Calamus*, p. 43.

any one. . . ."[1] All this was rather sad; but on hearing this buzzing of the flies which accompanied his slow, elephantine step, Walt could have repeated to himself the words of his poem:

> I am more resolute because all have denied me
> than I could ever have been had all accepted me.[2]

But the much-enduring man had, outside of himself, motives for not being disturbed. He was no longer alone as in the first days. His two loyal friends, O'Connor and Burroughs, did not remain silent: O'Connor obtained from H. J. Raymond, editor-in-chief of the New York Times, who nevertheless reproved Whitman,[3] the right to greet in his journal the new edition of *Leaves of Grass*,[4] and Burroughs dedicated to the poet an enthusiastic study, which the Galaxy, of December, 1866, published. Of all the testimonies which allow us to see the poet in the glorious serenity of his autumn, there could be none more complete or truer than the pages written, at different times, by the congenial and friendly colleague, John Burroughs. They are essential notations from life, in which Walt Whitman of the Washington years is portrayed. This article was but the prelude of homage which John Burroughs meant to render to his great comrade. In 1867, after having lived for four years in his daily intimacy, he brought out a little volume of a hundred pages, entitled *Notes on Walt Whitman as Poet and Person*, where, in a very simple form, far removed from the flamboyant manner of O'Connor, but with accent of faith and of deep sincerity, the poet was painted in his person, his race, his habits, and his work; the leading ideas of the sketch were penetrated with light and justified by a solid and penetrating intel-

---

[1] *Calamus*, pp. 44–45.
[2] *Leaves of Grass*, p. 251.
[3] Bliss Perry: *Walt Whitman*, p. 176.
[4] New York Times, December 2, 1866. See *Camden Edition*, VIII, p. 189.

ligence. In presenting boldly this little monument, the author was not merely presenting himself as the defender of a misunderstood man; he expressed in his Preface: "Although Walt Whitman, as Poet and Person, remains yet comparatively an unknown, unregarded figure upon the vast and crowded canvas of our age, I feel for reasons attempted to be set forth in the following pages—that I am in some sort called upon to jot down, while they are vivid upon me, my observation of him and his writings."[1] And he added further on, with a sure foresight: "There will come a time when these things will be invaluable."[2]

Burroughs, like O'Connor previously, hailed in Walt Whitman a universal genius, who had to suffer the fate of great discoverers, repudiated by their time, and in whom, for the first time, was incarnated America and Democracy. Although devoid of all emphasis, the homage was integral; the friend, without caring for incredulous and stupid mockers, published his faith and compiled the first document which enables us to-day to know the real man which was Walt. His courage was as sure as his insight, in a time when Whitman did not count in America a single champion, except two or three personal friends, and saw himself kept on the index by all the literary men and their followers. The modest *Notes* of Burroughs was the first volume of a series which later was increased little by little in the course of years, and promises in our day to reach unusual proportions.

In the very country which Walt glorified, incomprehension persisted, despite the advertisement of O'Connor and Burroughs. Something was however slowly preparing for him, far away on the other side of the Atlantic, in the old mother-country. The few copies of the first two editions of *Leaves of Grass* which had reached England were passed almost unnoticed; in the meantime a friend of Ruskin, Thomas Dixon, who acquired in a sale a small lot of the edi-

---
[1] John Burroughs: *Notes*, p. 3.
[2] *Id.*: p. 5.

tion of 1855, sent a volume to William Bell Scott, who himself read it to William Michael Rossetti. Interest in the American poet was thus aroused in a little circle of fervent artists which included such personalities as the two Rossettis and Swinburne. And when the edition of 1860 appeared, it met passionate admirers among literary and university youth; a second time was proved the curious destiny of this book, written by an artisan for artisans, and recognized only by intellectuals, written by an American for Americans, and scarcely noticed but by foreigners.

From that time Whitman had in England a small group of partisan enthusiasts, of whom he had no knowledge till they made themselves known. Interest in his personality and his book was fairly awakened in some groups, in 1866, for Moncure Conway, who had been the first to come, at the advice of Emerson, and to find the poet at home, shortly after the edition of 1866, and who was so astonished to meet a man tranquil and sweet instead of a fierce and bellicose giant whom he was expecting to encounter, published in the Fortnightly Review[1] a well-meaning article, but showy: "Mr. Conway's article is as impudent as it is cordial, it is a mixture of good and bad,"[2] wrote Walt to his mother, when he sent it to her. He did not like the journalistic amplifications and all his life took great care to be presented in the light of exact truth.

But English admiration was about to reveal itself more worthily. W. M. Rossetti, who conceived the idea of publishing *Leaves of Grass* in England, communicated with Walt in order to discuss details of the publication which he projected. Letters were exchanged in which was strengthened a warm friendship between the two men. Walt was full of confidence in his judicious friend; he consented to the idea of a selection of poems. It was in this form that the volume appeared in 1868—the

---

[1] *Fortnightly Review*, October 15, 1866, p. 537.
[2] *Camden Edition*, VIII, p. 186.

FIRST VICTORIES OF "LEAVES OF GRASS" 229

publisher J. C. Hotten—with the title: *Poems of Walt Whitman*. It comprised a hundred pieces, the Preface of the 1855 edition and an introduction, in which W. M. Rossetti declared outright that the author of *Leaves of Grass* "realized the greatest work of our period in poetry." In the minds of Walt's first English admirers this selection represented the necessary stage of initiation with the view of a future acceptance of the whole book, and perhaps they were right, since the effect produced by this volume was undeniable: it assured the reputation of Walt Whitman in England, and won him the enthusiastic sympathy of a new generation of poets, critics, and artists, who naturally admired him according to their own particular point of view, a little exclusive, somewhat literary, but their homage comforted much more than what was offered many a time, in his own country, by gross and puerile scribbling.

A short time after the publication of this volume W. M. Rossetti received several letters from a young man, who declared himself already a passionate admirer, for many years, of the great American;[1] it was John Addington Symonds, who had become the correspondent of Whitman and one of the first among the small company of faithful friends. He was an Oxonian of exceptional intellectuality, whom a feeble constitution doomed to a lamentable existence unceasingly menaced by neurasthenia. When his friend, Frederick Myers, read to him, in 1865, passages of *Leaves of Grass*, Symonds experienced, he tells us, to the very marrow of his bones, an electric shock. The enormous vitality of the book revolutionized this ardent soul in an infirm body, and later Symonds nourished himself with these verses to the point of declaring later that Whitman had more influence on him than Plato and Goethe and for that matter any masterpiece except the Bible.[2] This was one of Walt's most brilliant conquests that of this university man, whose

---
[1] H. H. Gilchrist: *Anne Gilchrist*, p. 183.
[2] *Camden's Compliment to Walt Whitman*, p. 73.

intellectual and aristocratic prejudices he had overthrown. Symonds decided not to publish his study till after Whitman's death.

Upon others the volume edited by Rossetti produced the effect of an illumination: notably upon Charles Kent, editor of the Sun, who published in his journal an enthusiastic review of it.[1] The same year the poet Robert Buchanan soon proved himself the indefatigable champion of Walt Whitman in England, devoted an essay to him,[2] and Swinburne, in his book on William Blake, established a parallel between the verse of the painter-poet and those of the American. But the acceptance which filled Walt with pride and joy was the one, unexpected and significant, of an admirable woman who became his "greatest friend."

Anne Gilchrist, widow of the author of *William Blake* and a friend of Rossetti and Carlyle, was a woman of large and sane superiority, open to the highest speculation, yet keeping herself profoundly feminine and maternal. She read the *Poems* edited by W. M. Rossetti a year after they appeared, and its impression was such that she immediately asked him to lend her the complete edition of *Leaves of Grass*. The original work with its crudity only increased her enthusiasm, and in a series of letters to the friend who helped her to know the man entire, she poured out all the fervour which she felt toward the poet who awakened in her a whole world of new emotion. "In regard to those poems which raised so loud an outcry," she writes, "I shall take courage to say frankly that I find them also beautiful, and that I think even you have misapprehended them. Perhaps indeed they were chiefly written for wives. I rejoice to have read them. . . ."[3] These letters of a woman seemed so beautiful to W. M. Rossetti that after counselling with his

---
[1] H. H. Gilchrist: *Anne Gilchrist*, p. 183.
[2] Robert Buchanan: *David Gray and Other Essays*, p. 203.
[3] Bliss Perry: *Walt Whitman*, p. 189.

friend to publish them, he sent them to America, where they appeared, anonymously and lightly retouched, in a Boston review, the Radical, in May, 1870.[1] In a Puritan community, this *Judgment of an English Woman on Walt Whitman* could not fail to make an impression. No one had as yet dared to speak with such sane freedom of the great pagan. In reading the eloquent pages of this unknown woman, who "having been a wife and a happy mother, learned to accept everything with tenderness, to feel something sacred in all,"[2] and whose conscious enthusiasm spread like a flood, the friends of the poet were in transport. As for Walt he experienced, at that moment, one of the gravest and intensest joys of his life—as strong, if not more so, than at the time of the letter from Emerson and the plea of O'Connor. If that woman were near him! How she understood him in his entirety, how she was herself revealed unreservedly throughout this testimony, with all the spontaneous warmth of a soul rich and congenial. She was truly of her race and came forward to justify him. And what a prop for his despised book this luminous plea dared by an extraordinary woman, a respected mother—what answer to his detractors! The soul of Walt dilated in reading these moving pages: it was like a whiff of strengthening air which came to him from the other side of the Atlantic. He always had more faith in the intuitive comprehension of true women than in the reasoning intelligence of dialecticians, and the issue proved him right. He was happier than if he had sold at a single stroke a thousand copies of his book. "Have you read the article?" he asked his friend Miss Helen Price whom he met on the street, declaring immediately that it gave him great pleasure.[3] Two years later, he again repeated to W. M. Rossetti that nothing in his life as a poet had comforted him so much as

---

[1] Reprinted in H. H. Gilchrist's *Anne Gilchrist*, pp. 287-307.
[2] H. H. Gilchrist: *Anne Gilchrist*, p. 289.
[3] Bucke: *Walt Whitman*, p. 31.

"the warm appreciation and friendship of that true, full-grown woman."[1]

A little later, Anne Gilchrist communicated directly with Whitman; and it was the beginning of an affectionate correspondence, in which these two beings, so close in temperament and intuition, reflected all the respect, all the confidence and admiration which they felt one for the other. Six years after the publication of her letters, Anne Gilchrist went to America, and the bond which was formed between them was strengthened by the personal contact of the man, whom she found not only in perfect accord with the image which she made of him, but greater perhaps than his book. And Walt likewise always spoke in touching and grave words of his admirable friend. When he lost her, in 1885, he wrote to her son Herbert, in expressing the desire to keep for himself only the letters which she had written him: ". . . Among the perfect women whom I have known (and it was my unspeakable good fortune to have had the best possible for mother, sisters, and friends), I have known none more perfect in every relation than my dear, dear friend Anne Gilchrist."[2] And piously, toward his seventieth year, reviewing the affections of his life, he wished to commemorate "the noblest of his friends (to-day buried in an English tomb) in dedicating a poem to her dear memory."[3]

Decidedly there was a glimmer in the horizon. Farther even than the bounds of the English language, an approbation came to Walt Whitman. In that same year 1868 the poet Ferdinand Freiligrath published in the Allegemeinen Zeitung of Augsburg a study of the Poet of Democracy, sowing thus the first germ, which was to fructify beautifully from his revelation in Germany. In the world a little nucleus of admirers was formed. Little mattered what was beyond in Europe, and that America remained deaf to the call of

---

[1] Bucke: *In Re Walt Whitman*, p. 72.
[2] H. H. Gilchrist: *Anne Gilchrist*, pp. v-vi.
[3] *Leaves of Grass*, p. 397.

her poet; once admit any part, the book had enough power in it to propagate itself and to make the tour of the globe. One day it would end perhaps by offering itself, encircled with glory, to American eyes, at last opened.

About fifteen years had thus passed since the day when, shy and proud, Walt put his viking ship afloat, shaped entirely by his own hands.[1]

---

[1] This chapter gains new significance by the publication of the *Letters of Anne Gilchrist and Walt Whitman*, edited by Thomas Harned, 1918, Tr.

XIX

THE STRICKEN OAK

DECIDEDLY, there was a bit of a change in the situation of the poet: this could be seen in the testimonies which he received during the last year of his stay in Washington—a period for him of very great literary activity. Then from 1868 to 1872 his name appears here and there signed to a poem in various reviews and friendly journals.[1]

There was more: Walt was invited by the American Institute of New York to recite a poem on September 7, 1871, at the opening of the fortieth annual exposition of national industry.[2] The poet accepted and read, in a hall heaped with specimens of produce, merchandise, machines, and implements, his *Song of the Exposition*. The following year it was the United Literary Societies of Dartmouth in New Hampshire which invited him to deliver the Commencement Poem. The choice of a man objected to by men of good standing, for an academic solemnity, may appear singular enough: indeed it seems, according to recent avowals, that the author of *Leaves of Grass* had been chosen by the students to annoy the faculty.[3] "Everything went off well," the poet wrote to Peter Doyle, the summer of 1872, the summer he spent in Brooklyn. He recited the poem: *As a Strong Bird on Pinions Free*.[4] He profited by his stay in New England, whose quiet green villages he loved, to cross Vermont to Lake Champlain and to pass a day or two at Burlington

---

[1] *Camden Edition*, X, pp. 178–179.
[2] H. Traubel: *With Walt Whitman in Camden*, pp. 326–327.
[3] Bliss Perry: *Walt Whitman*, pp. 203–205.
[4] *Leaves of Grass*, p. 346.

where his "dear sister Hannah" lived, far from her people—not happily married.

The year 1871 was for the poet singularly rich: three volumes, issued in Washington, bear this date. Especially a pamphlet entitled *Democratic Vistas*, the first work in prose published by Walt since he became a new man. It was on one of his favourite themes, or rather one of the aspects of the only great theme which filled his life: the justification of the Democracy of the New World by a new Literature which should be equal to the exigencies of the race and the time. Till then he was solicitous only to exalt the Individual and the American Nationality and to leave in shadow some of the frightful realities which his country exemplified, realities which he knew better than any one: now he threw a flood of light on these enormities—the ignoble greed of riches, vulgarity of manners, political corruption, meanness of ideals. These he stigmatized with an enormous verve and resentment. Had Walt lost then at Washington, among the bureaucrats, his joyous and boundless optimism? Never, for he affirmed anew, with as much entirety as in his Preface of 1855, his unshakable confidence in the destiny of a race, called according to him to surpass all others; but, that she might be worthy of the great opportunities which her immense territory and the energy of her people offered her, there was need of great Writers, sprung from her, like Homer from Greek soil, and who would address themselves to her soul to awaken and sustain this soul, to exalt and show it the way. There were needed these precursors, source from which the higher moral, spiritual, religious life, of the mass was to be fed, that it might not sink under the enormous materialism which it possessed. And projecting his looks far from the terrifying sadness of the present the author enumerated the real splendours of the future continent, such as he glimpsed it and as it ought to be. The article was admirable in strength, spirit, accent; it was at once an examination of the national conscience, an outline of high sociology, a pamphlet, an act of lyric faith. The man gave himself to it wholly, and verily revealed himself with the fervour of a prophet. He had worked on it many years;[1] and these pages, which will one day be a classic, where Walt Whitman spoke with so much fervour to his people to avert them from the danger which threatened them and to point to them the remedy, passed unnoticed in America. "No one reads it, no one calls for it," he wrote the following year to one of his English admirers.

The second publication of that year was a collection of verse entitled, *Passage to India*, in which, among some old poems, appeared twenty-three unpublished pieces. These were not, as one soon sees, merely a sprout of *Leaves of Grass* whose trunk strengthened each season, projected new branches: but, when he published them, these hundred and twenty pages represented in the poet's mind the first stage of a second volume of verse which was henceforth to accompany *Leaves of Grass* and where, after having sung the plenitude of living, he included the thought and emotion of his old age. The poem which gave its title to the collection proved that his inspiration had not weakened, and it will remain among his more absolute pieces: the poem is founded upon two recent events, the cutting of the Isthmus of Suez and the completion of the transcontinental railway. It describes in words of religious cosmic joy the emotion of a soul which after having made the circuit of the earth and becoming enraptured with the consciousness of its unity—the Orient, cradle of humanity, bound at last to the Occident, fulfilling the vision of Columbus—takes its flight beyond.

There was finally a fifth reappearance of *Leaves of Grass*. No sooner was one edition ready than the poet planned changes, new architectural arrangements. As much as Walt lived, his book lived with him, and consequently kept evolving. This time *Drum Taps* was definitely incorporated with the main work, which contained but thirty new pieces.

---

[1] *Camden Edition*, VIII, p. 231.

A little later, following his particular method of juxtaposing before fusing, he made a second impression in which appeared as annexes the collection of *Passage to India* and the *Song of the Exposition*, which had already been published in pamphlet by Roberts Brothers, of Boston. Enlarged by this new story, the edifice acquired proportions more and more imposing: it amounted now to two hundred and sixty-three pieces, distributed in groups or separate. Materially, the volume was attractive in appearance and was offered perhaps as the most beautiful edition published up to this time.[1] However, like the preceding one, no firm protected it and it entered the world on his own responsibility. Walt championed it to the extent of becoming his own publisher.

Some requests came, from beyond the sea especially; the sale was very modest, considering that for five years this edition was on the market.[2] Nevertheless the author wrote that his "book went admirably." Some dozen copies sold sufficed to fill the candid and confident soul of the Good Gray Poet. It was not a success, far from it. But did not Walt have infinite patience within him, an unquenchable fountain of patience, cosmic so to speak? Does the plant wither when the rain tarries in coming and does not the seed wait in silence that the season revolve for its germination. . . ? Never a complaint escaped him of the ingratitude or indifference of men. In the depth of his being was perpetuated a silent contentment which passed all the contentment of the earth. It was to his disposition that he owed that confidence and that patience too strong to be uprooted by external events.

Moreover, despite the small sales, or even none perhaps, of his books, it was perceptible that the portion of the ground already won was broadening by a slow but continuous progress. The little phalanx of his admirers insensibly grew about his book, without any one noting it in the indifferent

---

[1] Bucke: *Walt Whitman*, p. 146, and *Calamus*, p. 88.
[2] Bucke: *Walt Whitman*, p. 146.

world. But Walt kept account of it, and this slender form of popularity satisfied him; that constant advance, was it not significant? The luminous pages of Anne Gilchrist disposed some people to revise their first impression. A second edition of John Burroughs's *Notes*, supplemented by new pages, appeared in 1871, and, the same year, Swinburne addressed a thrilling salutation to his great confrère: *To Walt Whitman in America*[1]—famous poem where the better note of the great artist and libertarian vibrates. Tennyson, to whom Walt, his junior by ten years, sent *Leaves of Grass*, acknowledged it in very friendly words: "I am in contact with many of your works," he wrote in July, 1877, "I have read them with interest and I can see that you have a generous nature and worthy of being loved;" and the aristocratic poet invited the Manhattan bard to come to him, should he ever cross the Atlantic. The following year he sent him a signed photograph, and, from that day, very warm epistolary relations were established between them.[2] Edward Dowden, author of a life of Shelley, a professor in Dublin, rendered a significant homage to the new poet in his essay on the *Poetry of Democracy*.[3] Other articles, notably of Buxton Forman,[4] the Shelleyan, and of Roden Noel,[5] letters, appreciations came regularly from old England, who rejoiced in the expanding of her language in free, unlooked for, splendid flowers, juicy with the substance of a new soil. It was not to be wondered at that these litterati who made a cult of Shelley, the great pagan soul, should feel powerfully drawn to this other and more modern and greater pagan who had risen on the shore beyond the Atlantic: just as it was not strange that Walt had found his first American admirer among the devotees of Emerson. Despite enormous divergences, invisible relations exist between these three individualities.

---

[1] A. G. Swinburne: *Songs Before Sunrise.*
[2] Donaldson: *Walt Whitman the Man*, pp. 223-226.
[3] Westminster Review, July, 1871.
[4] Buxton Forman: *Our Living Poets.*
[5] The Dark Blue, October and November, 1871.

At this time Whitman was introduced in Copenhagen by Rudolf Schmidt who, not content with affirming his admiration,[1] translated into Danish *Democratic Vistas*. There was still something better: Revue des Deux Mondes[2] dedicated without reserve twenty pages to a man whose "repugnant materialism," "detestable" instincts, "grotesque" jargon and the manners of one escaped from Charenton[3] did not, however, justify the ignoring of some gifts which, regrettably, had to be recognized. However circumspect and sown with reprobation was the homage, Walt could be proud of his victory. In France he found likewise a fervent admirer in the person of a descendant of Lucien Bonaparte, born in Ireland, Charles Bonaparte Wyse, who, some years afterward, adapted in Provençal, a dialect which especially fascinated him, some portion of *Leaves of Grass*.[4] In America, on the contrary, advocates were still few.[5] It must be said that in the course of his pilgrimage through the sad fields of public indifference it was far from the continent that the author of *Leaves of Grass* reaped the greatest number of admirers.

All the same, it was not without a certain satisfaction that Walt, in 1872, made a list of his foreign disciples on the last page of a little book, which he published at the same time as his Dartmouth College poem, *As A Strong Bird on Pinions Free*, and various new pieces, among them *The Mystic Trumpeter*. This poem he recited at the request of his friends, in his last years, and the pathetic lines addressed to conquered France, to comfort her in her distress. At this time Walt, who had the sensation of engaging in a battle in which he might be defeated, believed it still serviceable to his cause to republish the anonymous articles on himself.[6] He

---

[1] For Ide og Virkelghed, February, 1872.
[2] The Bentzon: *An American Poet*, Revue des Deux Mondes, 1872.
[3] The French equivalent of Bedlam. Tr.
[4] Donaldson: *Walt Whitman the Man*, pp. 215–220.
[5] Joaquin Miller became a Whitman follower now. See *Calamus*, p. 93.
[6] Bliss Perry: *Walt Whitman*, pp. 206–210.

would not abandon his book, which was himself, at a time which he considered as the going into action.

During this Washington period Walt did not cease to show the external signs of a magnificent health. His bright complexion and his youthful manner proved, in spite of his gray hair, the active man brimming with life that his contemporaries have painted for us. Nevertheless he noted well, by certain fleeting symptoms, that he no longer enjoyed that perfect physical equilibrium which, up to his prostration in the summer of 1864, had given him the assurance of being invulnerable. Time and again he complained of pains in the head and dizziness.[1] Walt had not eliminated from his system the poison of the wounds he so long dressed.

In August and September, 1869, these disturbing illnesses became more intense. "It is difficult to know exactly what it is and what it may do," he writes. "The doctor says it comes from the hospital malaria, that poison of the hospital which my system absorbed for years."[2] It was the following year that he began to wear glasses for reading and writing. The prostration returned at various times and was more or less acute, but his powerful constitution always conquered: when he felt ill he nursed himself in his own way and refused to take drugs. In 1872 he still suffered from his insidious illness: he passed a part of February, March, and the beginning of April at Brooklyn with his mother, then he returned there in June and July, and experienced a new attack. It was with these auguries that he journeyed toward the year 1873, the year he was fifty-four. Year 1873: fatal time, dolorous date, written as the lightning flash in this proud life, now utterly shattered. . . . The first of January he fell very ill; but this passed as before. The twenty-third, after a series of little repulsed shocks, came the supreme and definitive attack which he described to his friend Doctor Bucke. He was reading Bulwer's *What Will He Do With It?*

---

[1] *Camden Edition*, VIII, p. 180.
[2] *Calamus*, pp. 53-56.

at his office in the department. He rose to go to his room and one of the guards noticing how ill he looked accompanied him home, and after a sleep of several hours he found that he could move neither arm nor left leg, nor raise himself, nor make a movement. He thought the attack would pass.[1]

It did not pass indeed, for, this time, the man was felled. The man marvellously alive, who to his forty-fifth year had not known an hour of sickness and who gloried in it so openly, saw a period brutally placed at the foot of the chapter of his boundless, alert, joyous years. Ended the long road jaunts with Peter Doyle, ended the fine parties at the edge of the Potomac. . . . Walt was to be an invalid always. In spite of intervals of improvement he was never again to be the man he had been. After some admonitory rumblings the storm suddenly broke upon the great oak, breaking half its branches. And before the catastrophe one experiences an emotion, as if one looked at the falling of a wing of a great building: it was in truth the glorious edifice of his vitality, the enormous and splendid figure of the Good Gray Poet, now collapsed under a stroke of fate, now the lamentable moment which opens a new chapter in his life, that of old age and suffering.

The attack of January 23rd kept Walt abed for three weeks. His serenity never forsook him—not more than it forsook him for the twenty years which were left him to live his impotent existence. He wrote regularly to his mother—the exact truth, neither better nor worse. These letters of the sick Wound Dresser to his mother—which report his condition day by day—are a veritable poem of sweetness, tenderness, fortitude, whose every strophe one might detail; slowly, very slowly the use of his limb and his left arm was partly recovered. He did not complain: he had all that he wished— "little extras and the superfluities" as he wrote his mother. His friends kept themselves posted, the newspapers having

---
[1] Bucke: *Walt Whitman*, pp. 45–46.

announced that Walt was very ill; the doctor visited him every day. His close friends, like Peter Doyle, Charles Eldridge, Burroughs, Mrs. O'Connor, came to the sick man. Peter Doyle especially was made nurse and did not leave during his free hours. He brought to the recluse the air from without, now that the good day of the comrades, their coming and going, was never to be again.

Thus the weeks passed, a little monotonous. "I have tacked your picture on the wall, at the foot of the bed," he writes to his mother, "the one I like—it looks as natural as can be—and is quite company for me—as I am alone a good deal (and prefer to be)."[1] Soon he was able to be lifted, and to spend some hours in his room near the stove. Later, on February 17th, he could go downstairs and walk fifty feet supported on the arm of a friend, and thus breathe draughts of air. It was the seclusion which especially oppressed him, for he did not suffer.

His appetite was fair and he had no appearance of an invalid. Only the "distress" in the head, resulting from the stroke, caused him torment. Relief from this was impossible. It was indeed hard for a man of his strength, but he had no reason to complain. To heed him he was as well as possible and ought to deem himself devilish happy that his condition was not worse. His mind was perfectly clear and his good humour unalterable. Little by little and with much difficulty he ventured farther in the street, and even lifted himself into a tram. One day he went as far as his office, but he could not work. Soon spring came, the invalid saw the grass become green again and the buds of the willow swell. In the middle of April Doctor Drinkard, who attended him and in whom Walt had every confidence, tried treatment by electricity.

In May, when he was passing some hours of the afternoon at his office, and waiting with patience for the great healer,

---

[1]Bucke: *In Re Walt Whitman*, p. 77.

time, to put him on his feet again, a grave, sudden uneasiness interrupted his recovery. Previously, in February, he had the deep sorrow of losing his "sister Mattie"—his sister-in-law Martha whom he loved tenderly, the wife of his brother Jeff, the engineer; and in writing to his old mother, his sorrow for her death is seen to be deep. Who would have said that now, at this critical hour in which his own life was already broken, a second stroke, otherwise terrible, was prepared for him?

His mother, who, in September, 1872, had left Brooklyn to live in New Jersey with her son George, whose business had prospered since the war, was approaching then her eightieth year. She was suffering from rheumatism and, since the commencement of May, was feeling worse. Grave apprehension crossed Walt's mind. "Dear Mother; I am very uneasy about you—it is very afflicting to have the nervous system affected that makes you always discouraged, that is the worst—Mother I fear that you may be much worse than you say—I think of it night and day. . . ."[1] He proposed going to her, as soon as his strength would allow him; the first day of June he would be with her. The date was too distant, alas! May 20th he was called to her bedside and left immediately, despite his condition. The 23rd his mother died.

Words are weak to suggest the anguished hours which Walt passed at the death bed of his mother who had been the great love of his life. The humble farm mistress of the Long Island village, the carpenter's companion, the fecund mother, with magnificent heart to whom he proudly claimed himself indebted for his most intimate qualities, had been the most potent influence in his career and with her going was broken the strongest tie which bound him to a life long since painful and burdensome. Feeble as he was at that moment the emotion might prove fatal to him. Blow upon blow, he was struck to the heart of his physical life, then

[1] Bucke: *In Re Walt Whitman*, p. 90.

to the heart of his heart. And the supreme, heartbreaking farewell shows itself in the strophe which, later, he dedicated to her:

To memories of my mother, to the divine blending maternity,
To her, buried and gone, yet buried not, gone not from me,
I see again the calm benignant face fresh and beautiful still,
I sit by the form in the coffin,
I kiss and kiss convulsively again the sweet old lips, the cheeks. the closed eyes in the coffin,
To her, the ideal woman, practical, spiritual, of all faith, life, love, to me the best,
I grave a monumental line, before I go, amid these songs,
And set a tombstone here.[1]

---
[1] *Leaves of Grass*, p. 376.

PART SIX

THE INVALID

CAMDEN (1873–1884)

XX

THROUGH ABANDONMENT AND SORROW

AMONG human experiences there remained one which Walt Whitman had not yet sounded by living it: this of physical suffering and of sorrow. Nineteen years of invalidism, from the time he left Washington till his calm and sweet release, brought him this bitter completing of his education. To some the splendid physical man that they knew past his fiftieth year was still more beautiful while enduring with so much simple valour the trial of physical suffering. From the disabled body another aspect of the man emerged and developed, a Walt more intimate, who proved the continuation and the crowning of the first, the Walt, alive and sauntering, so glorious in his triumphant health, now lost forever.

If his physical downfall was irremediable, the sight of this shattered athlete who did not deny a syllable of what he had championed when brimming with vitality was perhaps worth these nineteen years of infirmity. When one sees him persist in flying from the great mast of his ship the pennant of confidence and optimism which he raised in middle life, one better understands the real meaning of Walt Whitman. He, the invalid poet, was about to enter a period of supreme affirmation and apotheosis. It is one of the great sages of modern times who, from a wretched corner of New Jersey, seems to beam on the world in all the brilliancy of his Olympian presence.

For Walt has, unknown to himself, quitted Washington forever, and Camden, a workingman's suburb, separated from Philadelphia by the Delaware, one which no "poet" would have chosen to shelter his meditations, was the har-

bour where he was soon to anchor. The sudden death of his
mother was a hard blow to his broken constitution. This
almost simultaneous disappearance of the "two best and
sweetest women whom he had ever seen and known, or expected to see," above all that of the dear one to whom he
was bound by the most intimate fibres, came at the very
worst period of his illness. A few days after he tried, for
change of air and escape from the heat, to reach the New
Jersey coast but he broke down in Philadelphia and had to
be brought to Camden, to his brother George.

Months, lugubrious years opened then for the poet, weak
and worn by prostration. He entered upon the only really
wretched period of his life; its serene radiance was suddenly
darkened. Oh, the sorrowful and heavy history of the interminable weeks of impotence and of deadly weakness!
Subject to repeated attacks, his head in a whirl, moving
about with extreme difficulty, passing sleepless nights, this
great liver was being apprenticed to bodily torment. He
occupied the second story of his brother's house, the room
where his mother died, and watched the slow days pass,
seated in her great mahogany arm chair, hearing from his
open window the homesick roll of the trains which crossed
fifty or sixty rods from his home. In the less weak intervals, when he felt the strength to move, he boarded a tram
which passed the door, took the Delaware ferry and passed
an hour at the Mercantile Library. True to his instinct he
took no medicine and looked after his own diet. His appetite was good and he let nature work unaided. Toward
the end of the summer his brother left 322 Stevens Street
to live at 431 in the same street, a fine house which he had
built, and Walt left the room where the gentle Louisa Van
Velsor had died in the presence of her two sons, and followed
his family in this removal.

Throughout the heavy melancholy of the empty, inactive
hours, although at times mortally, profoundly sad, he was
somehow supported by an invincible and marvellous hope.

Despair never touched the big-hearted solitary who was to draw for nineteen years inexhaustibly from the supply of stoic patience which nature had given him. Not once the shadow of a sacrilegious malediction or blame of life for its malign persecution, even at the height of his distress. He waits simply, compelling himself to put from him his black thoughts and to preserve his good temper. The heroic ingenuousness of these words which he threw in the face of his sorrow, as if to forbid its access to his intimate self! "I am feeling decidedly better these last 24 hours—guess I shall come out in the spring with the frogs and the lilacs—I keep a bully good heart, take it altogether."[1]

It was to his dear Washington friend, to Peter Doyle, that he wrote these words. Not only did he feel the bitterness, howsoever cruel for a being of such abundant vitality thus cut off from the joy of the open air and the intoxication of free rambles, he was hungry for tenderness and companionship, suffered keenly from loneliness. At Camden he was without a real friend and had scarcely a visitor. John Burroughs who had left Washington and was preparing to build his country house at Esopus, on the Hudson, came many times to comfort him with his dear presence. From time to time the mail carrier brought a letter from faithful Mrs. O'Connor, who proved herself outside the persistent and deplorable break between Whitman and her husband. But how insufficient these fugitively offered breaths of affection for such a heart! It was this lack of congenial friendship which kept the atmosphere about his arm chair lugubrious and heavy. Through Peter Doyle he reached his comrades occasionally; he could not, ill as he was, mingle with the crowd, his great friend, and make new acquaintances. He who not long ago, in the hospitals, had reanimated with the flowing radiance of his superb health thousands of sufferers, experienced in his turn the need of

---

[1] *Calamus*, p. 140.

being invigourated by affectionate and communicative presences, to be nursed and consoled like a little child. Despite all his courage and his good humour, the letters of the great solitary allow us to penetrate beneath the "nothing new" which he uses as a refrain, or by some more precise confession, for instance, that "it is pretty glum around and over me sometimes";[1] showing of what heavy hours his life was then woven. More than the days the "long cold evenings"[2] weighed upon him, succeeding the joyous ones at Washington, when he went with one or with a group for charming walks by moonlight.

Certainly Walt did not want for anything in the house of his brother George and of his sister-in-law who proved attentive and generous to the invalid. But the atmosphere of the house was not what his lungs needed: the brotherhood of blood which united them was not seconded by that other brotherhood, which alone unites men, and makes of the most remote beings a true family. The Colonel who "believed in pipes but not in poems"[3] had never understood his brother, who once said of him, "We have the feeling of brothers one toward another; but George does not know me. It is possible that I do not know George also."[4] At any rate Walt, who lacked nothing for material comfort, did not experience morally the feeling of home. He needed not only attention, he needed to be loved and understood: tenderness was to him like daily bread. He confided to Peter Doyle that the friendly presence and the magnetism needed are lacking here—"I come in close touch with no one. . . ."[5] He wrote again, at the time he was about to occupy the new house his brother had built: "I am truly well here, but my *heart* is blank and lonesome utterly."[6] What would he not have given to have

---

[1] *Calamus*, p. 107.
[2] *Id.*, p. 129.
[3] H. Traubel: *With Walt Whitman in Camden*, p. 227.
[4] *Camden Edition, Introduction*, p. lxxxii.
[5] *Calamus*, pp. 116–117.
[6] *Id.*, p. 118.

near him his dear son Peter, "his dear loving face and hand and voice."[1] "I think that if I had only the right quarters which I had in Washington, and a good wood fire, and you with me as often as possible, I would be comparatively happy.[2]" But that was a dream; fate chained him to Camden.

And then, he had one wound which did not heal. "Mother's death is still on my mind—time does not lift the cloud from me," he confessed two months after he had kissed her in the coffin. In August the same complaint escaped him: "I can put up with all but the death of my mother—that is my great sorrow which sticks—affects me as much now, or more, than at the time it happened. . . . I cannot still get used to it—it is the great cloud of my life, nothing which happened till then had such an effect upon me." Despite all, his optimism breaks out and he continues: "But I shall get over it, however, dear son (that is likely of course, it is not sure), and I shall return to Washington this autumn and we shall be together again. I hope you will find me the same, as I was when you went with me to the Baltimore station on May 2."[3]

He did not return to Washington that autumn nor the autumn following, nor the next, though the hope did not leave him till the summer of 1874. He remained titularly as employe in the department, the work being done by a substitute, paid by himself. But in July, 1874, he was relieved of his duties, after eighteen months' absence.[4] This time, it was the definite break with the old life and the beginning of his establishment in the labouring men's suburb where fate had stranded him. Then, in October, he wound up his business in Washington.

He did not seem extraordinarily affected by the new orientation of his life whose future was from that time enveloped in sombre uncertainty. He continued to live in

---
[1] *Calamus*, p. 132.
[2] *Id.*, p. 129.
[3] *Id.*, p. 109.
[4] *Id.*, pp. 154-5.

hope, "fortunately I have been stocked with a plentiful share of it."[1] Thus it was that he calmly accepted his situation. He waited. "Just one year ago to-day that I fell paralyzed, what a year it has been for me,"[2] he wrote in January, 1874. After long months, he knew himself doomed, that nothing better was to be expected; he then resignedly announced: "I had another violent attack to-day, but it will pass." Or better, "I have had a bad week enough but I still don't get flat. I am often thankful to be as well as I am."[3] O the excruciating and sinister breaking up of this physique, which was once as if cut from the same material as the cliffs and the forest! The pride of being strong and without physical blemish crumbled bit by bit.

The poor invalid remained resting in his arm chair, lost in his thoughts, with his dog Zip, his daily companion. He tried to work a little, when his painful head would permit. He began to collect his notes of the war and the hospitals; also a poem which he gave to the Graphic which honoured him with a very cordial article accompanied by a portrait. He was thus tying himself to life in revising his memories of a crowning epoch of it. He went out as often as he could for slow and short walks; it was then he began to be acquainted a little with the people who came his way, the ferrymen, the tram conductors and drivers, who were kind to the sick man. And this made a pretense of life; he was compelled in waiting for something better to deceive his hunger and to relieve his suffering.

He was even then but half way on the downward road. In 1875, the shadows still thickened about him. The preceding summer he wrote to Doyle: "It seems clear enough that there is no substantial recovery probable"; he admitted the possibility that he might not recover; he made a new will—left the large part of what he had to his feeble brother Ed, and the

[1] *Calamus*, p. 156.
[2] *Id.*, p. 141.
[3] *Id.*, p. 146.

THROUGH ABANDONMENT AND SORROW

rest to Doyle. "The time goes very tedious with me. . . . I get desperate at staying in—not a human soul for cheer, or sociability or fun, and this continued week after week, month after month."[1] This time the heroic sufferer seemed at his limit and breathed out the complaint of his heart stricken with loneliness. The great liver, the great seeker, the great lover, was in darkness, consumed by nostalgia, by the limitless sadness of not being able to live more, to be joyous, to love, to be loved. Sometimes the bitterness so filled him that he had no courage to put together the order of a letter when he had to send a simple line to his friend at Washington, and at the close of the year 1875, heavier still than the two previous ones, he wrote: "I have been very sick indeed, the feeling of death and dizziness, my head swimming a great deal of the time, turning like a wheel—with much distress in the left side which sometimes keeps me awake at night. . . . I have not been out for three weeks."[2]

To this distress of the solitary, disturbances of another kind were presently added. The allowance which Walt paid to the Colonel was using up the little wage-savings he made at Washington. These were fast diminishing. This prospective penury seemed to disturb him; what was he to do, invalid as he was and would probably be always? The possibility of dependence upon no matter whom was to him insupportable. He could count only on the meagre returns which the sale of *Leaves of Grass* was to bring him; he was ill and alone; his early death was assumed and the book agents in New York conducting the sale cheated him. Truly fate was filling his measure. And indeed who knows? The material failure of the book was perhaps the symbol and augur of its total failure as the bible of humanity, the gospel of the modern life. Despite his serene instinctive confidence how should Walt, depressed by suffering, his heart sick of loneliness, apparently forgotten by everyone, receiving no

---
[1] *Calamus*, p. 159.
[2] *Id.*, p. 163.

encouragement from without, not feel harrowed by lugubrious thought? It was truly from the depth of the sorrow of the titan chained on a Caucasus built of all his hardships that he wrote the poem—sent in March, 1874, to Harper's Magazine: *The Prayer of Columbus*, of Columbus come to the end of his voyages and venting his despair on the island where he was shipwrecked. "They tell me I have coloured it with thoughts of myself," writes the poet. "Very likely."[1] The discoverer of the moral continents of the future, the Spiritual Columbus who had furrowed with a bold prow seas of unknown humanity, used the analogy which was evident between his present condition and that of the old Genoese sailor—both assaulted by adverse winds, both saturated with misery, suffering, calumny, and ingratitude—and effused by the lips of the explorer the sadness of his own soul.

> A batter'd wrecked old man,
> Thrown on this savage shore, far, far from home,
> Pent by the sea and dark rebellious brows, twelve dreary months,
> Sore, stiff with many toils, sicken'd and nigh to death,
> I take my way along the island's edge,
> Venting a heavy heart.
>
> I am too full of woe!
> Haply I may not live another day;
> I cannot rest O God, I cannot eat or drink or sleep,
> Till I put forth myself, my prayer, once more to Thee,
> Breathe, bathe myself once more in Thee, commune with Thee,
> Report myself once more to Thee.
>
> One effort more, my altar this bleak sand;
> That Thou O God my life hast lighted,
> With ray of light, steady, ineffable, vouchsafed of Thee,
> Light rare untellable, lighting the very light,
> Beyond all signs, descriptions, languages;
> For that O God, be it my latest word, here on my knees,
> Old, poor, and paralyzed, I thank Thee.

---
[1] *Calamus*, p. 145.

> My terminus near,
> The clouds already closing in upon me,
> The voyage balked, the course disputed, lost,
> I yield my ships to Thee.[1]

The poet come to this extremity seemed journeying toward some fatal crisis which was smothering all the vigour left in him. But back of him legions of his race, from whom he had inherited a magnificent strength, invisibly sustained him in this terrible assault which was to be followed by many another; and it was decreed that he carry off the victory. The year 1876 was the beginning of a comparative recovery, slow, but sure. The most tragic moments were passed and the man insensibly began again to live in company with his infirmity.

To this unexpected renascence of the year 1876 one event strongly contributed. In the interval of suffering he slowly prepared a new edition of his poems: was it not now the only form of activity or approximating it which tied him to life? He discovered at Camden a little printing office, where the young printers were kind and respectful to him, and he entrusted them with the composing of his book, which he published himself.[2] Sometimes, remembering his first trade, he put his hand to the work. This edition elaborated in an unhappy time—the sixth and called the "Centenary edition" (the year of the centennial)—appeared at the beginning of 1876. It consisted of two volumes: *Leaves of Grass* conforms to the preceding edition, except some insertions, then a mixture of verse and prose entitled *Two Rivulets*, and including *Democratic Vistas, Notes of the War, Passage to India, Like a Bird on Pinions Free*, more than twenty new poems.

The supplementary volume, later bound with his verse, and proportionately enlarged by new pages, was the point of departure of the *Prose Works* such as we know it to-day, destined to accompany, emend, elucidate, the master work. In a preface, the poet allows us to see a reflection of the

---
[1] *Leaves of Grass*, pp. 323-324.
[2] *Calamus*, p. 161.

sombre epoch which he was passing through: "As I write these lines, May 31, 1875, it is again early summer—again my birthday, now my fifty-sixth. Amid the outside beauty and freshness, the sunlight and verdure of the delightful season. O how different the rural atmosphere amid which I now revise this Volume, from the jocund influence surrounding the growth and advent of *Leaves of Grass*."[1] Like a reaffirmation of pride and of youth and a recall of the beginning, the portrait which formerly signed the first edition of the book-gospel, the portrait—singular, unforgettable, a moment pushed aside—took again its place, never to leave it, "facing the poem in which the man of Manhattan sang the joy of his body and his soul."

The edition went on sale. Walt offered it for three dollars. Some copies were distributed to friends, to different journals, and to buyers of curios, as if he had produced something marvellous. At once a veritable flood of requests came from England, letters rich in admiration and commissions, containing whole lists of buyers. . . . Here is what had come to pass. Already the autumn before, W. M. Rossetti and Anne Gilchrist together found the way to buy in England a part of the edition which they already knew.[2] To the offer of material help Walt replied that although very poor he was not in absolute want, and that he was deeply cognizant of the generosity of transatlantic friends; he appreciated above all assistance under the form of the sale of his books.[3] When a review of the new edition appeared in the Daily News, Robert Buchanan immediately sent to that paper a retaliatory letter in which he exposed the tragic situation of the poet ill and helpless, whom he compared to a dying eagle, set upon by ravens.[4] A little later W. M. Rossetti prepared and distributed a circular in which he asked the admirers of the

---

[1] *Complete Prose*, p. 274 (Note).
[2] H. H. Gilchrist: *Anne Gilchrist*, pp. 223-224.
[3] *Complete Prose*, pp. 310-11.
[4] London Daily News, March 13, 1876.

poet to subscribe to his last volume.[1] And the response was cordial, prompt, unanimous; a select group of writers, artists, and intellectuals, clergymen, women of the aristocracy, high officials, were enrolled. Among a crowd of other famous ones there were Tennyson, Ruskin, Edward Carpenter, Edward Dowden, E. Gosse, G. Saintsbury, Hub. Herkomer, Madox Brown, Lord Houghton; and some subscribers sent twice, three times the price to offer more efficacious help to the old poet neglected by his own people.

All summer manna fell in Camden. Walt wept with emotion. After the cruel time which he had lived through this sudden coming of generosity did him a world of good. He felt, in his heavy veins, a new vigour come to him and now he became the happiest man on earth. "I was . . . poor, in debt," he wrote later—"I was expecting death (the doctor put four chances out of five against me). . . . Both the cash and the emotional cheer were deep medicines. Those blessed gales from the British Isles probably (certainly) saved me. That emotional, audacious, open-handed, friendly mouthed just-opportune English action, I say, plucked me like a brand from the burning, and gave me life again. . . . I do not forget it and I shall never forget it."[2] He said again to a friend: "Always I shall love old England. She comes to me now and always, when I think of her, as a great soothing affection."[3] And the requests continued, though abated toward the end of the year, addressed to England and Ireland. "It is very singular," the poet wrote to Peter Doyle, "how my books are in demand in Ireland."[4] He sold enough to meet the reduced need of his life. Walt was saved for a time.

In noting how different was the welcome which his poetical message received on both sides of the Atlantic, Walt

---

[1] Donaldson: *Walt Whitman the Man*, pp. 26-29.
[2] *Complete Prose*, pp. 519-520.
[3] Bucke: *In Re Walt Whitman*, p. 372.
[4] *Calamus*, p. 166.

could remember the new proofs of sympathy which came to him from his compatriots. In an article which John Burroughs sent to Scribner's Magazine of September, 1873, the editor cut out everything which referred to the wicked author of *Leaves of Grass*.[1] And when one of his first English admirers—Lord Houghton—then in America, came to visit him in Stevens Street in 1875 he declared that in all the orthodox literary groups which he met he was dissuaded emphatically from this visit—the Camden solitary was unworthy of it; Walt interpreted this ostracism in its true sense—as a flattering compliment.[2] The cutting appeal of Buchanan in the Daily News roused hot comments in the United States and wounded American conceit. Some journals of New York where Walt had a few of his most venomous enemies replied to the English accusation by covering him anew with sneering contempt the more when a handful of English æsthetes severely reproached America for leaving him helpless. The affair, all literary appreciation aside, was indeed noble, this treatment of a man sick and poor, who all his life had toiled! It was to such scrubs that the poet Joaquin Miller most passionately replied, in a lecture given in 1876 in Washington:

> Here in this proud capital, lived not long ago a great soul; an old man and an old man full of honor, with a soul as great as Homer's. . . . Grand old Walt Whitman. Even today he has the air of a Titan! Do not tell me that a man has consecrated for nothing all his youth and all his years to the pursuit of art, supporting poverty in the face of disdain. That man shall live I tell you.[3]

Engrossed in their enormous material tasks, too young to be sensible to a beauty other than that prepared by the easy versifiers, after the known masters of the Old World, the compatriots of Walt Whitman did not possess the peculiar faculty of comprehending their great man; and not seeing in

---

[1] *Calamus*, p. 110.
[2] H. Traubel: *With Walt Whitman in Camden*, pp. 31–33.
[3] Bucke: *Walt Whitman*, p. 213.

themselves and on their soil material for poems, they refused to recognize the man sufficiently mad to aspire to create wholly an original art. He was so in advance of his time and his race that only fine minds, trained, foreseeing, such as England possessed, were capable of knowing and saluting him. It was the old old history proved once again. Walt addressed himself to his own people, offered them their own image, which was reflected, heroic and divine, in the mirror of his art, and his own people remained blind and deaf; and it was from abroad, from the old world of intellectualism, of tradition and prejudices, that applause came, decisive and vindicating. The poet himself never directed the least reproach to his compatriots: "They owed him nothing: why would he present the note for wares which they had not asked for?"[1]

---
[1] H. Traubel: *With Walt Whitman in Camden*, p. 344.

XXI

THE NATURE BATH

OTHER influences were soon at work to strengthen the happy effect of this event and to lead the invalid to a real convalescence. After these gloomy years of enforced confinement Walt had an overmastering desire for the open air and the sun. And now that he was able to move about more freely he hastened to satisfy it. One day—it was the beginning of the summer of 1876—he went to a suburb in New Jersey, twelve or fifteen miles from Camden. The place was called Whitehorse, and in the neighbourhood was an old farm, occupied by the Stafford family, whose son Harry worked in a printing shop in Camden.[1]

From the autumn of that year the poet began to spend weeks, months, seasons, boarding with the Staffords, who became his close friends; and when they left the Whitehorse farm, he went with them to their new home at Glendale where the Staffords kept a grocery at the crossroads. Walt, who since his arrival at Camden had had for horizon only the melancholy trees of Stevens Street, and who, during the preceding seven or eight years, had known but the suburbs of Camden, found himself in a delicious place, "with primitive solitudes, winding streams, recluse and woody banks, sweet feeding springs, and all the charm that birds, grass, wild flowers, rabbits and squirrels, old oaks, walnut trees, can bring."[2] The nature nook was to finish what the active sympathy of his English friends began. The old man, thanks to the sun, the water,'the trees, entered into a "semi-renewal of the lease of life" as he said. Timber Creek—

---

[1]H. B. Binns: *Life of Walt Whitman*, p. 280.
[2]*Complete Prose*, p. 2 (Note).

the little stream which wound not far from the Stafford farm —made of the helpless invalid a man merry, revivified, still able, despite his permanent infirmity, to enjoy life.
Walt, at Timber Creek, spent all his time in the open air. He discovered a corner particularly wild; it was "a secluded little dell . . . originally a large dug-out marlpit; now abandoned, filled with bushes, trees, grass, a group of willows. . . . A spring of delicious water running right through the middle of it, with two or three little cascades."[1] There he established his private dwelling. Seated on a tree stump at the foot of a great oak among the mint, the cress, and the water iris, the sun sifting through the branches, Walt, a notebook on his knees, felt himself living in communion with luxuriant and wild vegetation, with insects, rustling leaves, the noisy little river, and wrote down his impressions. After the vicissitudes of his full life, the great liver saturated with humanity was face to face with mother nature which he had left, more than a half century, and he drank of it with delight. The old man heard, heard the divine music of eternity, the vibrant solitude, breathed the odours of the surrounding life, felt within him the pulse of the great present, prolonging the contact and his wonder. The invalid found himself at the fountain of all remedy and all comfort. "Away then, to loosen, to unstring the divine bow, so tense, so long. Away from curtain, carpet, sofa, book, from 'society,' from city, house, street, and modern improvement and luxuries—away to the primitive winding wooded creek, with its untrimmed bushes and turfy banks—away from ligatures, tight boots, buttons, and the whole cast-iron civilized life. Away, thou soul . . . thee singly for me day and night at least returning to the naked source—life of all—to the breast of the great, silent, savage, all-acceptive Mother."[2]

Before the permanent miracle of air, sky, trees, insects, the heart of the solitary of Timber Creek was flooded with

---
[1] *Complete Prose,* pp. 96–97.
[2] *Id.,* p. 77.

joy. He saw in them a great unnamable Presence which sometimes fused with his own. "Never before," he writes in his notebook, "did I get so close to Nature; never before did she come so close to me."[1] To regain a little suppleness in his limbs he spent an hour sometimes "exercising arms, chest, my whole body, by a tough oak sapling—pulling and pushing, inspiring the good air. After I wrestle with the tree awhile, I can feel its young sap and virtue welling up out of the ground and tingling through me from crown to toe, like health's wine."[2] An Eden joy renewed the child after his suffering.

In the glorious days of summer, in this Oegypan retreat, he celebrated a still more intimate communion with nature: "An hour or so after breakfast I wended my way down to the recess of the dell which I and certain thrushes, catbirds, etc., had all to ourselves. A light southwest wind was blowing through the tree-tops. It was just the place and time for my Adamic air-bath and flesh-brushing from head to foot . . . bathing in the clear water of the running brook . . . slow, negligent promenader on the turf up and down in the sun. As I walked slowly over the grass, the sun shone out enough to show the shadow moving with me. Somehow I seemed to get identity with each and everything around me, in its condition. . . . It was too lazy, soothing, and joyous—equable to speculate about. Deliciousness, sane, calm, Nakedness in Nature!—ah, if poor, sick, prurient humanity in cities might really know you once more! Men would know what purity is and what faith or art or health really is."

For years—till 1881—Walt continued thus his retreats to his little river. He was able to write to Doyle in 1877 that he was almost himself again—fat and red and tanned.[3] Not only did the poet owe to these unforgettable hours at

---
[1] *Complete Prose*, p. 97.
[2] *Id.*, p. 98.
[3] *Calamus*, p. 169.

Timber Creek his resurrection but we also owe them a collection of impressions. *Specimen Days*, in which the emotion of Pan thrills with an intensity which sometimes surpasses that of Thoreau—this collection Bucke describes truly as the "most luminous and vigorous invalid's journal" which was ever written. These notes, pencilled out-of-doors in the little valley or in the surrounding wood by the convalescing poet, are one of the gospels of life, and one of the purest testimonies of the communion of man with nature.

Walt during the years when his strength was slowly returning lived with his brother George at Camden. It was there in July, 1877, that he received a call from an unknown admirer, from Maurice Bucke, a Canadian doctor of Ontario who became his close friend and his biographer, and is now numbered among the great companions, the equal of O'Connor and of Burroughs. His portrait of Whitman at this period proves Whitman still a magnetic figure:

. . . Head and body were well and somewhat proudly carried. His ruddy face, his flowing, almost white, hair and beard, his spotless linen, his plain, fresh-looking gray garments, exhaled an impalpable odour of purity. Almost the dominant initial feeling was: here is a man who is absolutely clean and sweet—and with this came upon me an impression of the man's simply majesty, such as might be produced by an immense handsome tree, or a large, magnificent animal. . . .[1]

It would seem that the desolate solitude of his early sojourn in Camden was dreamed away for Walt. The previous winter a great joy came into his life: he saw face to face his dear friend, his soul-sister Anne Gilchrist, the noble advocate who pleaded with so much fervour the cause of *Leaves of Grass* in her open letters to Rossetti. She came for a stay of two or three years in America and settled with her children in Philadelphia, where one of her daughters studied medicine. There were then sunny hours for the

[1] *Calamus*, p. 11.

invalid near this rare woman; he passed a large part of his time with her, the time not spent at Timber Creek in the open air. Walt renewed an intimate comradeship which he had not had since he left Washington and he passed the winter in happy social conversation. Some echoes of these evenings come in Anne Gilchrist's letters to Rossetti:

> We are having delightful evenings this winter; how often do I wish you could make one in the circle round our tea table where sits on my right hand every evening but Sunday Walt Whitman. He has made great progress in health and recovered powers of getting about during the year we have been here: nevertheless the lameness dragging instead of lifting the left leg continues; and this together with his white hair and beard give him a look of age curiously contradicted by his face, which has not only the ruddy freshness but the full rounded contours of youth, nowhere drawn or wrinkled or sunk.[1]

Some weeks before Bucke's first visit Edward Carpenter crossed the Atlantic for the purpose of seeing the poet, who received him presently at Camden.[2] The author of *Towards Democracy* has given us the impression which was made upon him by the old man whose all-powerful magnetism was not enfeebled by years nor illness; a something of immense reserve in his personality. Like Bucke he made with Walt excursions to Philadelphia and like him noticed what real affectionate bonds united him to the people of the street, pedlers with baskets, porters, car conductors, who greeted him as they came from the ferry. An old Broadway driver who had not seen Walt for years grasped him by the hand, tears in his eyes, the expression of his joyful emotion on discovery of his old comrade. To his young, impressionable admirer Walt proved the living figure of his poems. The sweet presence of Anne Gilchrist, the warmth of her fireside, visits like Edward Carpenter's, such were the blessed good fortune which helped the invalid, strengthened by his frequent sojourns with nature, and thus were put definitely away the sombre hours which shrouded his life.

---
[1] H. H. Gilchrist: *Anne Gilchrist*, p. 230.
[2] Ed. Carpenter: *Days with Walt Whitman*, p. 4.

XXII

ACROSS THE CONTINENT

WHEN Walt recovered his health he was seized with an ardent desire for movement, air, shows, new impressions—as if to be recompensed for the periods of impotence and confinement which he had passed through. His infirmity permitting, he was resigned to drag his limb and to be no more than a damaged human machine, as valiant and happy as if he had still the superb health of old; he asserted his will to enjoy things to the full measure which fate granted him, and with a soul unshaken by bodily misery. It is an itinerant Walt whose tracks we are about to follow for this last big jaunt—then to return to roam no more.

Before the continental journey was undertaken, a series of excursions from Camden and back again were made, one to Baltimore in 1875 to honour Poe whose monument was then erected; that year he also visited New York where he was "lionized"; he returned the next year and was present at Bryant's funeral; he sailed up the Hudson to visit John Burroughs; his love of New York was intense as ever. "In old age, lame and sick, having reflected for years on many a doubt and danger for this republic of ours—fully aware of all that can be said on the other side—I find in this visit to New York and the daily contact and rapport with its myriad people, in the scale of the ocean and tides, the best, the most effective medicine my soul has yet partaken—the grandest physical habitat and surroundings of land and water the globe affords—Manhattan Island and Brooklyn, which the future shall join in one city of superb democracy, amid superb surroundings."[1]

---
[1] *Complete Prose*, p. 111.

These vacation habits grew upon Walt. The hospitality of the family of J. H. Johnston made him a home in the city; they lived opposite Central Park, and one of his favourite pastimes in the beautiful May afternoons was to sit in a Fifth Avenue stage watching the "Mississippi of horses and rich vehicles, by hundreds and thousands," a swift-moving procession. While the flow of carriages passed before the great lover of movement and of mass, he drew from a Park policeman comment on the American rich, "Lucky brokers, capitalists, contractors, grocers, successful political strikers, rich butchers, dry goods folks, etc.," exhibiting family crests on panels or horse trappings, suggestive of "soaps and essences" and a European garnish. Walt noted the comments of the policeman "as a doctor notes symptoms." He also watched the big liners leave for Europe, responding keenly to the crowds at the wharf. In quitting his dear New York his farewell words were: "More and more, the old name absorbs into me—MANHATTAN—the place encircled by many swift tides and sparkling waters. How fit a name for America's great democratic island city. The word itself, how beautiful; how aboriginal; how it seems to rise with tall spires, glistening in sunshine, with such New World atmosphere, vistas and action."[1] Three months later, after an interval at Camden and the Staffords, Walt, leaning on his invalid cane, started on his way. His old vagabond heart yielded to a great enterprise; he now felt equal to it. The future he did not know: perhaps there would come a day of total helplessness. He would travel thousands and thousands of miles toward the West on a longer journey than any he had made in twenty-five years. The poet left to discover the almost limitless regions which he had so often explored in his dreams, he was to tread the soil, meet face to face the people he had introduced into his poems, and to come near, more freely than in 1848, the immensity of the continent, its riches, its incomparable diversity, its unity.

---

[1] *Complete Prose*, p. 507.

In mid-September (1879) he left Philadelphia and reached Pittsburg, black with the coal smoke of factories, crossed Ohio, Indiana, Illinois, and stopped but one night in St. Louis; he continued his journey to the West. "What a fierce weird pleasure to lie in my berth at night in the luxurious palace-car, drawn by the mighty Baldwin . . . distances joined like magic. . . . On we go rumbling and flashing, with our loud whinnies thrown out from time to time; or trumpet blasts, into the darkness. Passing the homes of men, the farms, barns, cattle—the silent villages. And the car itself, the sleeper, with curtains drawn and lights turned down—in the berths the sleepers—on, on, on, on, we fly like lightning through the night—how strangely sound and sweet they sleep!"[1] is his note of it. He crossed Missouri and admired its pastoral splendour, made a stop in Kansas at Lawrence, and at Topeka; crossed the Kansas plains and into Colorado. At Denver, the city of the Rocky Mountains, he rested, having encompassed three-fifths of the continent.

There he was profoundly stirred. Denver and the gorges of Colorado intoxicated him with their marvels. He responded anew to the unspeakable magnificence of the scenery fulfilling and more than fulfilling his anticipations by its astonishing reality. Denver, a modern, busy city, between peaks and plains, immediately captivated him and for days he lingered in its beautiful streets breathing the pure air of the plateaus, and delighting in the streams of crystalline water from the mountains, visiting the smelting works where precious metals were piled in pyramids. He wished to end his days there.

In an excursion to the Rocky Mountains before the wild panorama of rocks, streams, valleys, snowy summits, before such a marvellous Walhalla this thought struck him: "I have found the law of my own poems." He felt a "new

---

[1] *Complete Prose*, pp. 132–133.

sense," a new joy spring up in him.[1] He was not crushed by these marvels, he had on the contrary the sensation of being in his element, among realities adequate to his instinct.

Denver was the limit of his journey. He went from there to Pueblo and on to Topeka; viewing plains of cactus and wild sage, and herds of cattle feeding. The prairies, oceanic levels of pasturage which occupied from north to south the middle part of the continent, were with Denver the most profound and most lasting impression of all his travels.[2] At Topeka he visited in prison thirty captured Indian chiefs. The assistants were surprised to see the sullen, silent prisoners respond to Walt's greeting. "I suppose that they recognized the savage in me, something in touch with their own nature."[3]

He was again overtaken by prostration, and was detained three months at St. Louis with his brother Jeff and two nieces. He lost no time in exploring the queen city of the Mississippi, its resources, people, products, environment. He saw the giant slaughter houses, the large glass factories, or lingered in the evening by the great spinal river. As he expressed himself to reporters who came to interview him, he was discovering the real America of which eastern cities were but the advance guard, and his faith in the future of his nation was increased twofold now that he had touched formidable realities which he had not till then been aware of. America to his mind was not yet conscious of the possibilities she concealed and one day surely a literature, poems, art, individualities, an average such as the world never saw, would jet forth from the colossal reservoir of plains, rivers, mountains. Everything up to this time which had been done in poetry in America was unauthentic and false, not in accord with the immensity of her resources. The era of great Natives, truly modelled on their own soil, was not yet come. They would issue and spread, after the pioneers and builders,

---

[1] *Complete Prose*, p. 136.
[2] *Id.*, pp. 132–140.
[3] Bucke: *In Re Walt Whitman*, pp. 382–383.

to carry on and perfect the work of the creators of indispensable material riches.

Whitman returned to Camden the first days of January, 1880, "in his average health and with strength and spirits good enough to be mighty thankful for," as the Camden Post reported. This journey to the West, late in life, was a last and solemn justification of the great Idea which had illumined his life and which fertilized his work. "Prodigious marvels, revelations which I would not for my life have lost," as he wrote to his great friend Anne Gilchrist.[1] This turn across the continent gave an edge to his appetite for pilgrimages, landscapes, people, and new places. Five months later he was in Ontario, Canada, the guest of his devoted friend Doctor Bucke who was head physician of an asylum for the insane. True to his literary instinct Walt kept a diary of his impressions of the asylum, the surroundings, rejoicing in the odour of hay, in the freedom of the prairies. With Doctor Bucke he made a slow exploration of east Canada, reached Toronto, and from there sailed on Lake Ontario and afterward the entire course of the St. Lawrence. He was alive to every suggestion of the ample, rich country revealed to him—faces, manners, scenery. Wild Saguenay above the mouth of the St. Lawrence was filled with a kind of "pagan sacredness." He marvelled at Canada as a land of waters, forests, snows, a land of happy men and women; not a privileged class only, but of the mass, great, healthy, happy. Later he thought Canada must become one with the United States.

After his long journey the little adorable woody corner of Timber Creek saw him most faithfully return to it. The tiny valley where in contact with nature he recaptured enough of strength and suppleness to be allowed a long absence, was to him like a fountain of health, to which he returned whenever he felt again the need to test the strength of his friends, water and trees.

---

[1] She had returned to England in 1878. Tr.

Doctor Bucke was now gathering material for his great biography. This meant a return to New York where with Bucke the poet spent several days of July (1881) amid the scenes of his childhood. They were for him a time of deep emotion. It was more than forty years since he had seen his birthplace and the burial place of his ancestors; and now in his sixty-third year, after a life of sorrow and of joy, he revisited the old Whitman farm lands, now for more than half a century in the possession of strangers, saw the well, the sloping kitchen garden, and the remains of the dwelling of his great-grandfather with its mighty timbers and low ceilings, and the Van Velsor farm, too, where as a lad he spent his vacations. Seated on an old grave of the burial hill of the Whitmans for many generations, Walt thought of his family history—three centuries concentrating on that sterile acre— and reflected on all the links which bound him to them.[1] He had come from there, sprung from this soil and this primitive humanity, solid and sane. Then he visited Huntington where the Long Islander which he had founded still existed and where old friends came to shake hands with him. He felt again the poet's old love of the sea, its immensity, the solitude of the shores where he breathed again the salt breeze, heard the same waves, bathed and sunned, and shouted Homer as of old. In returning he remained till August in New York with the Johnstons; his old habit of absorbing shows led him to the Harlem River and Washington Heights; he went to Madison Square to breakfast with his friend Pfaff, where the bubbling diversions of the Bohemians happened before the war. The two men thinking of the old time emptied "in abstract silence, very leisurely, to the last drop"[2] a big glass of champagne, to the memory of the jolly companions—all gone. Walt, that summer, passed again chapters of his life, lived again dear memories.

---

[1] *Complete Prose*, p. 4.
[2] *Id.*, p. 181.

XXIII

ANOTHER PERSECUTION

BOSTON as well as New York was visited in 1881. Walt had been invited in April by the young men of Saint Botolph Circle to give his lecture on Lincoln. He read his commemorative pages, and recited *O Captain, My Captain*. It was twenty years since he printed in Boston his third edition and he was unprepared for the reception given him by the cultivated audience which greeted him. There was something of poetic justice, too, in thinking of the reception of this man who had been scorned as a barbarian rhymester, whose burning verse, surcharged with the future, had long fallen unheeded upon the indifferent ears of his countrymen, and whose very presence now was felt as a benediction. "It was a scene which those present will long remember as pregnant with meaning to the whole of their lives." Another paper said: "He has been welcomed at Boston with open arms. Old and young, old friends and new, have gathered around him. The young men have taken to him as one of themselves, as one of those fresh natures that are ever youthful, the older ones, many of whom might once have been indisposed, now have grown to see the real core of the man in its soundness and sweetness and are equally hearty in their welcome. 'He is a grand old fellow' is everybody's verdict."[1]

Astonishing effect of the work of time, which must be preciously recorded, in the joy of foreseeing an acceptation beyond the limits of a club, a city, a country, and reaching

---

[1] Bucke: *Walt Whitman*, pp. 225–226.

round the world. . . . It was then well in Walt Whitman to persist in his tenacious effort to maintain amid silence or hooting the affirmation of an infrangible personality, to be at last recognized by a public formerly hostile. Walt's ship was moving into serene places since the terrible howling storm which assaulted its first venture. . . . The horizon was becoming serene, and a soft breeze caressed the sail. Was it a treacherous indication or an advance taste of the future? No matter; in spite of possible future storms, the breeze was sweet and welcome, the ship was advancing, advancing.

This visit was a prelude to an important event in the history of *Leaves of Grass*. Walt was preparing a new edition for 1881 and his Boston friend Boyle O'Reilley told him that the publisher James R. Osgood asked to see the new text. Osgood and Whitman had met long ago at Pfaffs; the flattering reception given to Walt from a public once hostile suggested to this publisher putting his name on the tumultuous book.

Walt answered this proposal in asserting previously his inviolable intention of publishing a complete edition of his poems; he thus anticipated the fundamental objection always provoked on the appearance of *Leaves of Grass*. Osgood decided to undertake the publication of it, and a correspondence followed in which point by point all the details relative to the make up of the book were determined. At last *Leaves of Grass* was to have a publisher. . . . Such fortune had fallen to the book but once in a quarter of a century—or rather partially, for the house had failed some months after the launching. "Up to the present," Walt could write, "the book in reality has never been published, all previous editions have been but reconnoitering, printed copies for enthusiastic friends."[1]

In discussing with his publisher the format, characters, make up, the poet with the minutia and niceness of an experienced printer formulated his wishes—a compact volume

---
[1] *Camden Edition*, VIII, pp. 276-286.

ANOTHER PERSECUTION

of about four hundred pages carefully printed on good paper—"solid, simple, not expensive, nothing fantastical." Details of profits of sales were agreed to, both in America and England. Osgood conceded everything in courtesy and good will.

Walt corrected his text at Timber Creek. "I have three or four hours every day," he wrote, "in arranging, revising, fusing, in rewriting here and there passages of a new edition of *Leaves of Grass*, complete in one volume. I do a large part of the work in the woods. I like to subject my pieces to the test of negligent, free, primitive Nature—the sky, the stars, the sun, the abundant grass, or dead leaves (as now) under my feet, and the song of some cat-bird, wren, or thrush within hearing. . . . Such is the library, the study where (seated on a big log) I have sifted out and given some finishing touches to this edition!"[1] All haste was impossible to Walt. How many times, before sending forth his ship for the first time he had altered, re-shaped, verified the parts. And at each new voyage it was overhauled from keel to mast. Now it was ready once more.

It was truly in a genial atmosphere that the invalid spent these months in Boston with the joy of summer and of the coming volume. When free from the printing house he went walking in Boston Common under the shady elms, where twenty years before he had had a memorable conference with Emerson; he went by tram to City Point, near the sea; he met the sculptor Bartlett, Joaquin Miller, and Boyle O'Reilley. But the richest memory of this visit was of some days passed at Concord. In September Frank Sanborn came to see Whitman in Boston, and invited him to Concord as his guest. At Sanborn's home Whitman met Emerson, Alcott and his daughter. The company discussed Thoreau, the various aspects of his life, while Walt studied Emerson who like himself listened rather than talked. He noted the "good colour in his face, eyes clear, with the well-known ex-

---
[1] *Diary in Canada*, p. 58.

pression of sweetness and the old, clear-peering aspect quite the same."[1]

Emerson invited Walt to dinner on the following Sunday. It was the first time that he saw Emerson in his own home. He was then seventy-eight years old; Walt studied for the last time that noble figure in an aureole of spiritual beauty. The occasion proved indeed memorable to the poet; to him this dinner, above all else, reiterated and sealed definitely the verdict of 1855.[2] Walt was driven about Concord, taken to the old "Manse," the battle-field, saw the statue by French, and meditated a half hour in the impressive cemetery, Sleepy Hollow, where Hawthorne and Thoreau were buried, and where later Emerson's grave was also made. He visited Walden Pond, Thoreau's sylvan home. He, like others, carried a stone to the cairn raised by pilgrims, remembering how Thoreau twenty-six years ago came to see him at Brooklyn. Concord gave a fine welcome to Whitman.

A writer on the Boston Globe interviewed Walt one day while he was reading proof of *Leaves of Grass:*

> It is now twenty-six years since I began work upon the structure; and this edition will complete the design I had in mind when I began to write. The whole affair is like one of those old architectural edifices, some of which were hundreds of years building, and the designer of which has the whole idea in his mind from the first. . . . To a casual observer it looks in the course of its construction odd enough. Only after the whole is completed, one catches the idea which inspired the designer, in whose mind the relation of each part had existed all along. This is the way it has been with my book. It has been twenty-six years building. Seven different times have parts of the edifice been constructed—sometimes in Brooklyn, sometimes in Washington, sometimes in Boston, and at other places,—and this edition is the completed edifice.

So many times did Walt believe he had given final form to his book that he must have been sceptical. He lived and his work lived with him, the substance of one passed into the substance of the other; he could not stop the growth

---
[1]*Complete Prose*, p. 182.
[2]*Id.*, p. 189.

ANOTHER PERSECUTION

of it, repress the mounting sap each returning season. And it is to be presumed that there was not to be a final edition while life lasted—triumphant proof that the book and the man were one. But the poet was right in saying that his structure was complete: the edition of 1881 is the book as we have it to-day, except the annexes of the ten years he was yet to live. This time the book was truly fused into one whole. One can see it unroll, vast and varied with its great spaces, its thickets, its glades, its mountains facing limitless perspectives, its rocks and plains, organically bound like a part of the planet. Walt was right, like a good workman, to float the flag from the top of his great structure. After a quarter of a century he saw at last the sum of his work. Such was the significance of the volume put out by Osgood. Its appearance was ordinary enough; the poet wished no ornament on the cover but this naïve emblem: a butterfly with spread wings poised on a hand.

For the first days of the sale, a movement favourable to it was set on foot. Some friends of Whitman, the leading journals and reviews received their copy. This time the reviewers were not insulting as in former times. The publisher wrote him on November 14th: "The book is going well." The house in England engaged in its sale cabled for another two hundred and fifty copies. For a book of its peculiar history, this could be considered a great success, and the winter sale promised a straight two thousand copies. Bad luck, after twenty-six years of struggle, seemed conquered this time.

But . . . there was a "but." It was decreed perhaps that the book was not to prove its worth except by surmounting obstacles in proportion to its vast measure. A cruel law—though really just and beneficent—doomed it to incessant trials and at the limit of them it would succumb and be either unworthy to survive or else succeed forever. In March, 1882, Osgood received a note from the Procurer of the district of Boston, Oliver Stevens, demanding that he suppress the edition. What was to be done? The literary circles of Boston contained enough people intellectually keen and free to welcome, if not with unrestricted enthusiasm, at least with interest and deference, such a work as *Leaves of Grass;* and the warm welcome which surprised the poet the previous spring proved it. There was also a group incensed as of old at the book. A society for the suppression of vice—the one which at the beginning of the century furiously attacked Thomas Paine's *Age of Reason*—a society, well entrenched, appealed to the Attorney-General of Massachusetts, Marston, and he enjoined his subordinate, Oliver Stevens, to notify the publisher of this warning. Thus Harlan of sad memory seemed to revive in this second public attack against "the most extraordinary bit of wit and wisdom which America has yet produced," to quote the words of Emerson's greeting. As a result of the conflict Osgood returned to him the plates and the printed copies remained in the storerooms. Both poet and author were satisfied with the transaction.

Thus Walt found himself again in the world with his book on his hands. So near to port, the contrary winds compelled him, once more, to turn back. Events seemed to prove these verses of the poet:

I too. . . . I also sing war, and a longer and greater one than any,
Waged in my book with varying fortune, with flight, advance and retreat,
    victory deferred and wavering,
(Yet methinks certain, or as good as certain, at the last,) the field the
    world.[1]

Whitman's friends hastened to his defense. Douglas O'Connor, incapable of remaining long in the shadow while a cause dear to his heart was being fought, at once came to the rescue, with the same ardour of battle as in 1865. The good cavalier forgot the unhappy quarrel and in a flamboyant letter published in the New York Tribune he branded Os-

---
[1] *Leaves of Grass,* pp. 9–10.

good-Marston-Stevens as he had branded Harlan.[1] Maurice Bucke, who was completing at this time the biographical essay, pleaded vigorously his cause in the Springfield Republican. The majority of the voices in the literary world was in favour of him. Later Osgood bitterly regretted the want of courage which made him submit to authority. He was severely censured and his cowardice produced a more serious moral damage than a law suit. He would have sold a hundred thousand copies in a month and no one to molest him. This was all very well; but in the meantime the book disappeared from sale, after some months in the market, and the inquisitors ostensibly triumphed.

In the midst of these diverse clamours Walt preserved his confident placidity. However annoying, even disastrous (he was at the moment poorer than ever) the affair was for him, he displayed neither animosity nor discouragement, his eye fixed on the future, seeing perhaps the victory long deferred and uncertain perchance, "certain or nearly certain in the end." Was he not accustomed to storm? He saw his book and his cause disputed on all the trifling grounds of public opinion and he declared with the phlegm of a true man: "If I have a cause, this has happened to help me. If I have no cause, this cannot harm me." And he retreated to Timber Creek.

The good apostles in trying to suppress the sale and circulation of the great book of life only helped, by the marvellous justice of things, in propagating and spreading it. And the proof came suddenly, brilliant and retaliatory. Walt transferred the plates of his book to a publishing house in Philadelphia, Rees, Welsh & Co., the predecessor of David McKay. In September a complete edition was immediately struck off. Three thousand copies were sold before the end of the year; and the sale continued, though lessened, the following year. The money was placed to Walt's account who since the sale of the edition of 1876 had scarcely any money.

---
[1] Bucke: *Walt Whitman*, pp. 150–152.

Almost at the same time as this edition, known as the eighth, the poet entrusted the same house with a volume of prose which was to accompany *Leaves of Grass* and propagate the new aspect of his personality. In July, down in the New Jersey woods, he wrote in his notebook,"If I do it at all I must delay no longer; the resolution came to me this day, this hour, (and what a day! what an hour just passing; the luxury of riant grass and of blowing breeze, with all the shows of sun and sky and perfect temperature, never before so filling my body and soul)—to go home, untie the bundle, reel out diary scraps, and memoranda, just as they are, larger or small, one after another into print pages, and let the mélange's lackings and wants of connection take care of themselves. . . . At any rate, I obey my happy hour's command, which seems curiously imperative. May be, if I don't do anything else, I shall send out the most wayward, spontaneous, fragmentary book ever printed."[1] The volume he called *Specimen Days* and *Collect* and is the same as the present edition not including *November Boughs*, which followed later—and he describes it as a huddle of diary jottings, war memoranda of 1862-65; nature notes of 1877-81 at Timber Creek, with Western and Canadian observations, and with these *Democratic Vistas*, different prefaces and articles published in review. Whitman also re-edited his early pieces in defense of abolition and temperance—this to prevent others from reissuing these crude and boyish pieces.

The prose work had never a large sale, and was eclipsed by the master work which accompanied it. Incongruous and full of skips and jumps—hurry and crudeness telling the story better than fine work, these marginal notes of his life reveal him intimately, help us discover the what and why of his work, and make a magnificent unity of his thought and his effort. Not a line of *Specimen Days* but exhales the powerful aroma of his individuality.

---
[1] *Complete Prose*, p. L.

XXIV

DAWN OF GLORY

THESE twin editions make a positive period in Whitman's history. In proportion as his structure kept rising, the circle of his readers slowly, very slowly grew. One by one, by successive starts, Walt saw people come to him. He imposed himself by the cool obstinacy of his will and now he was somebody in the family of universal poets, despite denials and repulses. It was not to the masses, however, that his prophetic words pertained: he saw them unaffected and obtuse, and they were to be so long after him. He won only individuals, but, it is true, the most noted individuals of his time.

In 1878 his faithful friend John Burroughs, the first of his biographers, devoted some new pages to him in his book *Birds and Poets:* his study *The Flight of the Eagle* is one of the largest and truest of Whitman appreciations. The same year Robert Louis Stevenson published his Gospel according to Walt Whitman;[1] its irony and dilettantism concealed a real admiration which he dared not wholly confess. Edmund Clarence Stedman, in summarizing the work of the *Poets of America*, gave a large place to Whitman, and his criticism in Scribner's Magazine in 1880 is masterful. At this time William Sloane Kennedy, a journalist in Philadelphia, already a devout champion, published in the Californian his first praise of a revered work. The homage of Sidney Lanier must be also noticed who in a touching and beautiful letter declared to Whitman that though they were in absolute disagreement in their conception of art, he was

---
[1] New Quarterly Review, October, 1878. Re-edited in R. L. Stevenson: *Familiar Studies of Men and Books*, p. 91.

one of his most fervent admirers. In all the great English reviews the personality of the man with the "barbaric yawp" was discussed; the conspiracy of silence was at an end. The Critic published his portrait with autograph verses in 1883. Walt "accepted all this, as the river receives its affluents," naturally, without humility or pride, with a soul calm and serene.

In England his place was steadily won since the burst of admiration in 1876, and a notable group regarded him as one of the great figures of the age. Between Tennyson especially and the singer of Democracy a deferent and sincere friendship was expressed in particularly cordial letters. Walt was fully alive to the high esteem of the poet laureate, though he felt a real aversion to his art, and this aversion he expressed—it was the time long ago when he first sent his ship afloat—in an anonymous article in which he proclaimed in strong words the essential difference between the poetry of the Old World and the poetry he announced for the New.[1] Despite this instinctive antipathy he saw in Tennyson the representative of a society still half feudal and his lyrical expression of it the most finished and the most glorious; the affectionate, delicate, truly noble homage from the Lord of Haselmere to this solitary and haughty man who would not disturb himself for kings seemed to him a sign of the times; he saw in the greeting of the knighted poet, steeped in aristocratic traditions, a greeting, through him, to a man of the American people. To Doctor Bucke who visited Tennyson in 1891 (his letter of introduction being from Whitman), he said: "Whitman is a vast something. I do not know what. But I honour him."[2]

An outstanding event of these years was the publication in the spring of 1883 of *Walt Whitman* by Maurice Bucke— the outgrowth of a profound knowledge of the man and his work, and of an enthusiastic devotion to both. Burroughs

---

[1] Bucke: *In Re Walt Whitman*, p. 27.
[2] *Camden Edition, Introduction*, p. lxxii.

previously—in the *Notes* of '67, completed in '71—had but very slightly sketched the biography of his great comrade. This time the most exact facts, a chronological abridgement of Whitman's life, an investigation of his origin, documents, dates, closely establish the starting point and character of his work. Whitman, extremely solicitous to see himself written in the light of truth, not only helped in the task by procuring for his biographer facts and indispensable suggestions, but he himself at the request of Bucke prepared the first twenty-four pages of the book.[1] He did not have the repugnance the ordinary writer experiences of being the simple placer of his wares to be offered to the world in his own word—as he superabundantly proved in publishing continuously anonymous articles on his work and his personality. And if he was almost indifferent to being lampooned by the press, it would have been supremely disagreeable to him to see his actual self denatured in the pages of a friend. From the standpoint of intimate veracity, the biography of Bucke remains the source, the classical epitome to which it will always be necessary to refer in order to evoke a living real Walt Whitman who by all the ample simplicity of his being reaches beyond the growth of commentaries which year by year are more vigorous and more detailed as to the inwardness of his book and the contour of his life. All those who later inquired into the circumstances of his life or who discussed the depth of his personality he invariably sent to the pages of Bucke; and at the very last he vividly declared to his friends celebrating his last birthday: "A stack of books and essays has been devoted to me, and Doctor Bucke's is the only one which expounds and explains me as much as can be done."[2] The book was ornamented with two portraits of the poet—one of which so distinguished had been engraved by Anne Gilchrist's son Herbert—the other of his parents, and with three engravings of Joseph Pennell

---

[1] Ed. Carpenter: *Days with Walt Whitman*, pp. 36–37.
[2] Bucke: *In Re Walt Whitman*, pp. 311–317.

of the West Hills Farm and the two burial places of the Whitmans and the Van Velsors. Walt wished to appear in the midst of his own people, the Long Island farmers, and to look out on the verdure and sea of his island. O'Connor collaborated, for his famous pamphlet of 1865, *The Good Gray Poet*, reappeared in it entire, preceded by a long letter in which he renewed his old plea.[1]

Such as it was with its shortcomings and its uncouth composition this sincere book of Doctor Bucke's remains worthy of the poet whom it promulged on the world's stage as a definitively accomplished force. The book was contumiliously received by some of the leading magazines. Now among buyers of rare books, a first edition costs thirty dollars. Walt day by day gained ground. In foreign lands his name continued to expand. *Leaves of Grass* was being translated into German, Russian, Italian, Danish. Walt was making himself a place—if not his place, which other centuries alone would accord him—and it was not in the power of any one to take it from him. The book had parted for the unknown and wonderful world journey which it is pursuing in these days.

Walt became for the remainder of his life a resident of the little town opposite Philadelphia on the Delaware. Little by little the forbidding chill of the place which he felt when he sadly declared that he did not know a soul became pleasant and familiar, now that he walked leaning on his cane, in the neighbourhood of his house; just as in Chestnut Street his big high felt hat made his tall figure conspicuous in the crowd. Every day he came limping to breathe the air of the street and the river, and to inhale the walking crowds, interested in sights and scenes, talking with the passersby, quick to join in conversation, to hear news, to listen, rejoicing as in the days when he was freefooted, in the movement of the street and the public

---

[1] See Lafcadio Hearn's letter to O'Connor—a fine criticism of *Leaves of Grass* in Bliss Perry's *Walt Whitman*, pp. 239-244. See also Bucke's *Walt Whitman*, pp. 193-194, for other authorities on Whitman. Tr.

place. "How are you, Mr. Whitman?" was the greeting he met. And with his sweet smile, the old man replied: "Good day, good day, how are you?"

Tram riding, beyond the great joy it always gave him, was now compulsory because of his lameness. His favourite drive was to go to the city by tram to the Market Street ferry. When he was equal to it, he mounted the front platform beside the driver who gave him his high stool; and there, his back against the bus and feet on the ledge, he went for miles and miles, absorbing the life of the street in a kind of silent contentment, of exaltation and of reverie. All along the route the singular old man of patriarchal appearance was now known as he was before in New York, and all loved him, without understanding the real "Mr. Whitman, the poet of Camden."[1] Walt was decidedly like the genius of the profession; in all the big cities he lived a secret sympathy always attracted him to it. It was during the winter of 1880-1881, which was a severe one, that Mr. George W. Childs appointed Whitman to make known to him the conductors and drivers in Philadelphia who needed overcoats. Walt's work was to measure the fellow, who later received a garment to fit. Walt found this singular occupation easy.[2]

The Delaware River and the sights along its banks were to him a deep joy, intense as on the first day. It was something of a substitute for the amplitude of the ocean he so insatiably enjoyed in New York. His artist eye, his instinct, supersensitive to all the emotion of nature and humanity, caught there all the delight in the strong, somewhat heavy, but harmonious, flight of the gulls on the water, the coming and going of steamboats, which he could name easily, the sail-boats when with all sails loose they passed amid sky and waters shining in the sun and appeared to him like a thing of indescribable beauty which no poet could put into words—the quays, the flocks of crows above the ice and

---

[1] Donaldson: *Walt Whitman the Man*, pp. 39, 40, 42.
[2] *Id.*, p. 43.

snow, the boats crashing through the ice, the lights on the shore and water, the high chimneys of the distant factory vomiting its flames in fantastic reflection, the moving poems of the heavens, the lovely moonlight nights, the splendid nights of winter and spring when he spent hours and hours, his soul intoxicated, looking at the stars whose names and position all his life he knew, the stars which he numbered with the silent adoration of a lover! Sometimes beneath the stars he felt under the spell of an enormous sweet emotion, such as this whose memory he fixed in his notebook:

> Venus, nearly down in the west, of a size and lustre as if trying to show herself. Seeming maternal orb—I take you again to myself. I am reminded of that spring preceding Abraham Lincoln's murder, when I, restlessly haunting the Potomac banks, around Washington City, watched you, off there, aloof moody as myself.
>
> As we walk'd up and down in the dark blue so mystic,
> As we walk'd in silence the transparent shadowy night,
> As I saw you had something to tell, as you bent to me night after night,
> As you droop from the sky low down, as if to my side (while the other stars all look'd on)
> As we wander'd together the solemn night.[1]

And the ferry, Camden ferry, after those of East River. . . . Now he knew well all the environs and the ferry itself with its queer scenes—the waiting room, with its picturesque and changing crowds, women, farmers, workmen, children, its hum of conversation, laughter, the many scenes on deck. Lizzie the waiting room woman, Phil the newsboy, Charley the stove tender, and outside, vehicles, teams, rattle, cries, colour, bell ringing, steam whistles.[2] The joy of all this is described in *Specimen Days*.

Sometimes when he felt the need of a change of air he went to Glendale to the Staffords, or to a cape of the Jersey Coast. It was at Cape May, listening to the voice of the waves, that he wrote the poem *With Husky-Haughty Lips O' Sea*. De-

---

[1] *Complete Prose*, p. 118.
[2] *Prose Works*, pp. 124, 128.

spite his illness he was cheerful. True he was always threatened with returns of his prostrations, but now he joyfully accepted his part, and despite his helpless leg and his constrained life, he was active, convivial, interested in the life of the world. New friendships were knitted into his life; besides Maurice Bucke, Kennedy, and Robert Ingersoll, he met real affection from the family of Pearsall Smith.

At this time, too, a young man who often passed Stevens Street made the acquaintance of the poet and used to talk to him. Later he wrote the recollection of Walt at that time: ". . . My nebulous impression then was of a large man, of generous nature, magnetic beyond speech. . . Although I was not ignorant of his books, nor was I inclined to underestimate their gravity, what he had written seemed dwarfed by the eminent quality of human attractiveness."[1]

This youth was Horace Traubel, soon to be in the first rank of friends and intimates of the poet during these last years given him still to hear reports of the world and to absorb them joyously.

---
[1]Bucke: *In Re Walt Whitman*, p. 113.

PART SEVEN
THE SAGE OF CAMDEN
Camden (1884-1888)

XXV

THE INVALID AT HOME

For more than ten years Walt had been stranded in Camden "to die there," as he said, and during this time he had lived with his brother George. The Colonel had to leave Camden and Walt had to find a new home. The idea of having a "shanty" of his own often came into his mind. Now the cherished idea had to be carried out. He had never had a home of his own: at sixty-five it was time to enjoy this new experience. For about two thousand dollars he could buy a suitable house; and he found one not far from Stevens Street. George W. Childs, the benevolent millionaire, advanced the sum, which the poet repaid little by little. One fine morning Walt found himself a property owner.

The house he came to live in was close to the river in a rather prosaic and retired part of Camden, 328 Mickle Street. He settled there at the beginning of the spring of 1884, not to leave it till death. The rather wide street where he lived was lined with large trees; one grew opposite his windows, and the houses round about in the diversity of their fronts and their unequal height gave a somewhat provincial look to the street. The small two-story house itself the poet called his den. To some it gave the impression of the cabin of an old sailor. But Walt had chosen it and liked it and began now to organize anew his life there. Little by little a semblance of order was introduced. Mrs. Mary O. Davis became his housekeeper and a devoted one. Her presence always animated the house and gave the old man the intimate impression of home.

It was in the little room on the lower floor that he passed his days. About him was heaped an arsenal of reviews, page proofs piled on chairs or spread on the floor. On the wall were portraits of his mother and father and a small canvas—brought two centuries before from Holland—a picture of one of his maternal ancestors. Pictures of his friends were on the mantelpiece. Walt sat in his great arm chair before the open window, a book or writing pad on his knees. It was there that he worked and received his visitors. There were flowers in the window, and a canary in its cage sang sharp, joyous notes. Walt had his dog with him, but between the bird and the poet there was a special intimacy: its trace found its way into these verses of *Leaves of Grass:*

Did we count great, O Soul, to penetrate the themes of mighty books
Absorbing deep and full from thoughts, plays, speculations?
But now from thee to me, my caged bird, to feel thy joyous warble,
Filling the air, the lonesome room, the long afternoon,
Is it not just as great, O Soul?[1]

While he worked or dreamed, the life of the quiet street was near: neighbours came and went, passersby stopped a moment before the window, and from his arm chair he replied gaily to their greeting and sometimes he conversed with them. And the old man, who had been at home in the great world, all at once experienced a special feeling of comfort. He had found a shelter suited to his years.

His mode of living, according to the strong phrase of his friend O'Connor, was "the immemorial poverty of goodness and genius." The profits which he derived from his book, having received the royalties of two or three previous years, amounted to an insignificant sum. From time to time periodicals like Harper's Monthly, the Century Magazine, or the Critic, accepted a short poem or some pages of prose, and paid him generously. It was truly wonderful to receive fifty dollars for a piece of twenty-three lines or ten dollars for less than a quatrain; but this happened rarely, and these occasional windfalls were not sufficient for his maintenance.

---
[1] *Leaves of Grass,* p. 386.

THE INVALID AT HOME

But the old man was not worried: he thought perhaps of the lily of the valley, and he was right. Throughout his life he had lavished succoring affection and had sung the miracle of it; he published his *Leaves of Grass* to create ranks of Comrades. And now in his days of infirmity, noble hearts responded to the appeal, and were firmly determined not to let the Sage of Camden suffer. He had many rich friends in New York and Philadelphia. They formed an invisible guard, and watched over the little house to forbid the approach of poverty.

Walt asked nothing himself. He left it to his friends to discreetly apprehend his needs.[1] Charity out and out he would have coldly refused. His dignity remained intact and supreme. His English friends sent sums of money from time to time. In a preface to an English edition of *Specimen Days* he put on record his gratitude to the overseas' donors to whose generosity he was indebted for "very sustenance, clothing and shelter. And I would not go to the grave without briefly, but plainly, as I here do, acknowledging— may I not say even glorying in it?"[2] The Pall Mall Gazette in 1886 contributed a good sum to his support; Sylvester Baxter tried to obtain a pension for his work as "voluntary nurse" but he did not succeed.

The settlement of the poet in Mickle Street was followed by another decline of his strength, already irreparably imperilled. Whatever had been his past suffering he had still a heavy load to bear. In July, 1885, he suffered a sun stroke; he recovered from that to find himself weaker, and with a new disturbance of his tottering constitution. Walt slowly went down the fatal descent which the catastrophe of 1873 pushed him. He lived in his thought and kept his optimism, in a serene waiting for what the future held for him. The great regret of the old man, since his isolation, was his incapacity even to move with a cane. He had to give up his

---

[1] W. S. Kennedy: *Reminiscences of Walt Whitman*, pp. 22–23.
[2] *Complete Prose*, pp. 433–434.

favourite promenades to the ferry, the river, to Market Street, to mingle with the crowds and, what was hardest of all, to pass long days anchored in his arm chair. To remain like an old ship high and dry, while he heard the currents of life move, and their odour come in whiffs, unable even to moisten the keel, it was indeed hard. The clearer his head remained the more perfectly conscious was the invalid of his corporal lethargy. His friends, who found him in his great chair, silent and thoughtful at moments, but never breathing a murmur against fate, understood all the same the immense, unspoken desolation which his courage and even his joviality concealed.

Again his good friends planned to restore the great recluse to the open air. They bought a horse and buggy for him and he was able to go jaunting again, sometimes alone, sometimes with his little friend Bill Duckett. This gift of his friends replaced in a way his vacillating legs, and enabled him to take delicious drives through the woods and by the river, sometimes in Philadelphia. It is to John Burroughs again, who came every year to spend a little time with his old friend, that we owe the picture of one of these drives which they made together in 1887: "Bye and bye Walt had his horse hitched up, and we started for Glendale to see young Gilchrist, the artist. A fine drive through a level farming and truck gardening country. We drove briskly and saluted every person we met. . . . Walt knew the history of many prominent houses on the road. . . ."[1] And indeed the beautiful drives would end some day, even before the final day, as the fine walks had ended. . . . But awaiting them was a benediction.

Once more, it was a new aspect which Walt's life took on in this retreat in Mickle Street. It was not the fact perhaps of his living in a little house which is so characteristic of this period as the semi-claustration to which his diminished strength condemned him. Despite the buggy and its pleas-

---

[1] John Burroughs: *Whitman*, p. 54.

ure his life was concentrated more and more about the arm chair in which, without collapsing, his great body stagnated; and to this new phase corresponded a special development of his intimate being. He was deprived of expanding in space, and he deepened within himself, dreamed with an intensified soul, prolonged his meditation in which he reviewed, as if to give them a final retouch, the great themes of his life and of all life. He became filled with thoughts of eternity; a new expression lit up his face; the circles of his psychic life were enlarged. In short, the atmosphere about him completely changed. Whereas the greater part of his time heretofore was spent among his friends of the populace, the nameless workmen of the street, and of the shop, the people he was now in contact with—and how much he may have regretted it perhaps—were for the most part intellectuals. In this new setting there rises an incomparably great, majestic, and simple figure of the seer, the patriarch, the sage and the old man of young heart, free from the rancor distilled by old age, an extraordinary figure, calm, silent, solitary, radiant, immeasurable, who lit up the room in Mickle Street and as such he remained to be forever materialized in admirable portraits which are equivalent to surpass works of art.[1] The Titan stricken in his body, but in full possession of his intellectual faculties, thinks leisurely in his home, allows his thought to voyage through space and on the track of conjectures; judges, concludes, reëxamines the meaning of his work, and renews in the ardour of his imagination the innumerable journeys of the man intoxicated with health that he once was. . . .

How sweet the silent backward tracings!
The wanderings as in dreams—the meditation of old times resumed—
    their loves, joys, persons, voyages.[2]

---
[1] See the Critic, October, 1902, p. 319, and the Century, November, 1905, p. 82.
[2] *Leaves of Grass*, p. 387.

XXVI

THE SOUL OF WALT

WHEN Walt, in answer to Maurice Bucke's invitation, went to Canada in 1880, the latter profited by this leisure to study complacently the physical and moral aspects of the poet, that he might the better write his biography. Among the notations accruing from these weeks of intimacy there are precious ones, which can give us a theme of a complemental examination of this great disconcerting figure who escapes you just as you think you grasp him, and by imponderable attributes escapes all analysis. Walt was more than sixty, and some new characteristics or rather those more apparent than before were written on his countenance. Paralysis and his confined life without changing the continuity of his essential self subtly influence the further development of his individuality.

Curiously the face of the poet retained the same brilliant ruddiness as when he sauntered every day along Broadway; and with hair and beard now white as snow, the contrast was very striking. His cheeks were still smooth and full, his lips, under the cover of the heavy moustache, full and strong as ever; and the heavy-lidded eyes had an expression of repose and drowsiness without lassitude. It was the fleecy aureole which lit up his face, and his trailing limb at first view gave him the appearance of an old man of eighty; yet when scrutinized closely, he had the look of childlike frankness. "His face is the noblest I ever have seen," said Bucke.

Already in 1878, John Burroughs confirmed his first impression in declaring: "After the test of time nothing goes home like the test of actual intimacy, and to tell me that

Whitman is not a large, fine, fresh, magnetic personality, making you love him, and want always to be with him, were to tell me that my whole past life is a deception, and all the perception of my impressions a fraud. I have studied him as I have studied the birds, and have found that the nearer I got to him the more I saw. . . . His face exhibits a rare combination of harmony and sweetness with strength—strength like the vaults and piers of the Roman architecture. He does not make the impression of the scholar or artist or *litterateur*, but such as you would imagine the antique heroes to make, that of a sweet, receptive, perfectly normal, catholic man, with beyond that, a look about him that is best suggested by the word elemental or cosmic. It was this, doubtless, that led Thoreau to write after an hour's interview: 'that he suggested something a little more than human.'"[1] Likewise, in spite of his age, his precarious life and his illness, Walt always manifested the same scrupulous neatness as in health: his clothes, worn or torn, his total personality, physical and moral, exhaled an exquisite perfume of purity. He spoke without gesture or vocal emphasis. He avoided arguments, preferring to all constructive reasoning and elaborate logic the simplicity of acceptance, praise, persuasion. His old curiosity he retained, making him an "intense listener."

Years of illness, the apparent monstrousness of the stroke which smote him, the passionate attacks, even poverty, did not fill him with acrimony, disenchantment or rancour. "When I first knew Walt Whitman," writes Maurice Bucke, "I used to think that he watched himself and did not allow his tongue to give expression of a feeling of fretfulness, antipathy, complaint, and remonstrance. After long observation, however, and talking to others who had known him many years, I satisfied myself that such absence or unconsciousness was entirely real."

He was punished bodily and in his poetical work, yet he

---
[1] John Burroughs: *Birds and Poets*, pp. 215–216.

preserved a soul as clear as if fortune had sprinkled flowers uniformly in his path. This optimism was not the effect of a heroic will, but as an attribute natural and inevitable, perhaps the result of an interior life in perfect equilibrium. He had made the complete round of things and avowed himself neither morose nor blasé. His obstinate good humour was stronger than disaster, his composure marvellous. Interior emotions were never reflected on his physiognomy of the "unaffected animal." At certain moments, we are told, his face, nearly always lighted by benevolence, appeared imprinted with august seriousness, and then, "there was an air of power spread over it which made one almost tremble."

With the advancing years, his simplicity of manners, his habits and tastes, which had always been remarkable, were accentuated. Perhaps no one ever saw, to such a degree, a human being so purely himself, nothing but himself, imperturbably and simply himself, without foreign alloy, as a mountain, a tree, or an animal. Walt Whitman was in this respect a veritable prodigy of ease and naturalness. He was astonished to be so little astonished. He was invariably the same man, everywhere and with everybody. Walt was simple, and this simplicity was not an attitude, but the attesting of the fundamental ingenuousness which was allied in him with the highest genius.

He said one day to his friend, Anne Gilchrist, that none of his friends knew that he was a poet. No prestige had the power to affect him. It was this absolute independence of manner, of taste, of attitude, this obstinate and tranquil insubmission to the artificialities of social convention, which all his life made him as much the butt of waggish jokes as his invariable open collar, his ruddy cheek surrounded by white billows of hair and beard, his ample clothes of a bygone age, his giant proportions, and the very particular joyous atmosphere which enveloped his entire person. With the same tranquil front with which he received praise or blame for his work, Walt let pass the jests, the caricatures, parodies, malign insinuations, and continued in the same way—perhaps amused really. He proved, with his naïveté and his slowness, the ideal target for the shafts of men of wit, he who had so little.

In 1884, Edward Carpenter, who came again to see his friend, found him the same man as in his preceding visit, though weaker and perhaps slightly reduced; and in studying the august features of the old "Northman, enchained on his throne," he was more strongly impressed than ever with the singular extremes indicated in his face. He discovered in him the irreducible stubbornness, mingled with an intense thirst for affection and a universal tolerance, with an excessive prudence and calculation blended with candour, and always the same indomitable savagery of the old falcon, neighbouring with the infinite, the all-enveloping tenderness which made the base of his character.[1]

Walt Whitman, in fact, offers multiple astonishment by the riches of contrasts of which the unity of his character is woven. He encompasses a world of opposites: as soon as you seize and fix his essential traits, other characteristics at least equally important immediately solicit you. And one hesitates to translate him, thinking that, at best, he will escape you, that he has neither commencement nor end, that he is not one to be grasped.

You will hardly know who I am or what I mean. . . .
Failing to fetch me at first keep encouraged,
Missing me one place search another,
I stop somewhere waiting for you.[2]

The union in him of the complementary characteristics of the Whitmans and the Van Velsors does not explain the enigma he offers us; it is perhaps for the future to grasp fully such a type of complete man. Among so many strong extremes the most striking is revealed when studying Walt

---
[1] Ed. Carpenter: *Days with Walt Whitman*, pp. 35-38.
[2] *Leaves of Grass*, p. 79.

in his daily life; you discover that he is alternately close to the common run of men, to the verge of being one of them, and formidably isolated by his superhuman proportions. This contrast is not revolved in naming him a kind of archetype of the average man, and nevertheless part of the explanation is suggested by that. "I imagined," he confided one day to Bucke, "a life which should be that of the common man in average circumstances, and nevertheless great, heroic." The "average" with him was not the equivalent of "mediocre," but the state even of the "sublime": a perfect democrat—not of attitude or of word, but of daily practice—he balances the qualities of the mass, his share being largely the inappreciable intellectual faculties which belonged to him individually: he included all the attributes of daily humanity, and besides, that "great something," presence of which Thoreau and Tennyson respected without being able to define, and which was not what one commonly calls genius. Nature did not make him expiate the superiority he was endowed with, in marking him, as so many very great men, with what may be called bizarre inaptitudes, defects *vis à vis* of the average man; but prodigiously generous to him, she placed him as high as the highest peaks, and instead of the snow and the bare rocks corresponding to his altitude, he preserved all along the sides the vegetation of the warm, shady valleys sprinkled by farms and by harvesters. It is thus that Walt Whitman is a new type of humanity, a product *sui generis* sprung from the soil and from the Democracy of the New World.

How explain that the least vain of men, the most indifferent to criticism and opinion, was the same man who, all his life, edited and circulated in friendly papers articles and notes in which not only his cause, but his character, was defended, his history and doings, his intentions complacently described? Walt, who never catered to a great man and who when questioned as to his work, spoke of his "pomes" or his "pieces" with such real simplicity denying them all sublime

THE SOUL OF WALT

intention and considering them only as efforts of new poetry, declared, however, to Bucke that not one of his most enthusiastic admirers such as O'Connor or Burroughs valued *Leaves of Grass* as much as he himself did. For his cause remained constantly in his eyes the great cause; and his physical and moral being were identical with his cause. All his life he was seen exposed to erroneous interpretations, and he published these notes on himself to reëstablish things finally right. He wished to be painted in the light of truth. The marvel was that this great, calm pride and this enormous conception of his personality, this limitless faith in his destiny permitted him to maintain himself in his daily associations with ordinary people, the most ordinary among them, not on the surface, but intimately—yes, the most common and the most natural of the sons of earth.

And in proportion as you encompass him, the contrasts multiply, overwhelm you. Close to his natural freedom and his communal fervour was a strong tendency not to open the folds of his intimate being. This natural reserve could indeed, with a man so closely related to nature, be ascribed to the innate prudence of the animal. Or rather, the sentiment of his dignity, which was strong, forbade him to deliver the key of an inaccessible sanctuary. You might see at once the same individual who joyously welcomed the victories of science and the application of the modern spirit, keep exclusively for his own use the most primitive things, the good strong things blessed by time: his sheet-iron stove and old utensils a provincial grandmother would not have tolerated. You might hear the inveterate dawdler, who always declared a magisterial disdain of money, glorify the spirit of business, the industrial and mercantile activity of his race, as one of the necessary and splendid qualities of humanity. He wrote in *Democratic Vistas:* "I perceive clearly that the extreme business energy and this almost maniacal appetite for wealth in the United States are part of amelioration and progress, indispensably needed to prepare the very results I demand. My theory includes riches and the getting of riches, and the amplest products, power, activity, inventions, movements."[1] And elsewhere in a note found among his manuscripts: "In modern times the new word Business has been brought to the front and now dominates individuals and nations (always of account in all ages, but never before confessedly leading the rest as in our nineteenth century); Business—not the mere sordid, prodding, muck-and-money-raking mania, but an immense and noble attribute of man, the occupation of nations and individuals (without which is no happiness), the progress of the masses, the tie and interchange of all the peoples of the earth. Ruthless war and arrogant dominion-conquest were the ideals of the antique and mediæval hero; Business shall be, nay is, the word of the modern hero."[2]

Walt had boldly addressed the individual above the law as the sole authentic sovereign of the earth, exalted the outlaw, the rebel, the criminal, and from the same heart he dedicated a little poem to Queen Victoria and another to old Emperor William I: and he said of presidents to someone who spoke to him of Cleveland: "He has read my *Leaves*, someone says, and did not think ill of them. I like to know all about the Presidents. They stand for a good deal, to my thinking. I've a fondness for their messages. . . . I have a hope that they'll run their administration as they run banks. Why not? I don't wish to debase the office, nor abolish it as Moncure Conway says he does. No, no; the President is the one man representing every inch of the Republic. He's worth keeping if only as a figure-head of our national democracy, the solidarity of the nation. So say I, at any rate, and stick to it."[3]

It is easy to see that Walt was not a simple renegate nor an irresponsible: despite the singular radicalism of his poem, he

---
[1] *Complete Prose*, p. 215 (Note).
[2] *Diary in Canada*, pp. 72–77.
[3] Bucke: *In Re Walt Whitman*, pp. 367–369. See Whitman's poem, "Election Day," *Leaves of Grass*, p. 391. Tr.

was not in reality more revolutionary than he was conservative. Never did this impassioned lover of the modern, this mad exalter of young America, which he adjured to be only itself and to reject models from beyond the sea—omit among his Adamic intoxication of singing a new continent, to send a memory to the past, and the masters of long ago. Throughout his work this pious sentiment is inscribed among wonder and prophecies; and at the last banquet with his friends, his first word was a homage to "powerful comrades" which had gone before. He finely adjusted the scales to evaluate the part of the past which entered into the formation of the future and to know with marvellous foresight the secret of their harmony.

How often has the poet been reproached with the grossness and vulgarity of his instincts. How many times apparent inelegance was declared unworthy of a poet or an artist? It is true he was a man of strong, common instincts, but none who knew him well would doubt the extreme finesse of his taste. Miss Helen Price has recounted an instance of his delicate sense of colour in fruit, of motion in fishes; and others of his sense of religious exaltation in the presence of the great truths of nature.

It is easy to say, too, that Whitman did not have a rational and deductive brain and that his purely intellectual faculties were not reascendant: there is some truth in this, but what is to be made of the extraordinary acuteness of vision, of the talent of master analyst which is evident in certain pages of *Democratic Vistas* in which he bares the vices, defects, cancers, the monstrosities of American society, or better still the analytic criticism of Carlyle and Emerson? It was rarely that he employed his critical sense; nevertheless, he could always formulate definite truths without flourish.[1]

And such are the contradictions which the man presents no matter from which side he is viewed. He has to be ac-

[1] Whitman is an admirable critic: his book talks are among the best of their kind and are found in his prose works, and in Traubel's *With Walt Whitman in Camden;* Burroughs thought him the best critic in America. Tr.

cepted thus. He does not explain himself: he is exposed, with his antinomies, his sudden breaks, his incoherences. He was aware of them and in recognizing them as neither proud nor humble. Like life, like nature, and like truth, he was made of contradictions, which of themselves resolve into a superior equilibrium. For if there was one thing in him which was to be trusted, it was the perfect poise of his character; and because of this the monumental impression felt in his presence was accounted for. He was the living confirmation of the truths which are tried and not proved.

What silences all the doubts and what is proved from all questions is the sovereign grandeur with which the old man is clothed helpless in his arm chair in which his massive and haughty figure seems to defy decay. He had said:

> I announce myriads of youths, beautiful, gigantic, sweet-blooded

and he had himself been one of them. But he also said:

> I announce a race of splendid and savage old men.[1]

And this also he saw illustrated in himself. After all, it was enough to look at him, to grasp his hand, to hear him say words of welcome, to have the most satisfying explanation of his work and of himself. By his physical proportions the massive amplitude and absolute symmetry of his figure, the colour of his skin, the timber of his voice, his manner, Walt Whitman appeared a true prodigy of harmony in power. This son of farmers, this artisan seemed as far from current humanity as the latter is from the primates. In a group of superior men, his natural superiority was proclaimed without his saying a word. Surely he had never been so beautiful since the time when old age and illness had transmuted into august majesty the manly strength of his years of health. The young barbaric god was little by little transformed into a majestic being which

---

[1] *Leaves of Grass*, "So Long," p. 381.

from the little house in Mickle Street lit up the world or began again his voyages of long ago among men and scenes. He does not diminish so much as we grow to his stature. A visitor, in 1877, after an interview with the poet, recorded his impression of him as: "the most *human* being which I have ever met." O'Connor already has given a particularly happy expression of his friend: "To call a man like him good seems an impertinence. In our sweet country phrase, he is one of God's men." And John Burroughs thought him a new type of humanity, precursor of an age when the individual, after having passed the crucible of future democracies, shall blend in equilibrium the fundamental qualities of the antique man, and the spirit of enterprise and research, the sensibility of the modern man.

Walt Whitman to those who knew him best is described as Oceanic, Adamic, Cosmic; he suggests that vast repose, that divine monotony of the tides and of eternity, felt in the foundations of his character, more akin to water, soil, wind, rocks, than is permitted man to be, all in his being affirmed supremely man. From his immense serenity a perpetual incantation of Erda pronouncing before the Voyager the words of earth, seems to rise, sweet and strong, all enveloping, drawing you toward the circles of the great All. . . .

Old age, calm, expanded, broad with the haughty breadth of the universe,
Old age, flowing free with the delicious near by freedom of death.[1]

[1] *Leaves of Grass*, p. 126.

XXVII

DAYS IN THE COTTAGE

WALT now worked two or three hours a day, by fits and starts. When he was active, he always wrote the motifs of his poems in the open air, among concrete realities. This source was now almost cut off from him. Inspiration also came at long intervals and was generally brief. The period of the out-of-doors was at an end since the old man was sequestered. He busied himself in collecting from his notes the impressions of his former life, evolving his conclusions, glancing backward over travelled roads. Despite the chary benevolence of the literary world toward him, some reviews and journals welcomed his verses or bits of prose which he sent from time to time. The Nineteenth Century published in 1885 a group of short pieces, *Fantasies at Navesink*, and in 1888 the New York Herald paid him generously for whatever he sent.

He explained one day to a friend his method of composition. When he was struck by an idea which offered the theme for a piece, he revolved it slowly in all its aspects, then, once definitely adopted, jotted it on paper which he slipped into an envelope. He did not trouble himself as to the form it should take, nor its possible bearing. He remained expectant of new suggestions and abandoned himself entirely to the outcome. As soon as some development of the mother-idea came to his mind, he made a note to be put with the first one; on the day when he judged the subject sufficiently developed and the idea ripe, he emptied the contents of his envelope and set to work. He always used his knees as a writing table; his pen was generally a large goose quill, and to jot down the impression of a

DAYS IN THE COTTAGE

moment any paper within reach would do—wrapping paper, envelope, or newspaper margin, etc. He was never provided with notebooks. For his prose pages he kept notes, review clippings, or no matter what document which he carried between two pasteboards held by a thread, with the collective title well in view. His poet arsenal was made up of an infinity of similar bundles, piled near him.

Walt was never a great reader except at certain periods of his youth, when he was eager to advance by all the means at hand. The mountains of extracts and commentaries found after his death prove, however, what enormous sums of varied knowledge he accumulated all his life. He had read in his own way, but he had read few books through. Bucke remarked that when Walt took a notion to enter his library at London, he would have a dozen volumes about him and pass from one to another, without the shadow of system, reading here and there. The supposition that Walt lacked method would have been contradicted by the examination of some of his innumerable notebooks where were found pinned, pasted, or inserted in surprising order, treasures of information gathered from all sources throughout his life. He had a book of citations and reading extracts. Surely a scientist or even a literary man would not have practised the fantastic method which he followed in the course of this slow and incessant search in all directions at once, but it must be recognized that from his point of view it was richer in results than if Walt had from childhood formed the habit of the mental discipline of the college.

The little house would have been searched in vain for a library. Walt owned in fact but two or three dozen books which never left his shelf. On these he was nourished, and he could recite pages of them. They were Shakespeare, a Bible, translation of Homer and Dante, poetry of Walter Scott—whose fiction he adored, with that of Victor Hugo, Leconte de Lisle, and George Sand and Fenimore Cooper—an Epictetus, an Ossian, an Omar Khayam, a venerable copy of

Consuelo which he cherished, and the work of Felton on Greece. Mixed with papers could be found a Burns, *Confessions* of Jean Jacques, selections of American literature by Stedman, Spanish literature by Ticknor, Prose Writers and Poets of Germany by Hedge, the works of Fauriel and Ellis on the poetry of the Middle Ages. This alone proves the catholicity of his sympathy. Aside from these worn-out volumes, and some of which were almost one with his life, it could be said that the poet cared very little for books in general. New books he received in large numbers: after casting a rather indifferent glance at them he allowed them to lie on the floor or gave them to his friends. Toward the great moderns, his curiosity was qualified. If he knew fairly well Carlyle, Emerson, and Tennyson, the little that he had read of Ibsen, Ruskin, Tolstoi, or Browning was not enough to hold him long; Hugo was not known to him except by perhaps a hundred verses, but that was enough for Walt to hang his portrait framed in black near the window of his room, to prove his respect for the great poet of France.

If books in general tempted him little, dailies and periodicals had an attraction for him that age could not weaken, perhaps because they reflected the life of his time and because facts were more to him than philosophy. Every day he followed the big dailies and the local sheets, and kept clippings of them. He enjoyed especially illustrated journals, and when a friend entered with a magazine under his arm, he asked to look at it. He had experienced the world and knew its entanglements, and he manifested the same interest as before for actuality, the business of the country, international events. That great insatiable appetite for living every-day humanity could never be diminished in him. When a visitor came to see him, the news of the day was one of the favourite subjects. Even with his enforced seclusion he still proved himself an American of the nineteenth century, part of his time, and curious in following its orientations. His natural clairvoyance, his multiple experience, his profound knowledge of men always free from acrimony was seen in his judgment on contemporary events. In 1870 he followed with keen interest the vicissitudes of the Franco-Prussian War. He denounced Napoleon III but the French people had all his sympathy.[1] He honoured Victor Emmanuel; he had deep esteem for Frederick III, but not for his successor. Some of his opinions show a particularly lucid intelligence. In 1873 he foresaw the expulsion from Cuba of the Spaniards—realized some years after his death. Many times he announced the inevitable absorption of Canada by the United States. He had the intoxication of his race and believed in its expansion: what is called to-day American imperialism could find in him more than an argument and an anticipated approval. He always declared himself a free trader and advocate of political rights for women. Strange, too, this impenitent celibate considered marriage and the family the fundamental foundations of the Republic. He also thought the world was too much governed. Religious, social, literary polemics usually found him uninterested. He was very categorical and even vehement in affirming his tendencies, yet he showed limitless indulgence toward individuals. Without pretending to be an eclectic he was too conscious of the rôle devolved upon each one in the enormous economy of the world not to yield to men and doctrines full and exact justice. He had no need to reread Epictetus to be persuaded of the immanent and final equity of the universe; he carried the instinct of it within him, reflected in every line of his face.

He had to beguile the monotony of the days by a semblance of activity. Some were too heavy and he could neither read nor write. Now he remained still, his glance wandering, listening to the sound of the quiet street or weighing his thoughts. In such moments a pleasant word or the spirited face of a friend did him good. Too often one came to see him to tell him of trouble or to engage in the discussion of

---
[1] *Calamus*, p. 73.

grave questions; it was carefree and bright presences suggesting good fresh air which he most needed to escape the heavy hours. One of his invariable occupations was to send a word of remembrance to his friends. Often it was a postal card with some simple, affectionate words telling his occupation at the moment, his state of health, generally in an optimistic way. The loving hearts, the great companions whose tenderness he tested, were never absent from his thought, and to his last moments it was his preoccupation to keep intact the bond of affection which united him to the little phalanx. When he did not feel inclined to write to each one separately, he sent news to one of them asking him to communicate it to a second and so on. Very often instead of writing he sent to his favourites a paper, a review, an illustration. When his name or some item concerning him appeared in a journal, his first care was to procure some dozen copies which he sent to them. He discovered at Camden a curious little printing shop which attracted him. He used to have printed there "memory leaves" which he sent to his friends—a more direct message from him—made in advance of their formal appearance in a magazine.

In the years before 1888 the old man could at least count on the invariable return of some pleasant hours each week, his Sunday visit with his excellent friend Thomas Harned, brother-in-law of Horace Traubel, the young comrade whose devoted pure affection was unforgettably established. Walt called this house his "other home," so much did he find himself at ease there. "Every Sunday when I get up, I say to myself: I believe that I will go to-day to Tom's." And he came regularly, not by habit, but because he loved the household, found himself in congenial company, expanded in conversation and good cheer, and proved himself the best of company. During these delightful reunions Walt would recite favourite poems, never his own. Before the portrait of Lincoln on the wall he sometimes lifted his glass saying "I drink to you." With his unusual independence of manner, his disdain of convention, he yet proved on these occasions the perfect gentleman that he naturally was. Never the least vulgar expression came from him, even when men were the sole company.

One of the attractions of the Harned home for Walt was the children. He was their natural companion. Between the fine old man and children the bond was marvellous. Sometimes the very little ones were affrighted by his great beard and his natural majesty but a word from him and they were won. In Mickle Street the children coming home from school always greeted him when they passed the window. They brought him flowers in their season. During a time of extreme pain, when the least noise caused him suffering, he would not allow the nurse to drive them away.

The occasions were rare that Walt, besides the Sunday dinner at the Harneds', indulged in eating with friends. His health would not permit. After 1885 his strength gradually declined. He was able to make two visits to Glendale where he had written the beautiful nature sketches of *Specimen Days*. Ordinarily he passed his days at the window of his room, seated in his big arm chair, a wolf skin thrown over the back, dressed in loose gray, cuffs of his shirt rolled back disclosing his strong hands, well proportioned, his workman's hands always clean, lying on the arm of the chair or holding pencil and paper. Flowers sent by friends were the life now in the shadowed room. Sometimes in the beautiful evenings he came to sit on the sidewalk, under a tree near the house, stayed there, alone or with a friend, to breathe the fresh air. Passersby stopped to talk to him, children played round him; it was still a way of mingling with the life of the street. But soon he could only with difficulty move from room to room.

Recluse as he was, he inquired the news and when he learned that any one about him was in need his good heart responded to it. Though simple as he was and removed from people, a certain curiosity, blended with consideration and benevolence, concerning the white-bearded invalid, brought many from the neighbourhood to the door. By public rumours it was known thereabouts that he was a poet, and this profession badly defined, eccentric, intensified the uncertainty of his neighbours. Of his goodness at least more than one had positive proof.

PART EIGHT
THE SETTING SUN
Camden (1888–1892)

XXVIII

A NEW ASSAULT FOILED

It was a few days after celebrating with his friends his sixty-ninth birthday that Walt suffered a severe prostration. It was at the close of a wonderful evening with his friend, Doctor Bucke, an evening passed by the river watching the sun in his red triumphal setting:

Shot gold, maroon and violet, dazzling silver, emerald, fawn,
The earth's whole amplitude and nature's multiform power consigned for once to colors;
The light, the general air possessed by them—colors till now unknown,
No limit, confine—not the western sky alone—the high meridian—North, South, all,
Pure luminous color fighting the silent shadows to the last.[1]

He did not feel the chill of twilight till he returned to his room. Then he was overcome, hurled to the floor where he remained motionless for hours, unable to call for aid. Later he was able to reach his bed. The next day he had another attack, followed by a third at noon.

Under these repeated assaults, the great giant this time staggered. Doctor Bucke and Doctor Osler came. They found the patient on the sofa of the little room, momentarily unable to speak; his whole body shook. Presently he was able to mutter: "This will pass soon, and if it does not—all is well." During the entire week the poet was between life and death. His remarkable self-mastery and tranquil courage never left him. His dear friends expected his death any moment. He himself in these redoubtable hours visualized the last one, and it was then that he pencilled verses of farewell to his

---
[1] Walt Whitman: *Leaves of Grass*, p. 400.

poems, the heart of his heart, calling them by name, like dear friends who circled about his bed. . . .

Now precedent songs, farewell,—by every name farewell. . . .[1]

On June 12th there was a ray of hope. Doctor Bucke was forced to leave almost sure of the result of the attack. Fate did not mark that hour and still once more Walt foiled the assault. He was persuaded that he owed this to the affectionate presence of Doctor Bucke; but he owed it perhaps to his wonderful constitution. Another attack in his enfeebled state would surely be fatal; waiting he survived, and with his humour and his splendid calm he summed up the situation: "The old vessel is not longer fit for the voyage. But the flag is still at the mast and I am still at the helm."

Unspeakably slow was his convalescence, with its ups and downs, its continual relapses, its train of suffering, its strict confinement. For weeks and months he had periods of lethargic heaviness, of deadly lassitude when it was impossible to write a letter, when speech was painful and difficult. Paleness and fatigue proved the gravity of the crisis. Perhaps he might pull himself out of the "ditch." He was not sure of it. He was happy that his head was clear and his right arm of use. "Now that I am reduced to these two things, what great blessings they are," said the invulnerable optimist. He had not lost his gently ironic gaiety during these sombre hours. He had been an invalid for more than fifteen years, subjected to every torture and to a slow dissolution when he should normally have enjoyed long, joyous, healthy years, yet he not only did not regret a single minute of his spending himself freely in hospitals, but he proudly rejoiced in his experience without which he would have lost "something infinitely more precious." To Kennedy who sent him roses from Massachusetts during the summer he wrote in mid-October: "It is dark, I have had my dinner and am sitting near the fire and gaslight, anchored and tied to

---
[1] *Leaves of Grass*, p. 403.

my old big democratic chair and room, the same as all summer, now in the fall and soon the long winter and (if I live) probably through all. . . . Upon the whole get along and baffle lonesomeness and the blues; God bless you and the wife."[1]

Toward the end of another year lamentable complications set in which caused him frightful suffering day and night; Doctor Osler would not leave his patient, giving his service free. In reality, Walt, though conqueror of the attack, declined visibly. The enemy, the lurking enemy, made a great leap in the dark toward his prey; if he was not able to seize him yet, he would do so soon. The old man knew it, and looked ahead, ready for the final attack. He had scarcely need to repeat with the sage: "What is good for you and nature, is good for me," that peace might dwell in him.

This illness overtook him in the midst of the preparation of a new volume which he wished to put out that year. The proofs of it he received on May 31st. During the terrible week in which his life "was not worth a cent" he tried in his lapses of ease to examine the proofs, which his friend Horace Traubel brought him from the printer. Once more Walt knew the joy of seeing a limitless affection, a fresh and marvellously comprehensive devotion respond to the appeal which all his life, all his work proclaimed. In this critical hour, afflicted as he was, what would he have done, even with all his heroic will, without the dear friend who every evening came to discuss with him the details of the book, and who became from this moment the indispensable auxiliary, the *alter ego*, with whose help he could comfortably arrange his last publication. Traubel had been at one time a printer and the two men understood one another fully. Walt, always slow in his corrections, was kept back by weeks of drowsiness when it was impossible to read a line; and though the uncertainty as to the future and the determi-

---

[1] W. S. Kennedy: *Reminiscences of Walt Whitman*, p. 59.

nation to complete his book were a daily incentive, the work appeared endless. His manuscript was not entirely re-edited and he lacked the strength to put the last touch to his notes. Still the work progressed in spite of weeks of lethargy, and Walt wrote: "Traubel is unspeakably faithful and good. . . . I would have been able to do nothing with the printing without him. . . ." And he, during these unforgettable hours passed with the poet, interpreting his least gesture, listening to his vivid conversation in fits and starts, could measure the royal reward—which he never sought—of his trusty devotion, of his tender, exalted faith, of his nights passed after the day's work, in reviewing proofs and attending to all correspondence.

During these months of daily coöperation Traubel recognized with what minute care Whitman set about the preparation of his volume. No matter how trifling the difficulty, he never decided off hand; he gave everything its time, to be weighed for and against. Without refusing advice, he wished no decision taken without his consent. He asked about the overseer, the printers, and charged his friend to take them either a silver piece or a portrait to pay them for trying to suit him. He was solicitous of the material appearance of a volume; he would not tolerate, for example, that a chapter end at the bottom of a page and to avoid offending the eye, he did not hesitate to sacrifice a paragraph. Nothing was left to chance. He might be deceived in the end, and acknowledge his error, but not regret it.

Faithful to its title, *November Boughs*, after a very laboured parturition, appeared in mid-autumn 1888, with the name of the publisher, McKay. It was a collection of verse and prose in which were unified the different critical or autobiographic bits which he published here and there since 1882, and grouped under a single title, *Sands at Seventy*, about sixty very short poems—the longest did not fill a page. Close to notes on Shakespeare, the Bible, Burns, Tennyson, and memorial bits from his notebooks, he put there, such as it is with its dross, an essay planned for a time on Elias Hicks, the Quaker preacher; he with his parents had heard the old man preach. *Sands* is inscribed to the memory of a man or an event, or perhaps the meditations on the great thought of death, anticipated, invited, caressed, without any complaint or despair, rather with a latent exultation. Like a snowbird, singing amid desolation, from the depth of "old age land locked within its winter bay," "held by sluggish floes," "with gay heart," he still made his song heard.[1] It was no longer the time of the great hymn of maturity, running free like a river: age, confinement, physical suffering had touched his inspiration. . . .

As I sit writing here, sick and grown old,
Not my least burden is that dulness of years, querilities,
Ungracious glooms, aches, lethargy, constipation, whimpering *ennuis*,
May filter in my daily songs.[2]

But if the ampleness of the previous poems is no longer found, their emotion seems intensified by the gravity of the hour and the closeness of the unknown. And how, through these bits made from odd verses, which resemble remotely the fragments of Greek tragedies collected from their dramas, the mighty personality of the man vibrates! It was like a prolonged farewell, like words tender and grave which friend repeats to friend on the threshold, after having clasped him in his arms, amid "the shadows of nightfall deepening," postponing severance, garrulous to the very last.[3] The portrait which accompanied *November Boughs* seemed one of a good god with hoary hair, resting under a tree of his Paradise, his limbs stiff with the fatigue of the day.

Horace Traubel was not at the end of his labour when this work was done. Walt was determined to prepare his complete work from 1855 to 1888, verse and prose, in a single

---
[1] *Leaves of Grass*, p. 394.
[2] *Id.*, p. 386.
[3] *Id.*, p. 404.

volume. It was the "great book," as he called it, whose output was to be limited to six hundred copies, each containing an autograph. This formidable quarto of 900 pages, of rather clumsy appearance, appeared a little before Christmas; the author sold it off hand, and gave it as a "personal" and "authentic" edition. Once more he was his own publisher. There was something characteristic and simple in this quaint way of distributing literary merchandise which suited him: it was one of the primitive and strong notions which he piously kept as a personal custom, amid the complexities of the modern civilization which he admired so deeply. After his intimate friends received their copy, affectionately dedicated, Walt was ready to meet orders which arrived from time to time from Asia or Australia, as well as England or even the continent. The number was sufficiently within bounds that he could without much effort make his sales by drawing directly from the big package placed in his room. In reprinting his poems, despite his great weakness, he persisted in revising the entire work to get rid of slight faults of punctuation or spelling which had escaped his vigilance in the previous volume. With these corrections and *November Boughs* which was added to this, the text corresponds to the eighth edition. As soon as the "great book" appeared, Sylvester Baxter, a warm admirer and a friend, proudly greeted it in the Boston Herald.

From the other side of the Atlantic it was plain that his place was already won. An English reprint of *Specimen Days* was made in 1887, in a collection edited by Ernest Rhys, followed the year after by *Democratic Vistas;* the poet wrote prefaces to both; and *November Boughs* appeared in Glasgow the same time as in Philadelphia. In 1889 a partial translation of *Leaves of Grass* for which Knortz and Rolleston had not found a publisher in Germany, even in offering to pay the cost of the volume, was brought out in Zurich with Schabelitz.[1] For years before this Luigi Gamberale published an

---

[1] H. Traubel: *With Walt Whitman in Camden*, p. 18.

Italian version of the book the title *Canti Scelti*. For the first time a trial in another language was given it: was it already being proved that before finishing its career *Leaves of Grass* would be translated into every language on earth? The cosmopolitan following was advancing, never again to halt.

From France, two men joined it with generous applause. First it was Leo Quesnel in 1884, in Revue Politique et Littéraire, an enthusiastic, suggestive, and comprehensive study in which the man was viewed in his essential character and which remains in a brief form, after a quarter of a century and the many new judgments which it inspired, one of the most absolute presentations of the poet and his work. The second, four years later, announced a still more brilliant testimony whose amplitude was not marked only by the large number of pages which it filled. It was Gabriel Sarrazin with the essay—*Renaissance de la Poésie Anglaise*. Walt Whitman, when he had this translated by a friend in January, 1889—he read no language but his own—experienced one of the great joys of his life. He was seized to his very depths by emotion for this magnificent insight—the unity of his character and his book understood by this Frenchman far away, as he had been when the letters of Anne Gilchrist to Rossetti appeared, twenty years before. And the first reaction persisted. He insistently alluded to Gabriel Sarrazin, when he wrote to his friends at this time, proving how deeply he was touched. In thanking Kennedy for the translation, he said: "His piece is like a great, great tradewind hurrying the ship into port." Months later he resumed, "It is a marvellously consoling page for me—coming from a man who proved himself so evidently a Frenchman from Paris, armed from hand to foot, with a penetrating eye, with a sharp scent and ear, plunging to the very depth of criticism." And in September he added: "The Essay of Sarrazin seems the boldest stroke which has been struck in my behalf up to this time."[1] From this time, Walt placed

---

[1] W. S. Kennedy: *Reminiscences of Walt Whitman*, pp. 61-73.

his admirer in France with the great companions of his work, O'Connor, Burroughs, Bucke, Anne Gilchrist—small, precious phalanx in whose escort he would appear to posterity. He sent to his new friend, then in New Caledonia, the "great book," which just appeared, and an affectionate correspondence sprung up between them. It was "marvellously consoling" in fact—not alone for the poet himself—to see the advanced French thought adhere to this modern gospel of the New World, communicating to it, very far from all dogma, a wonderful expression of humanity and nature.

All this was like a breeze come to refresh the invalid in his solitude and inactivity, and brought him a mystic response to the desperate appeal, wild and yet tender, which he threw out. The world was no longer deaf as before. When his friend Carpenter published his poems *Towards Democracy* the old bard could feel the indirect homage which they implied. And soon he receives from England a new response, in the pages of *The New Spirit* of Havelock Ellis, a book big with new signification and of which the critic power does not weaken the wonderful inspiration, a response unrestricted, free and generous as he loved, and such as one of the elect could formulate, combining the sensibility of the artist and the power of a scholar and philosopher. One day he said to Traubel, in his picturesque language: "I like frank people, those who detest or those who love, the yes or the no which one does not misunderstand."

There is a little poem in *November Boughs* in which the secluded, motionless man is painted:

In some unused lagoon, some nameless bay,
On sluggish, lonesome waters, anchor'd near the shore,
An old dismasted, gray and batter'd ship, disabled, done,
After free voyages to all the seas of earth, haul'd up at last and hawser'd tight,
Lies rusting mouldering.[1]

---
[1]*Leaves of Grass*, p. 403.

Now his friends could mount the narrow stairway of the little house to see Walt in his room, his holy of holies, his fortress, his den, his solitary domain now and always, and where he lived like an old captain sheltered in his cabin.

A poem, that room. . . . The little parlour below where he had worked up to this was already a fine confusion of newspapers, manuscripts, and "of everything under heaven": but it was nothing beside his room since it became his only "workshop." The bewilderment of visitors in the presence of the extraordinary bric-à-brac, in the midst of which the great incorrigible Bohemian lived, was easily understood; all the same, it was only the first impression and after some minutes all this queer and indigent chaos was transformed in contact with the reigning-presence which it surrounded. In heaps, in bundles, in stacks, by the seats, crammed in baskets of loose papers, between the legs of tables and chairs, under the table and stand, were heaped the numberless manuscripts, letters, clippings, which Whitman had accumulated since his youth and which he kept with the inextricable daily confusion, old reviews and new, books, proofs, nameless things, mixed with the wood for his winter fire. When one took in from the threshold the heterogeneous heaps in which the poet seemed to be blockaded, the first feeling was that of the aftermath of a cataclysm. Then courageously, without daring to place a finger on an old letter or a page of yellow manuscript, one was compelled to make a way among these dusty reefs to the arm chair where the smile of the master was the royal welcome. Under this apparent desolation there was a singular order: the master of the house alone had the secret of it. These mysterious timeworn bundles, which contained carefully classified notes, documents, letters, belonging to some business or some work in preparation, had perhaps the air of being piled pell mell; however, any time that Walt needed a page, he left his chair with effort, went toward a corner of the room, and taking by the end the heavy cane he leaned on, harpooned with curved handle the pack in which he was certain to find it. It was marvellous to see with what dexterity he operated, even in the dark. Whether by foresight, or whether he possessed exactly in his head the map of this archipelago of papers, he astonished his friends each time, however accustomed to these *tours de force*, by the sureness of his eye and the immediate success of his search into the indescribable confusion. He refused absolutely that any one help him in foraging among his papers, for a strange hand would inevitably transform into real disorder this methodical and disciplined disorder.

There it was, in the midst of this arsenal, that the old man worked, meditated, ate his meals, and received visitors. He had about him, within reach of his cane, this countless number of notes, which after his death astonished his literary executors by their unsuspected riches, and in which a half century of life was accumulated. "Wherever I go," he says, "somewhere—winter or summer, city or country, alone at home or travelling, I must take notes." And all of them were classified, ready to be used some day. Some sheep could easily have nestled among the piles, but was it not simpler and more convenient to have all these treasures scattered about him than to pack them in drawers or boxes? His room had a floor, therefore he used it.

In certain aspects this famous room is identical with the man and with his work: it is like his poems, in which ordinary people see but chaos, in spite of the admirable order found there for himself and for others. Only it must be understood what one means by "order." For instance in the great notebook which he always kept near him and where the addresses of buyers of his books were written there was no index; no alphabetical order helped one to find them: he however found this practical and clear. In these surroundings with which the most modest workman would not have been content, the great old man was happy, now that he was forced to live indoors. There surrounded by books, which he re-

A NEW ASSAULT FOILED

read incessantly without ever wearying of them, by his notes from which he formed from time to time the subject of an article, by his commonplace gewgaws, before a good fire the crackling of which he loved, he lived in a manner perfectly adapted to his needs. "Some friends are surprised," wrote Horace Traubel, "to see him living in the midst of such simplicity. But he finds in this room all that a home can contain of happiness and sanctity. There is not probably in the whole world a workroom like this one." Seated in the imposing rocking chair which the children of his friend Donaldson gave him for a Christmas present, timbered as by some stout ship's spars, the old Northman commanding it filled the room with his magnificent presence. A timeworn look, a scent of old oak attach both to the chair and the person occupying it.[1] And when the aureole of his white hair lay against the wolf skin, spread as a protection against cold, the extraordinary beauty of his face was still more striking. Immediately that threshold was crossed some visitors were astonished at this beauty; they felt then in the presence of a sovereign of the invisible world whose bright welcome and placid good humour could not make them forget his indescribable majesty. No disagreeable musty odour came from that invalid's den, in spite of the litter there: Walt kept the windows of his room constantly open, even as he kept his curiosity concerning the present awake. With the odour of old things which filled the poet's room was mingled something of the alert and the living.

Such was the absolute confinement till the close of the year. It was then that Warren Fritzinger, a son-in-law of Mrs. Davis, came to be Whitman's nurse. He was an old sailor and had already been three times round the world; that was indeed a recommendation with the poet, who was fascinated by all which concerned the sea. This man remained with him to the last. To insure his wages, some friends of Whitman, who were devoted to him, assumed the sacrifice—

[1] *Complete Prose*, p. 521.

heavy for some of them—of a monthly contribution. Walt was not a difficult patient and demanded little of the nurse: when, during the day, he tapped with his cane on the floor of his room, it was usually to send him for an outing. Upon his features was imprinted the weight of the last crisis. Not only was there discernible an expression of lassitude, but his pink cheeks had become pale and somewhat sunken. When he felt too weak to sit in his arm chair, he remained in bed and received his friends. If not he rose at eight o'clock for his breakfast and to read the morning papers. It was painful to see when he dragged himself, with the help of the furniture, the wall, and his cane from room to room, and to think what the splendid form had been before the stroke which had levelled him. The stubborn old man did not wish to be helped and meant to be sufficient for himself as long as an atom of strength was left him.

The buggy and bay horse, now useless, had been sold. Done the fine rides through the woods, to the riverside, along the suburbs. No more would Walt go to be refreshed by the wind, carried by his trotter. However bitter the privation, he had to be resigned to it. And after all was it right that he should complain, for though entirely broken in nearly all his branches, he still put forth a proud trunk.

XXIX

MEDITATION AT TWILIGHT

IT WAS not only the phases and happenings of a decline already evident that suggest the touching sight of these last three surviving years during which the man overwhelmed, ravaged, dying a little more each day, calmly resists and maintains his head high and clear above the wreck, while around him the little phalanx of his friends draws closer, to be near at the end. This largeness, this heroic simplicity, this emotion made up of these last moments, it is not perhaps given to translate them except by certain portraits taken in 1890 and 1891; it is enough to understand them to see that never was Walt so beautiful as at this august hour, in which death, invited with a grave joy, advances toward the stoic old man ready to welcome him with his good smile and to reach him his strong hand saying: How are you, mighty one? I am waiting for you. Here I am Walt Whitman the artisan who has sung his race, obeyed the inner call. . . . Wherever you lead me, I have faith in you and I wish to continue with you the wonderful voyage of my early life! Perhaps death hesitated in seeing so much light still about his white hair, so much human pride in the face of this man. . . . No matter, she was not afraid of him, she was his Comrade, the last comer and not the less dear.

To the middle of July, 1889, Walt had not seen once the sky above his head; he could scarcely leave his room. One whole year of imprisonment was completed by bereavement, the death of dear Douglas O'Connor who died at the age of fifty-seven. The seclusion had been still harder than at the time of his first attack, despite his being used to it and the faithful friendships which surrounded him. It was then that his friends planned a way to procure again for the invalid the joy of fresh air; one day Horace Traubel went to Philadelphia for a fine wheel chair. The slow vehicle, pushed by a faithful hand, took the place of the buggy, which itself had replaced the jaunts afoot. It was not perhaps the most exhilarating means of locomotion, but he blessed this last resource; life was lovely and good since he could still, with body in ruin, go to taste the breeze and to feel humanity about him. Walt was wheeled toward some peaceful part of the riverside and remained there an hour silently absorbing the surrounding spectacle. He had never been a great talker, and the gossips had always annoyed him, but now the intervals of silence lengthened. Even before a friend, he often remained without speaking a word: nothing was more grateful to him than the silent communion in the warmth of a dear presence. He said one day to Traubel: "I think that men in proportion as they understand one another end by saying nothing; a look and all is said." Not a morose silence, rather a serene and confident gaiety. And he observed himself, studied his progressive dissolution, without ceasing to declare himself grateful. He was happy to be "well" enough, to preserve intact his mentality—to be able to put the last touch to his work, and to see himself understood by a small number of choice spirits. If relief of pain came after a bad week, if a happy incident occurred or the sun smiled, immediately the ray of joy reached his friends in writing. "I write but little—someone send me fruits. . . . I have sold fifty copies unbound of the big book for three dollars each. . . . Have had many visitors, talked some. . . . I hear the noise from the streets, the peddlers; pretty little children come—heaps of letters some of them queer enough."[1] The worst indeed would have had to unite their studied cruelty to exhaust his good humour.

A little after his first excursion in the wheel chair, the thirty-first of May came round: to his friends this anniver-

---
[1] W. S. Kennedy: *Reminiscences*, pp. 64, 66, 67.

sary was especially worth celebrating, it was Walt's seventieth birthday. These fraternal love feasts repeated year after year knit the bonds of affection between those who were determined not to let his name be lost, to hand it on to posterity as a sacred trust. It took the form this time of a local celebration: a group of "citizens of Camden," lawyers, merchants, functionaries, gave a banquet to the poet. The largest hall in the village was chosen: it was decorated with flags, and an orchestra was ready; at the fixed hour only the hero was lacking, whose presence was not announced till the close of the dinner. But Walt was still so weak that his friends were anxiously asking themselves whether he could appear for the toasts, especially with the violent storm raging outside. He came; and at the moment, when the arm chair with the surprised old man in it appeared at the door, all the guests rose in silence, then cheered by sustained applause. Camden's famous citizen answered the homage by waving his hat. He was wheeled to the head of the table and there before a large basket of flowers and a bottle of champagne he listened to the president's introduction. "My friends," Whitman said, "though announced to give an address, there is no such intention. Following the impulse of the spirit (for I am at least half of Quaker stock), I have obeyed the command to come and look at you, for a minute, and show myself, face to face; which is probably the best I can do. But I have felt no command to make a speech; and shall not therefore attempt any. All I have felt the imperative conviction to say I have already printed in my books of poem and prose; to which I refer any who may be curious. And so, hail and farewell. Deeply acknowledging this deep compliment, with my best respects and love to you personally —to Camden—to New Jersey, and to all represented here you must excuse me from any word further."[1] Then he heard all the speeches with the same ease as if he were of the guests come to honour another man; when a passage especially

---
[1] *Camden's Compliment to Walt Whitman.*

pleased him, he applauded by tapping on the table with a bottle placed in front of him.

Numerous were the friends who Walt, with his poor weak eyes—those gray-blue eyes with heavy lashes which had so many times scrutinized human faces—could only distinguish mistily; friends from Philadelphia, young writers, journalists, scholars, editors, even a judge, all one with the Camden citizens. Still more numerous were the absent admirers who from England, America, and everywhere sent their greeting on the seventieth birthday of the poet: a real variegated bouquet, which the old man breathed with a delight not less than of the basket of flowers from which the snowy head lifted itself. From John Burroughs to Gabriel Sarrazin all the scattered members of his spiritual family were named that evening. And it was possible also to see a symptom in the fact that the important newspapers sent reporters. After the last toast one of the guests intoned a song, from memory, with the poet's help; then he left the hall, the basket of flowers on his knees, his chair swaying with the crowd of guests who came to shake hands with him. Surely Walt was happy this evening: however, with his dislike of public homage, he expressed regret for the intimate celebration which Thomas Harned gave him the year before. There was perhaps a little too much of effusion and demonstration in the Camden compliment.

One of the practical results of the seventieth birthday dinner was the gift to the jubilarian of a purse containing a subscription, more than one hundred and twenty dollars. To this he added a sum of his own in the bank to be used as he needed it. Another fruit of his seventy years was a special edition of *Leaves of Grass*, the ninth—limited to three hundred copies—small in size, morocco binding; the six portraits or ornaments gave a particular stamp of elegance. The poet sold it for two and a half dollars with the same simplicity which he offered some of autographed portraits—"all well enveloped" for three dollars. Was he less a great

MEDITATION AT TWILIGHT

man, because he was an agent? To these poems he annexed *Sands at Seventy* which made part of his last collection, and the volume closed by a page of prose from *Sands at Seventy—A Backward Glance o'er Travell'd Roads*. This time it was the last step before the really final edition, the conclusion presently reached by the incessant changes through which this unique book, enriched at every renewal, had undergone for thirty-five years.

A backward glance over the travelled road. . . . How many times the old man had glanced and lingered during the long days of seclusion, now that he worked and read little. What a road, what a journey! One summer day, in the flower of his strength, he began his enormous task not without having measured his strength; and he ventured with the candour of his enthusiastic and meditative faith. How had he dared? He asked himself now whether he accomplished his great design: to take up the challenge which Democracy and modern Science seemed to throw at Poetry.[1] For it was certainly in this spirit that he put his living self in a book, in order that America might study herself in the mirror of one great Individuality. Twenty years of incomprehension, of furious disdain or ridicule, of efforts to suppress his work, followed. He had, it is true, in the dawn of the first day heard the glad greeting of Emerson (those marvellous words of strength and light which surprised him), and two or three companions, much later, magnificently defended him. But these were lost in such a desert of ignorance and malignity that often, despite the robust faith in him, he had doubted the future. . . . Yet he had never lost courage and he always persisted. . . .

After patient years and years, here and there some listeners answered. O the noble pages of Anne Gilchrist and the affection so tender to a solitary soul of his friends in England! And he succeeded after thirty years of struggle in which he fought unarmed, his soul Gospel locked in

---
[1] *Leaves of Grass*, p. 427.

his breast. Like a talisman he had a little army of enthusiastic friends and defenders, the most faithful and convinced, such as never fell to a precursor; and thanks to them the great goal, to know that he was heard and understood, was reached. And in blessing fate which procured him these friends he thought sometimes if he deserved detraction, he certainly was not worthy of such splendid friends.

And after all, the masses were not won. . . . He had said to his countrymen:

Take my leaves America, take them South and take them North.
Make welcome for them everywhere, for they are your own offspring.[1]

America had not taken them and fully disdained them. He remained misunderstood except by men of letters, original artists, exceptional people. It is possible to mention a few advocates such as the original planter of Alabama who for years was nourished on *Leaves of Grass*, almost neglected his farm, and who travelled a thousand miles to see face to face "the man who had done the most for him after Christ;"[2] or that noble woman of Detroit who read to her children the great book of life to educate them. But these were eccentric people, those apart whom the mass would have shunned. What antagonism between the crowd and himself, that the aversion of the latter was so tenacious, that custom could not overcome the surprise, occasioned particularly by his queer form? What variance? He came from the masses by his whole being; he remained his whole life, more than any poet in the world, in contact with the masses, he addressed himself exclusively to the masses, he exalted the masses in poems cut by them into his flesh; and the masses did not recognize their blood. He remained for them unintelligible. It was as if he had made some

---
[1] *Leaves of Grass*, p. 20.
[2] W. S. Kennedy: *Reminiscences of Walt Whitman*, pp. 18–21.

great discovery in the most occult corner of the field of science, forbidden to the crowd, he who had plunged into the heart of everyday humanity, who had but translated universal and primitive emotion. What was this mysterious law which led men obstinately to reject a nourishment prepared with their more intimate needs in mind?

And this interdiction he saw confirmed not only by the public, but by the American literary world. The great publishing houses persistently ignored him—and he was obliged always to be his own publisher. The verse which he sent for thirty years to the reviews had been generally returned; some of his poems had thus made the round of the periodicals of the country without finding a single harbour. The most recent example was that of Harpers' who refused his copy four times in succession; and he found himself rejected by all the great reviews of his country. He knew it now and sent nothing more. All the insults, all the deception, all the rebuffs that a blackballed writer could endure he had experienced one time or another. The bulk of the comprehensive articles which had appeared on his book in the American press—aside from the devout appreciation of an O'Connor, a Burroughs, and a half dozen comrades —were those which he was obliged to publish and circulate himself in friendly papers, whether in New York, at Washington, or at Camden, for the purpose of explaining and putting an end to the misunderstanding which kept the public away. As for the famous writers, from beginning to end, they were massed against him. He had no need, in order to know the measure of their sympathy toward him, that Edward Carpenter for instance reported that Lowell said he found nothing in Whitman; Longfellow that Whitman might have been a poet if he had sufficient education, and that Oliver Wendell Holmes admitted that he had talent but that instead of vying with nature, decking her with garlands, etc. It was true that he did not understand professional literary men and that their antipathy toward him arose because they and he were made for different purposes. No matter he remained a Solitary, though his work can find its final justification only in one vast communion.

He reviewed these memories without bitterness and even without sadness. He indulged in no grief. He complained to no one. He had his choice when he began. The ingratitude of an age attracted him no more than physical infirmity, as a theme for sighs. He accepted it, reflecting on the secret reasons which in the thought of the cosmos could justify it. He was not without reproach and he knew well that many things in his work deserved the most violent attacks of his enemies.[1]

There was left then to be finished in silence the work of time. The question which an American review put—"In a hundred years will Walt Whitman be considered a great poet or will he be forgotten?"—was surely a delicate one, and no one will be able to answer before a century or even more. However distant might be the issue, he could wait and his work after him. He did not know more than another the secret of the future, though from the first day to the last no one had been persuaded as strongly as himself, and without possible illusion of the enormous new Sense of his book: but all the same he seemed to discern some encouraging sign. Had he not learned that in England his book had won an unlooked-for victory, at Oxford as well as among workmen,[2] and that even the peasants of Schleswig knew his name? And the young men who came to see him or who wrote to him, from all parts of the world, to tell him what he had been to them? And in Boston were there not signs of a change of opinion? These white spots in the horizon were they forerunners of the dawn? . . . Yes, in truth he believed he saw success in the future. . . . It was true that he had not won much up to this, but he had gained a

---

[1]Bucke: *Walt Whitman*, p. 59.

[2]The Honourable Mr. Francis Nielson, M. P., at the Whitman Centenary dinner in Chicago, stated that Shropshire workingmen read *Leaves of Grass* in 1880. Tr.

foothold. . . . He had understood certain aspects of the world and he thought that the report which he drew up would last. . . . And, inspired by this certitude, he could trust the century. He would have his hour, when the time came. One day perhaps humanity, in search of the word of the past which would help it to continue its route, would find itself confronted by his work, and suddenly the illuminating thrill would seize it. Till then it was not in the power of an individual to suppress his name from the world's list since some had pronounced it with limitless affection. These words which in a black day of his life he put into the mouth of Columbus, could he not repeat now that the horizon was clear?

And these things I see suddenly, what mean they?
As if some miracle, some hand divine unseal'd my eyes,
Shadowy vast shapes smile through the air and sky,
And on the distant waves sail countless ships,
And anthems in new tongues I hear saluting me.[1]

After all, had he not tasted the kind of glory to which he could aspire by the vastness of his undertaking? Could it be accepted without discussion? The incessant struggles which he had endured, the fury of the attack directed against his work, had they not been providentially sustained to establish its greatness and truth? Were not his very enemies a witness, as much as his most exalted admirers, of his undeniable contribution as Precursor? The immortality of his message—he could not prove it, but he felt it as the indestructibility of his soul. He had above all the same serene, instinctive, ineradicable confidence in his personality and his work, a confidence against which all the logic of the world would have blunted its edge. . . . Surely, if the fight had been rough, the fruit which he was permitted to gather, at this close of the day, was worth all the conflict which he had to sustain. . . .

---

[1] *Leaves of Grass*, p. 325.

XXX

HOUR OF APOTHEOSIS

A SERIES of Lincoln anniversary memorials sometimes in Camden, in Philadelphia, and even in New York were ovations to Whitman as well as pious tributes to Lincoln. His last visit to New York in 1887 was more than an atonement for years of neglect—being as it was a dramatic compliment to him of American men of art and letters—Stedman, Lowell, Mark Twain, John Hay, R. Watson Gilder, St. Gaudens; Andrew Carnegie made his *Triumphant Democracy* real by donating liberally to the poet of Democracy.

Because, in 1889, Walt had not been able to celebrate the Lincoln anniversary, he determined the following year to conquer his weakness and perform this pious duty; it was perhaps for the last time. The meeting was to be on April 15th, at the Contemporary Club of Philadelphia, and a few days before the grippe confined him to his bed. His friends persuaded him not to attempt the impossible; but the great volunteer was not of this mind and refused to be interfered with. Truly, they did not know "the full measure of his stubbornness."

At the appointed time the old man arrived at the meeting in a cab. His daring was finally justified since all passed well. The very presence on the stage of the old dying athlete, come himself to pay tribute to the memory of the hero of the Union whom he compared with Moses, Ulysses, or Cromwell, was still more affecting than his words and imposed silence for his faults. His voice still had all its strength and the same charm of melody. Sometimes the speaker stopped reading his speech a moment to throw in a sentence or glance about the hall; and when he wished to indicate certain passages, he turned about in his arm chair and repeated them in a most fervent tone, his face uplifted. From this massive ruin, tottering on the brink of the grave, there was the same radiance as of old; and the light from which it came was more intense in proportion as the old tenons were loosed from their mortises.

The month following there was another anniversary when Walt for the second time crossed the river—his birthday, which his friends had come habitually to celebrate by a banquet where in the warmth of the great communal Individuality they arranged themselves, believing they felt a fresh breath of victory, charged with the promise of the future. They were young men most of them who sat round the table this year, spread in rooms of the Zeisser restaurant. The event of the evening was the improvised speech of Robert Ingersoll, come on purpose from New York, his day in the law court finished, and who, facing the poet, spoke marvellously for three quarters of an hour directly at him finishing each period by these words "I thank you for that." Walt passionately listened; his friend was superb and "never was he so proud, so fully justified as on that evening." However Ingersoll forgot, in the warmth of his materialist conviction, to mention a very little thing perhaps not at first glance discoverable in *Leaves of Grass*, but which for him the architect was the invisible substructure of the edifice. It is the faith in the survival of human personality. Ingersoll replied, developing the reason of his attitude, and a dialogue followed in which the poet and the free thinker expressed their views touching on immortality; neither convinced the other. Walt remained with his instinct, and his friend with his logic; but the hour was one of Platonic beauty and every guest kept an undying memory of it. The real victory of Ingersoll was to draw into controversy, by the power of his word, him who never argued.

In the group of generous companions of this last period the orator of this evening soon came to be enrolled with much distinction. In October of the same year, before two thousand people in Horticulture Hall of Philadelphia, "Colonel Bob" lectured on *Liberty and Literature*, subject urged by a presentation of the work of Walt Whitman. Ingersoll did not hesitate to place his great popularity at the service of his friend, who not only gathered the moral benefit of the lecture, but the receipts also. In pleading the great cause of the poet, the lawyer was bold and combative, with slight professional tendency to declamation and effect: the best of his lecture was probably the citations interlarding it. Walt, in listening, experienced a deep joy and pride to be thus defended by a man so different from himself. That his book had been able to win the enthusiastic support of persons as different as O'Connor, Burroughs, Bucke, Anne Gilchrist, Sarrazin, Ingersoll—did not that prove it had a universal appeal? When Ingersoll had finished his plea Walt, who sat on the stage near his champion, rose and spoke these words to the public:

"After all, my friends, the main factors being the curious testimony called personal presence and face to face meeting, I have come here to be among you and show myself, and thank you with my living voice for coming, and Robert Ingersoll for speaking. And so with such brief testimony of showing myself, and such good will and gratitude, I bid you hail and farewell."[1]

Perhaps he had the presentiment of saying the last goodbye; it was his last appearance in public. There was a particular gravity in these words in which he gave his own presence as the supreme justification of the work his friend came to exalt; he wished to show once more before departing the surprising identity of himself and his book—of his book of which he delivered the key to those who would understand.

One day in July of the same year Walt received a visit from a young Scotch doctor, who told him that in the industrial city of Lancashire, not far from Manchester, was a

---
[1]Bucke: *In Re Walt Whitman*, p. 253.

group of young men for whom *Leaves of Grass* was as the Bible; he himself was one of them, and he came to bring the homage of his comrades. The following year another of the circle, J. W. Wallace, crossed the Atlantic in his turn for the same purpose. Doctor Johnston, as so many other visitors before him, was unforgettably moved before the grand old man, who received him royally; and in recounting his visits no other written testimony surpasses in vigour and closeness the portrait which he drew of him. Walt at seventy-one relives in it so vividly that we imagine ourselves in the little home in Mickle Street and we feel the warmth of a ruling presence.[1] Thus erect in his great chair, his forehead high and clear, Walt Whitman remained, battling decay. His chest and face were not more bent than his great affirmations were weakened under the weight of age and illness. He was inaccessible to remorse, to disenchantment, and to doubt; he confronted the approach of death without wavering or recoil. At seventy-one he was the same Bohemian Walt, intransigent, free from prejudices as when he gapingly strode along the streets of Brooklyn. He knew how to protect himself from all compromises and all subjections. He had avoided marriage though he firmly believed in it; when Doctor Bucke asked him why he remained a bachelor, he said he had no set purpose in it except, "an overmastering passion for freedom, unconstraint." To his most intimate companion of these last years, the irreconcilable individualist gave but one advice: "never ask advice of any one."

Eighteen years of pain and the most distressing situations did not affect his imperturbability. When in 1885 he learned of the death of Anne Gilchrist, he did not flinch, he did not utter a syllable. In a mood of peace and triumph he wrote to her son Herbert: "There now remains but a rich and sweet memory—nothing more beautiful, in all time, in all life, on all the earth. . . . I can not write anything like a letter today, I must sit alone and think." And when, four

---

[1] J. Johnston: *A Visit to Walt Whitman*, pp. 131-217.

years later, his dear friend, O'Connor, died, nothing in his manner would have led a stranger to suspect his infinite sorrow. "For some minutes he said nothing," Donaldson wrote, "to any one near him when the news came—and remained seated in his corner, his head bowed down. When he raised it, his eyes, usually dull and colourless, had a distant look and he remained a moment without speaking. After an instant in a deep voice he uttered these words: 'And what a friend.'" As if he had already experienced the eternal metamorphosis, he seemed at times, above his bodily decay, to grow immensely, to expand, to widen to his planetary proportions. And indeed he loved to compare himself, in his accumulated impotence, to "an old shell fish cast up high and dry on the shore sands, helpless to move anywhere." One thinks rather of some Creator in the midst of a chaos of papers watchful of the good order of the world, and knowing the fair and just laws of the world as they filter into his soul.

In his old days, and especially when he wore his broad-brimmed hat, Walt with his face deeply wrinkled and with still some pinkish brightness reminded one of the old Quakers. Though he was essentially earthy and his fortitude free from all austere rigour, there was a survival in him of his paternal race. It was not without cause that in *November Boughs* he paid tribute to the great Quaker preacher Elias Hicks, and that for a long time he replaced in his poems the regular name of the months with their number, according to the custom of the Friends. But the influence of the maternal line, the reserve of tenderness of optimism and of joviality which he received from Holland, was always there to prevent that inflexible Quaker from degenerating into sulky hardness and dryness either in his looks or in his attitude toward life. He wrote in 1890 to a friend: "Are you not a little blue?—it's no use—one has to obey orders and do duty and face the music till he gets dismissal and may as well come up to scratch smiling."[1]

---
[1] W. S. Kennedy: *Reminiscences of Walt Whitman*, p. 65.

In the middle of April, 1892, Walt propelled in his wheel chair, breathed the outside air after four months of imprisonment. The beginning of that year was full of sinister forecasts. The end was indeed not far. Darkness little by little weighed upon his sight and soon he would be half blind. According to an expression which he borrowed from Epictetus he was but "a tiny ray of soul awkwardly dragging here and there a great lubber of a dead body"; and the image seemed to him so adequate to his present situation that he had it printed at the head of the paper on which he wrote his last notes to his friends.

His nurse used to conduct the old man toward the banks of the river to study the magic of space, and to give his face to the caress of the breeze. "I saw a great schooner with four sails the finest I ever saw, poised on the water like a duck. That, I truly think is a poem, a poem," he said after one of these outings. That living poem, a great sail boat moving upon the water, he declared he was unable to describe, as he had the locomotive. The shipping quay was one of his favourite haunts at the twilight hour, when the freshness of the banks kept him within city bounds; he watched the boys play baseball, he breathed the air of the fields. He still thirsted for the great shows of the out-of-doors and a setting sun filled him with the same great and solemn joy as the show of the world awakened in the first man. Amid the planks and boxes of the Camden wharf his great body was shaken by the movement of the chair, but the head high, the great liver recalled by the earth, came to see the sun go down, and seeing them face to face, it might well be believed that the same royal apotheosis enveloped the disappearance of both. And the man reflected that obeying the same rhythm as the planets he would be born again like them, shining in youth at the day appointed by eternal laws. And while the delicious breeze of twilight refreshed his wrinkled face, an echo of a stanza he sang seemed to pass into the air:

You earth and life till the last ray gleams I sing,
Open mouth of my soul uttering gladness,
Eyes of my soul seeing perfection,
Natural life of me faithfully praising things,
Corroborating forever the triumph of things.

 . . . .

O setting sun! though the time has come,
I still warble under you, if none else does, unmitigated admiration.[1]

 Since it had been imprudent to take Walt far from his home, his friends rather than give up the celebrating of his seventy-second birthday planned a makeshift. This time they would come to Mickle Street to break the fervent, faithful bread of affection: the parlour of the little house was not large, but it would do to gather around the great Comrade. The precaution was wise, for the evening of May 31st Walt had to be carried to the table where thirty of his friends were guests. He spoke these words: "After welcoming you deeply and specifically to my board, dear friends, it seems to me I feel first to say a word for the mighty comrades that have not long ago passed away—Bryant, Emerson, Longfellow; and I drink a reverent honour and memory to them. And I feel to add a word to Whittier, who is living among us—a noble old man; and another word to the boss of us all—Tennyson, who is also with us yet. I take this occasion to drink my reverence for those who have passed, and compliments for the two great masters left and all that they stand for and represent."

 A perfume of intimacy and of joyous confidence filled the little room, predisposing the poet to avowals which all felt to be the last. At times one would have believed himself back at the symposiums of Greece, and when Walt with his slow, musical, selective speech made a remark, confessed his faith or explained anew the meaning of his book, one could not but think of Socrates exercising his power among a

---

[1] *Leaves of Grass*, pp. 374–376.

group of his disciples. He, invigorated by so many affectionate presences on this solemn sweet evening, spoke with vim and before leaving for his room thus said his farewell: "The chief thing is that we are here, that we are happy, and that we have a good time. I salute all of you—I send my love to each one of you—and to many, many others who are not here."[1] There were for the guests unforgettable blessed moments during this simple celebration, illuminated as it was by an Olympian presence. From that time, this presence would be missing at the anniversary banquets; before the return of May 31st the friends were called again for another celebration infinitely greater.

A word of congratulation from James Russell Lowell, born the same year as the poet, sent on their seventy-second birthday might be considered a sign of the times. Two months later Lowell died, and the poet sent to the Boston Herald a line of homage to the memory of him who had "faithfully worked," "according to the light of his own convictions."

What great names Walt left on his way! . . . Lowell, the last of a great group—Bryant, Longfellow, Emerson—and Whittier to survive him but six months. A great era of American literature was closed.

Before being felled by a last storm, the old tree gave once more its fruit. It was not without fear of repeating himself and in confessing that he had perhaps better keep silent that he put out, at this anniversary, a collection of verse and prose, in which to the notes and memories, he added a dozen or so of short poems, proofs of creative hours which he knew in the course of the last three years. The title of the collection, *Good-Bye, My Fancy*, was a true one; he himself felt that it was finished, that the sap would not rise again in the obstructed veins. But since a slight stream rose from the depths, he would receive and present it. Thanks to Horace Traubel, who the same month published in the New England Magazine moving, filial, and wonderfully searching

---
[1] Bucke: *In Re Walt Whitman*, pp. 297-327.

pages on Walt with whom he daily associated for years, he was able to conduct this new and last enterprise.

> After surmounting three-score and ten,
> With all their chances, changes, losses, sorrows,
> My parents' deaths, the vagaries of my life, the many tearing passions of me, the War of '63 and '4,
> As some old broken soldier, after a long, hot, wearying march, or haply after battle,
> To-day at twilight, hobbling, answering company roll-call. Here, with vital voice,
> Reporting yet, saluting yet the Officer over all.[1]

Nothing further remained but to add these last measures to the symphony of *Leaves of Grass*, and this final work the poet already undertook to complete in the last moments of respite left him. After that the work forever fixed was to go among men, to follow its destiny.

For many years the old man lovingly entertained the project of acquiring a home in some part of the forest. The time came to realize this wish. Walt would not wait longer. In 1890, Christmas day, he was taken outside Camden, to a new burying ground, where he chose the site of a tomb which he wished built. "I am not to die this moment," he said that evening to a friend, "I am but preparing the house needed for my old body." The site was delightful, at the incline of a hill, facing the sun, shaded with great trees: as he had always worshipped trees and sun, this was fitting. At last he would sleep the splendid sleep, near his own people, at least his father and his mother: for it was his intention to gather his whole family here, those dead and yet to die. In waiting, he was busy in having built the tomb and simple but durable monument which he planned: the work would take a good part of the savings of the poet, but Walt could once more in his life

---

[1] *Leaves of Grass*, p. 410.

prove himself a wonder. In May of the following year he visited the cemetery to take note of the work and returned satisfied. The house was prepared for the day when its occupant would come accompanied by his friends to take possession of the woody retreat under the trees.

XXXI

THE DELIVERANCE

ON DECEMBER 17, 1891, the old man was seized with a hard chill in the afternoon, took to his bed, and the next day the diagnosis proved that he had acute bronchial pneumonia. The final scene of the tragedy which lasted for twenty years was begun. Walt did not leave his bed except for his new home. Then the last complication set in. His friends were informed that all would soon be over. Walt was completely conscious of his condition; he did not lose an atom of his coolness and his quietude. On the 21st it seemed that the last hour was approaching, but a drink of milk gave him again a semblance of vitality. The sick man now wished to be left alone with the nurse. After three or four days all were apprehensive; the dying man was plunged into a kind of half-consciousness. Now he declared for the first time that the end seemed near. Doctor Bucke who had hastily come at the news of danger was also sure of this. It was evident that Walt at the end of his strength was sinking, and his most tender friend could do nothing to hold him back. . . . Medical aid was put to the utmost. Walt asked nothing but that he might go, begged gentle death, so belated in coming, implored her to put an end to his long suffering. His sweetness and gentleness never left him.

John Burroughs came, and remained ten days, watching for a last time the living features of his old companion, and in finding him as beautiful as ever, more splendid than he had ever been at the time of his glorious power with that expression of the unconquerable fighter in his face, could scarcely realize that he saw him on his death bed. On January 2nd the great patient had strength to sign a codicil to his will. The only complaint of Walt was that in these moments of intense suffering when he had not the strength to turn his head, he remained sound and was assailed by a flood of thought. Why did not death come to free the strong and clear spirit which persisted in a lamentable human ruin. . . .

The issue, however certain, was now averted to some unknown chance. The glorious human edifice was still to last three months. Walt had to submit. No one heard complaints during these weeks of survival harassed by cough, by pain in the side, by restless nights. The tortured man needed to be alone; he preferred his watchers in the next room rather than at his bedside. He still for some moments partook of the life of the world for he still asked for his newspapers and his mail; he still had words of tenderness for his distant friends, Stedman, Ingersoll. His old friend J. H Johnston of New York came to see him. His pen was at hand and from time to time he painfully traced two or three lines to Doctor Bucke or to his sister Hannah. There were long silences, and it was plain that he suffered intensely and uninterruptedly. Walt had at least a supreme joy before departing. The final edition of his books, the tenth, which contained as an annex *Good-Bye, My Fancy*, was completed, and he could hold in his hands the work forever finished, such as he would leave to the world with his last corrections. The volume (published by McKay) contained 411 pieces—ten or twelve thousand verses—making up the poetic total of his life. Walt wished that the first hundred copies, bound in heavy gray paper with the title in yellow, should be sent to his friends in gratitude for their affectionate support, unfortunately without the dedication or signature which his nerveless hand was unable to affix. In February, wishing to show that his heart was always with them, he wrote with trembling hand a collective letter, which was reproduced in facsimile and sent by Horace Traubel to all of Walt's correspondents in Europe and America.

This is his very last word, before all the cares of the world had submerged him, to send this farewell kiss to all those who supported the cause of *Leaves of Grass:* "February 6, 1892. I must send you all, dear friends a word from my hand—I am propped up in bed with pillows, deathly weak still, but the spark seems to burn bright always. . . . My health is not so bad as you might think, though my suffering the most of the time is intense. Again I repeat my thanks to you, friends in England, with all my heart, it is perhaps the last—in reaching you my right hand." And in a postscript he wrote this testamentary and prophetic thought—the last important word traced by his hand: "More and more it is seen to be true that the only theory worthy of modern times in view of a great literature, politics and sociology should combine all the best men of all the countries, not forgetting the women." To this letter was added a prospectus announcing the completed edition of his poems, the only one he wished to carry his name to the future. Later David McKay brought out the volume also complete, of his prose works, in the same form as *Leaves of Grass.* And the world then would possess all of Walt Whitman condensed in two volumes. One must thank fate that despite the suffering of these last hours he was able to put the final period to his work, which left his dying bed in perfect order, without uncertainty or gap, such as he wished to leave to eternity or to oblivion.

At the same time that he left to mankind his great Testament, Walt was careful to make known his last will to assure the integrity of his work, and the distribution of his temporal goods. He had made one will in 1888; the old was to be replaced by that of 1891, completed by a codicil which named as testamentary literary executors Maurice Bucke, Thomas Harned, and Horace Traubel. Then his all being disposed of Walt could leave with light and joyous heart. He had closed his accounts and found himself correct with himself and everyone.

And now, after so many delays, the inevitable hour was come. The fifteen days which the liberatrix needed to destroy his massive figure Walt passed in almost absolute silence, more tragic than the sighs which were evidence of his interminable dissolution. He wished to be alone; the great fighter was now intrenched within his interior fortress. Who would have thought that so much dregs still remained in the cup for his last moments! Death seemed to wish him to be gorged in it in proportion as he was filled with life. Walt knew death by long draughts during the weeks which were as centuries. It appeared, as well as life, to be for him multitudinary. "You would weep," wrote Traubel to Doctor Bucke, "if you were at his bedside, and saw this struggle and this heroism." There was something great in that forbearance, these victorious suffering hours which changed the sadness of his friends into a kind of joy, as before an exultant apotheosis. The grim ruler whose features he came closely to see was to him without terror, he had met death before when he lavished his care on soldiers; the horror of the last hours were a vain chimera. For he remained fully, entirely conscious; had had neither delirium nor coma. On May 17th the pen between his fingers was still able to trace these trembling and almost illegible lines to his sister in Vermont: "Unable to write more—here is five dollars—received your nice letter—God Bless you. W. W." And after that effort, the hand which traced so many verses for the future ceased forever its writing.

In the afternoon of the 26th, at half-past four, the signs of release were evident. Then Horace Traubel came in and Walt gave him his hand which his disciple held in his own, above the counterpane; the end came simply, peacefully, without spasms, without fright, without motion of the body. The dying man, who appeared not to be suffering, retained full consciousness. When the nurse changed his position he rolled his eyes an instant as if to thank him by a faint smile, the last service given him in this world, then remained lying very calmly, while his breath insensibly shortened. And like a breeze which passes or a petal which softly loosens and falls, the end came with the decline of day: it came so gently that no one knew at what moment the transition was made. In the last crisis, no words of pathetic adieu; the great liver went with the same ease, the same naturalness that he lived toward the beyond so often speculated upon in his serene meditation, to the kingdom of shade or light, none knows, but surely of royal repose. The shadow of a smile of content at gratitude to the nurse passed over his calm, wasted features, then later his hand fumbled as if searching for something and he was by invisible stages swallowed in the great All.

> At the last, tenderly,
> From the walls of the powerful fortress'd house,
> From the clasp of the knitted locks, from the keep of the well-closed doors,
> Let me be wafted.
> Let me glide noiselessly forth;
> With the key of softness unlock the locks—with a whisper,
> Set ope the doors, O Soul.
> Tenderly—be not impatient,
> (Strong is your hold O mortal flesh,
> Strong is your hold, O love.[1])

And now, evening was come and while rain gently fell, Walt remained dying in his room, his face in full repose. This time the great oak whose branches once swayed so gaily in the wind, peopled by singing birds, after the successive lightning strokes which broke its branches was brought to earth gently, lifted by its roots to the level of the soil; and lying there the king of the forest appeared still greater than when it was upright.

---
[1] *Leaves of Grass*, p. 346.

XXXII

A PAGAN FUNERAL

There remained the last rite, the burial of him who so confidently faced the end of the journey. To be worthy of Walt the ceremony must be one with the big simplicity of the man, and it was: never a funeral of the purer impress of humanity, of nature and of heroism, rounded the life of one of earth's immortals. On March 30th, at eleven o'clock, in the sitting room of the little house on Mickle Street, the body of Walt Whitman in an oak coffin strewn with flowers was half exposed that all might see the legendary figure which had for so long appeared to passersby framed by the open window or erect in the buggy and the wheel chair. Clad in the unchanging gray flannel with his broad shirt collar open, and his white cuffs turned back, the poet whose features death left unchanged looked ready to leave for his new home, his face as natural as on the day he allotted his burial.

Near the body resting among palms, sheafs, and crowns sat his brother, George Whitman, and for three hours a ceaseless procession crowded the narrow door and about the coffin; they were the crowd which came to salute a last time him who was so vividly nourished by them, the multitude of friends known and unknown, the unknown especially. All the elements of the community were represented in these thousands of visitors, men of the people and of workers en masse, artists elbowing policemen, scholars mingling with school children, doctors, ministers, lawyers, all curiously one in the same desire to look at the admirable countenance so serene in the bond of death. In one last "meeting face to face" as he loved them in life Walt offered again to the crowd the radiant enigma of that physiognomy in which nature placed the most absolute sign of the triumph of the race. John Burroughs who came from his farm to be near his dear old-time Comrade was more than ever struck with the perfect symmetry of the dead face so like the superhuman image of Zeus. Robert Ingersoll threw a quick glance at the coffin and turned away; Moncure Conway, in his turn, murmured these words: "How Rembrandt would have liked to have painted this face."[1] And in looking back at the strange man whom he came to find one summer day thirty-seven years ago in the suburb of Brooklyn, he said a little later: "I do not believe that Buddha, of whom he appeared an avatar, was more gentle to all men, women, children, and living things."[2]

At two o'clock, the hour for removing the body, the crowd continued to press about the door yard, as if the procession would last till evening, and access to the house would have to be forbidden. The old head, tenderly kissed by George Whitman, disappeared under the lid, and Walt with his family crossed the threshold of the little house he had entered eight years before. A magnificent guard of honour escorted him on his last ride:[3] that is to say the élite of his American companions and admirers, new friends and old ones, whose presence was most clearly the answer to the call of the man tormented by an incessant need of love. Outside a dense crowd which since morning had not ceased to grow blocked the house. And in the town, from the ferry to the cemetery, was a great crowd of people, come from their shops and their homes, to be at the burial of the great man of Camden. There was no sadness either of face or

---

[1] Donaldson: *Walt Whitman the Man*, p. 271.
[2] John Burroughs: *Walt Whitman*, p. 55.
[3] Immediately before the funeral car holding the coffin J. H. Stoddard, Julius Chambers, George W. Childs, Julian Hawthorne, Robert Ingersoll, Horace Furness, Daniel Brinton, John Burroughs, Lincoln Eyre, J. H. Johnston, Francis H. Williams, R. M. Bucke, Talcott Williams, Thomas Harned, Horace Traubel, Charles Garrison, Harry Bonsall, J. H. Clifford, Harrison Morris, Richard W. Gilder, H. D. Buch, Thomas Eakin, A. G. Cattell, Edmund Clarence Stedman, David McKay, Thomas Donaldson. Donaldson: *Walt Whitman the Man*, p. 272.

atmosphere. Along the streets pedlers arranged their stands or exhibited their baskets of fruits and sweets; the funeral of the great joyous liver suited marvellously his character, taking on the appearance of a fair. Would not Walt have been delighted thus to leave in the midst of a popular fête! Perhaps he would have found few in this crowd who could have called by name *Leaves of Grass* or explained who the man was who was being buried, but little mattered this ignorance. What was precious and touching was this collective evidence which without knowing it the average man bore to him who sprang from the people and kept them in his own heart. The same crowd continued throughout the entire way to the cemetery, and the friends of the dead man, in seeing all the silent faces watching the bard of Democracy pass, thought: "How fit, how touching all this is, how well it would please him."[1]

The procession reached the gate of Harleigh Cemetery, and moved toward a large tent decorated with palms, in which was a raised platform: the grave was some rods from the tent. The bearers laid the casket before the platform on which Thomas Harned, Daniel Brinton, John Burroughs, Francis H. Williams, Robert Ingersoll, and Maurice Bucke were seated. No show of sorrow, no funeral march; the preparation suggested rather a holiday. It was an ideally soft, fair day, sweet with the breath of early spring as though nature was tender to the man of tender heart and smiling to him whose smile was so luminous. The crowd filled the cemetery and alongside the hedge onlookers reached the very entrance of the grave. On every side, on the slopes near the open grave, a sea of attentive faces, an innumerable multitude reminded one of the crowds in the amphitheatre watching a Greek play. All these people had not quit their work moved by curiosity to hear Ingersoll or to be present at a new and strange ceremony; it must have been that they were

---

[1]Bucke: *In Re Walt Whitman*, p. 363.

forced out of their daily routine by some hidden impulse, perhaps by the vague, inexplicable feeling that the man whose white hair they had reverenced belonged to them more than to any one, relatives or disciples, and that they were his true family. On the slope, part of the swarming crowd, a man of forty years steadily watched the tent where the coffin rested, without appearing to understand more than those near him what these preparations meant. But what he did understand, what he felt rather, was the immense void in his heart at the sight of the coffin where lay the man who loved him more than a son, and who had so profoundly loved and understood him with his simple and true heart. And in the heart of Peter Doyle, the former conductor, separated from his great companion for life, the past infinitely throbbed.[1]

Then before the assembled multitude one of the friends on the platform, Francis H. Williams, arose and said: "These are the words of Walt Whitman." Then he read one of the stanzas in which the poet exalted blessed death, dispenser of supreme joys:

Dark mother always gliding near with soft feet,
Have none chanted for thee a chant of fullest welcome?
Then I chant it for thee, I glorify thee above all,
I bring thee a song that when thou must indeed come, come unfalteringly.

. . . .

From me to thee glad serenades,
Dances for thee I propose saluting thee, adornments and feastings for
  thee. . . .[2]

Then one by one the others rose to testify, in words of grave simplicity each according to his character and belief, what they themselves, the world, and the future owed eternally to the man asleep in the coffin. Though their voices trembled with emotion they had not come to the grave to lament, but

---

[1] H. B. Binns: *Life of Walt Whitman*, pp. 344–345.
[2] *Leaves of Grass*, p. 260.

rather to affirm their exultant joy that such a man had lived among them. When all had spoken Francis H. Williams rose again to read one of the sentences chosen from among the great religious books and prophecies composing the Bible of Humanity: "These are the words of Confucius, of Gautama le Bouddha, of Jesus Christ, of the Koran, of Isaiah, of John, of Zend Avesta, of Plato. . . ."

And when the last friend had spoken and the last sentence was pronounced, the extraordinary ceremony was finished. That was all, and that was great, simple, and natural and perhaps shall one day be the funeral of man as one coming closer from himself and from the truth of life. The consecration of the dead by the words of great genuises and of his friends was his liturgy, and more than the thundering notes of Siegfried's funeral march the aërial melody of that day of apotheosis stirred the heart. A feeling of triumph heightened the emotion of the friends surrounding the body while the motionless crowd on the hillside, too remote to hear, waited patiently the moment when the remains of the poet disappeared under the vault, as if in recollected expectancy of some marvel. It was Robert Ingersoll who said the farewell words. When he exalted with a voice whose usual power was weakened by emotion him who had sung, "the great and splendid psalm of life," and ended with this solemn thought: "Today we give back to Mother Nature, to her embrace and kiss, one of the bravest, most tender souls which ever dwelt in human clay," a great silence rested on the whole assembly, on all the hearts touched by an unspeakable moment, as if the soul of the dead were diffused into nature and the crowd; and before that bier, under the swaying, new-budding trees, symbol of the eternal regeneration, some thought they saw the day when the poems of the sage, left to time, would blossom anew through all the earth like the grass of the hill— they thought they heard the thrill in the odorous air charged with promise, the great salutation of the future before this grave.

The bearers again lifted their burden; the procession now moved toward the vault, along the crowded path. It was built on a shady slope, of three blocks of granite of an Etruscan simplicity, bearing as the inscription these three syllables which the future will have deathlessly engraved on human hearts before they are rubbed from the stone: WALT WHITMAN. All about an abundance of verdure, grass, wild plants, tufted branches, impetuous spreading of free vegetal life; young trees seemed attentively guarding the door of the house where he was about to rest in whose veins had run the same life substance which made them grow on this slope. The crowd was in double rows on both sides of the tomb and the coffin was carried between them and placed in the grave. Not a word was uttered while the coffin was lowered, but the moment Walt was within his house a little messenger of spring, perched on the tree shading it, gave out some trembling notes, then smothered his clear and exquisite melody. It was the wood which by the voice of its choristers seemed to welcome the new guest who came to sleep there. And now all was finished; the friends remained there a moment bent in mute emotion. All of them knew that they lived an ineffaceable hour of their life and time. And the crowd, held in spite of itself, lingered near the tomb of the divine old man about to be left to the silent freshness of the night.[1]

Walt was there where he should be. That wonderful physique retaken by the elements would be part of the earth which he had trod with firm step in loving it, of the air which had joyously filled his strong man's lungs, with the flowers, with the grass, with the herbs—gifts to him of so many joyous miracles. Truly the earth reclaimed her own. He belonged to it entire to the minutest cell. Yes, the earth hungrily reclaimed all of him. . . . And yet the man, who by a miracle of love, was transmuted into a

---

[1]Bucke: *In Re Walt Whitman*, pp. 437–452; Kennedy: *Reminiscences of Walt Whitman*, p. 47; Donaldson: *Walt Whitman the Man*, pp. 272–275.

Book, remains triumphantly beyond the reach of glebe, and wind and water, eluding tender death which soothed at last his long suffering, continues to haunt the hearts of men, indissoluble, everlasting. In going, Walt Whitman left us his "double."

THE END